THE UNFAILING PROMISE

THE UNFAILING PROMISE

RICHARD LEE

WORD BOOKS
PUBLISHER
WACO, TEXAS
A DIVISION OF
WORD, INCORPORATED

THE UNFAILING PROMISE

Copyright © 1988 by Richard Lee. All rights reserved. No portion of this book may be reproduced in any form, except for brief quotations in reviews, without written permission from the publisher.

Scripture quotations used in this book are from the following sources:

The King James Version of the Bible (KJV).
The New American Standard Bible (NASB), © The Lockman Foundation 1960, 1962, 1963, 1968, 1971, 1972, 1973, 1975, 1977.
The Holy Bible, New International Version (NIV). Copyright © 1973, 1978, 1984 International Bible Society. Used by permission of Zondervan Bible Publishers.
The New Testament in Modern English (PHILLIPS) by J. B. Phillips, published by The Macmillan Company, © 1958, 1960, 1972 by J. B. Phillips.
The Living Bible (TLB), copyright 1971 by Tyndale House Publishers, Wheaton, IL. Used by permission.
The New King James Version (NKJV). Copyright © 1979, 1980, 1982, Thomas Nelson, Inc., Publisher.
The Revised Standard Version of the Bible (RSV), copyrighted 1946, 1952, © 1971, 1973 by the Division of Christian Education of the National Council of the Churches of Christ in the U.S.A., and are used by permission.

Library of Congress Cataloging-in-Publication Data:

Lee, Richard, 1946-
   The unfailing promise.

   1. Christian life—Baptist authors. 2. Consolation.
I. Title.
BV4501.2.L4254 1988   248.4'86132   88-5731
ISBN 0-8499-0651-2

Printed in the United States of America

8 9 8 0 1 2 3 9 RRD 9 8 7 6 5 4 3 2 1

To my mother
ONGIE HITT LEE
whose life has shown me Jesus,
and
to my father
REV. WILLIAM B. LEE
who taught me to love God's calling

Contents

Preface — 9
PART ONE: *The Fiery Furnace* — 13

1. The Truth about Trouble — 15
2. Where Is God When We Need Him Most? — 24
3. Don't Dodge the Fire — 32
4. When Saints Get Sick — 41

PART TWO: *The Transformation* — 51

5. How to Master Your Mind — 53
6. Say Goodbye to Guilt — 62
7. You Can Handle Your Habits — 70
8. Dare to Tackle Temptation — 78

PART THREE: *Four Against Faith* — 89

9. The Way Out of Worry — 91
10. Facts about Fear — 98
11. Answers to Anger — 105
12. The Cure for a Bitter Spirit — 113

PART FOUR: *Out of the Depths* — 123

13. Up from the Pit — 125
14. Maintaining Moral Purity — 134

15.	How to Get Out of a Mess	146
16.	What to Do When You Feel Like Quitting	155

PART FIVE: *On to Victory*   165

17.	Claim Your Mountain	167
18.	Finding Perfect Peace	176
19.	Causing Heaven to Hear	185
20.	God Can Use You, Too	194

Preface

Broken promises. Everyone is familiar with them. We've all been disappointed at one time or another by someone who has failed to keep his promise to us.

It may have been the repairman who said he would be right over, but never showed up. The politician who forgot his campaign promise as soon as he was elected to office. The friend who said he was going to pay us back for the loan, but never got around to it. Or maybe that special someone we loved deeply who simply wasn't there when they promised they would be.

Times like these always leave us with feelings of frustration, emptiness, and disappointment. Why? Because promises mean so much to us, and there is little we can do about it when they are broken by someone else.

If you are tired of broken promises—good! That means that you and I have something in common. We both want to know someone whose word we can depend on . . . someone who will never let us down . . . someone whose promises are unfailing. That's why I have written this book: to remind us that there is Someone we can always count on—and that Someone is our eternal God.

That's a marvelous truth to hold on to—that our God will never fail us. Even when we are struggling with our own lives; when we are far less than we should be; when fear and doubt threaten our faith; when we are even failing in our promises to Him; God stands ever near, ready to forgive us and teach us how to regain our strength and confidently walk life's road again. That is His unfailing promise.

I would like to express my appreciation to Dr. Ed Hindson for his valued advice in the completion of the manuscript; my faithful secretary, Emily Boothe, for her tireless hours of typing; and Dr. Jim Black and Beverly Phillips of Word for their help and encouragement. Finally, a special thanks to my loving wife, Judy, whose faithful support means so much to my life.

Richard Lee

THE UNFAILING PROMISE

PART ONE
THE FIERY FURNACE

~~~~

Is his mercy clean gone for ever? doth his promise fail for evermore? Hath God forgotten to be gracious? hath he in anger shut up his tender mercies?

—PSALM 77:8–9

1

The Truth about Trouble

As I watched the evening news one night, there came the story of a little girl who lived in Toledo, Ohio. She was like most little girls in every way except one. Her parents noticed it when she was just a baby. It seemed that when she hurt herself, she never cried. At first they thought that she was just an unusually brave little girl, but after a while, they began to suspect that something was wrong.

Finally, her mother took her to the doctor, and after several days of examination it was discovered that the little girl had a rare disease of the nervous system which caused her not to be able to feel pain. The doctors cautioned her parents that she could never be left alone, for she could injure herself severely and never feel the pain. So you see, even pain can be a gift from God for our protection and good, while the lack of it can be tragic indeed.

But allow me to talk with you about another kind of pain, a pain that we all endure—the pain of trouble. Almost everyone has troubles Life is never so simple that one can travel its road without facing pitfalls and obstacles. Life is a journey, not a hundred-yard dash! The journey is often long and difficult, sometimes tedious, and sometimes treacherous. But in spite of its ups and downs, the journey of life is the most exciting adventure of all.

When life brings us the pain of trouble, we need to ask ourselves: Is it possible that this kind of pain can also be for our protection and good? We must identify our troubles, learn to benefit from them, and in turn bring about their solution.

Some troubles are easy to identify. If your car won't start in the morning, or your refrigerator stops running, you automatically know that you have trouble. But other troubles are not that easy to identify. Many times people know that there is something wrong in their lives, but they simply don't know what it is. Have you ever been angry and couldn't figure out why? Have you ever been filled with worry, and could not pinpoint what it was you were worried about? If so, you know what I'm referring to. Those feelings indicate unidentified trouble.

There is another kind of trouble that is more common to us. That is the kind that comes along and slaps you in the face, unexpectedly, unannounced, unprepared for, and unwelcomed. Nevertheless, it's there!

If you are struggling with either kind of trouble in your life, let me encourage you by reminding you that you are not alone in your struggle. The Bible tells us that Christ has promised us that He will never leave nor forsake us (Hebrews 13:5). You can depend on His promise. Then do not forget to realize that no matter how insurmountable your difficulties may seem, God is greater than all of them put together. I am convinced that God has a specific solution for every problem we face in life. He created us, understands us, and knows best how to meet our deepest needs. Whatever your troubles may be, they are not beyond the reach of God's love and the grasp of His grace.

HOW TO BENEFIT FROM TROUBLE

It has often been said that trouble will either make us better or bitter. The decision is really up to us. One of the most familiar promises in the Bible says, "And we know that all things work together for good to them that love God, to them who are the called according to his purpose" (Romans 8:28). Not only does God work in our lives through the blessings of His grace and goodness to us, but He is also actively at work through our problems and difficulties as well. That is the key to understanding how to overcome your problems. Once you realize that God is at work in your life despite your outward circumstances or even your inner turmoil, you can have the hope of a better life.

One of the great truths about overcoming trouble is that how we respond to trouble is far more important than the trouble itself. For it is our response that reveals our innermost character. Anyone can talk a positive line when life is going well. But when the problems come and the bottom seems to fall out of your life, what you do at that point reveals what you really are in your inner self.

Over the years of my ministry, I have observed many individuals and families who were cruising along the road of life, seemingly without a care in the world. They were healthy, happy, and prosperous in every way. They had good jobs, secure marriages, beautiful children, and everything seemed to point to the ideal situation in their lives. But when the storms of life came (and storms will come), the reality of their life and its values was put on the line. When life comes along and grabs you by the heels, turns you upside down, and gives you a good shaking with an authentic problem, you begin to understand what troubles are really all about.

Unfortunately, some Americans don't even understand what real problems are. They think that because they can't buy a new car, or a fur coat, or take a trip to the Bahamas, that they really have troubles. Whereas someone who has struggled with the deep problems of life will understand that such people don't actually have any real problems at all!

Herbert Casson once wrote, "The average man takes life as a trouble. He is in a chronic state of irritation at the whole performance. He does not learn to differentiate between troubles and difficulties, usually, until some real trouble bowls him over. He fusses about pinpricks until a mule kicks him. Then he learns the difference."[*]

The Bible is filled with examples of people whose lives seemed to be all together. Outwardly, everything was going well, and all of a sudden, the bottom fell out. I think of Job, whom the Bible described as the wealthiest man of the ancient East. He had countless herds and possessions and a wonderful family. But in one day, he lost them all. On top of that, he lost his health and was brought to the point of utter human despair. Here was a man who had done nothing to bring these problems upon himself. He was suffering despite being a good husband, father, and businessman.

I think also of Joseph, who was the apple of his father's eye. If there was ever anyone who seemed to have the right to give up on God and life itself, it was Joseph. Here was a teenager who had done nothing wrong, and yet had been sold into slavery and thrown into jail. But even in jail, Joseph became a model prisoner and rose to a position of leadership and influence. In time, he was able to stand before the Pharaoh of Egypt himself and was promoted to the position of top administrative assistant to the king. He is a beautiful picture of how someone overcame all of the problems and obstacles in his life and rose to the highest position of influence possible at that time.

---

[*] Quote taken from *The Supreme Philosophy of Man* by Alfred Armand Montapert. Used by permission.

Later, when Joseph was reunited with his brothers, they expressed concern about his intentions toward them. And he explained to them that though they meant their action for evil, "God meant it for good" (Genesis 50:20, NASB). His understanding of that truth was what enabled Joseph to endure all the injustice that seemingly had come into his life. Instead of being crushed by his troubles, he responded to them in a manner that made it clear that his ultimate faith and confidence in God was unshaken. He was not overcome with evil, but rather, he overcame evil with good.

Only when you and I learn how to face our problems in the way that Joseph faced his, will we ever be able to overcome them positively and effectively. The troubles of life are real. They exist in all of our lives. But in no way do they mean that God has forsaken us. Rather, God is at work in our lives no matter what our circumstances may be.

We should also *allow our problems to force us to God*. When children fall down and hurt themselves, they automatically turn to their parents for help. Perhaps you can remember such an incident in your life as a youngster. You were hurt and needed help, so you ran to a person that you knew loved you and cherished you. I can still remember my mother taking me into her arms and saying something to comfort me and soothe my hurts. That is the same way in which we should go to God with all of our problems and trials. He is the One who loves us and cares for us more than anyone else ever could.

Unfortunately, many people let their problems push them away from God. They become bitter and begin to question the love of God or even the existence of God. Bitterness will drive us from God. It will cause us to question His love for us and His commitment to us. It will also cause us to focus our attention on the experiences of others, instead of causing us to draw closer to God.

If we are really going to face our troubles and learn to benefit from them, we must allow them to draw us closer to God. Even the personal hurts and wrongs that others meant for harm must be handled in such a manner that they turn out for our own good. Often the very thing meant to destroy us will push us to the throne of God's grace.

Another truth is that *present troubles teach us to avoid future ones*. One of the proverbs in Scripture asks the question, "Can a man take fire into his bosom and his clothes not be burned?" (Proverbs 6:27). Unfortunately, there are certain lessons in life that we only learn once we get burned. While truth can be learned by precept, many of us only seem to learn it by experience. Once you have experienced the terrible consequences of sin, you will learn to avoid it in the future.

Life is a learning process. Along the journey of life God is continually teaching us through our experiences. One of the most foolish things we can do in life is to experience the consequences of our mistakes and not learn from them. Sin can be confessed and forgiven, but its effect still lingers in the memory, and hopefully it is the memory of the consequences of that sin that will cause us not to repeat it in the future.

Finally, our troublesome experiences *help us to give wise counsel to others.* No one can counsel you better than someone who has been through the same kind of difficulties. No one can help you get out of the valley better than someone who has walked through that same valley. I have found in my own counseling that I can help people better in relation to the problems that I have struggled with myself. Nothing bothers me more than to hear of people who are experts on everyone else's troubles, but have never had any of their own. Either they are not being honest about their problems, or they lack the wisdom to help people face the real issues of life.

If we can learn to respond properly to our problems and allow them to draw us closer to God, then our problems can be turned into spiritual opportunities for growth and ministry. As we learn to handle the problems of life, we begin to grow spiritually, and as we do so, we are better equipped to help others do the same. In so doing, we turn our difficulties into opportunities for serving the Lord. It is in this sense that you can really learn to benefit from trouble.

SEEK GOD FOR THE SOLUTION

If God is greater than our troubles and He can give us the wisdom to face our troubles, then it only stands to reason that we should seek Him for the solution to our troubles. As I have had to face the problems of life myself, I have found a simple process of seeking God to be very beneficial to me personally. Let me share it with you.

1. *Meditate on God's Word.*

The psalmist says, "Thy word is a lamp unto my feet, and a light unto my path" (Psalm 119:105). As we search the Scripture, we soon realize that it is God's manual for life. It is the key to successful living and the source of our understanding of God's wisdom. This book is filled with the answers to the problems of life. It can teach you how to know God personally, how to love Him intimately, and how to live a victorious and successful life.

Meditation is the act of self-discipline that enables us to concentrate our attention on the Word of God. It is one thing to read the Bible, but it is an entirely different matter to meditate or think deeply upon its truths. It involves more than just a casual reading of the Bible or the mere listening to a sermon. It involves the mental discipline of total concentration upon truths and principles of Scripture.

The Word of God has often been pictured as seed which must bear fruit in the heart of the believer. As we read the Word of God, the principles of God are planted in our hearts just as seeds could be planted in the ground. In time, those principles begin to come to fruition in our lives. As we meditate on those truths, they begin to grow in our hearts. That is the amazing power of the living Word of God, which is illuminated to our minds by the Holy Spirit.

You can plant a seed in the ground, but if it doesn't receive adequate nourishment, it will die. Unfortunately, many people take the Word of God and read it casually, never meditating upon its truths. In time, they forget the very things they have read and the seed of the Word fails to come to fruition in their lives.

If you really want to overcome the troubles of life, read the Word of God and quietly meditate upon its principles. As you allow the Spirit of God to illuminate your heart with the truth of God, you will discover that you are growing spiritually despite your outward difficulties. Once you begin this process, do not give it up. Keep disciplining yourself to seek God, and you will find all that He has for you.

2. Seek God in Prayer.

Prayer is communication between man and God. It is not the mere reciting of certain words or phrases which others have deemed appropriate for addressing deity. Real prayer is the heartfelt expression of one's inner being to the heart of the infinite and personal God Himself. As you read the Word of God, you may want to express its promises and principles back to God in prayer.

Learning to pray was one of the great concerns of Jesus' disciples. They went out of their way to ask Him to teach them how to pray. Their request seems to imply that effective prayer isn't always easy for everyone. As you struggle to find the meaning and purpose to the problems in your life, learn to pour your heart out to God in prayer. Talk to Him just as you would talk to any other real living person in your life. Do not worry about saying appropriate words and phrases, but pour your heart out to the Lord. Remember, that Jesus Himself said that it was the brokenhearted prayer of the publican which God heard, rather than the display of self-righteousness which was expressed by the Pharisee.

3. Obey the Principles of Scripture.

Once you discover truth, you must determine to obey that truth in your life. The Bible speaks clearly to the specific issues of life and tells us what to do to resolve our problems and difficulties. But knowing what the Bible says and doing what it says are two different things entirely. There are those people who know scripturally what is right and wrong for their lives, but they will not commit themselves to do what is right. Therefore, they can have no hope of solving the problems of life.

The Bible expresses truth in many different forms. It contains doctrinal statements, narrative stories, poetic expressions, and prophetic pronouncements. But in all of these literary forms, God Himself is speaking to us through the power of His Word. Because of this, we can know Him, know His will for our lives, and still fail to obey the truth expressed in His Word. If you really want to overcome your problems, you must be willing to obey the truth of Scripture.

4. Endure to the End.

Endurance is one of the great qualities of life. Just as an athlete endures the physical hardships of an athletic contest in order to win the victory, so we must be willing to do the same in our individual lives. In a sense, life is a marathon race. It contains many twists and turns and can only be won by endurance and dependability. As you run the race of life, no matter what difficulties and obstacles you may face, remember that he who endures to the end is the real winner. In His letters to the seven churches of Asia (Revelation 2-3), our Lord Jesus emphasized the importance of enduring to the end. He has also promised never to leave us or forsake us; therefore, we should have every confidence that we can finish the race of life well. As he faced the end of his ministry, despite all of its difficulties, the Apostle Paul said, "I have fought a good fight, I have finished my course, I have kept the faith" (2 Timothy 4:7).

You will never make it in life if you become a quitter. No matter what goes wrong—don't give up! When trouble comes our way the value of courage, persistence, and perseverance is demonstrated. I want to share with you the endurance of a man we all know. It is the story of his life that might somewhat surprise you. Here is his record:

At age 22—he failed in his business.
At age 23—he was defeated for the legislature.
At age 24—he failed in his business again.
At age 25—he was elected to the legislature.
At age 26—his sweetheart died, leaving him heartbroken.
At age 27—he suffered a nervous breakdown.
At age 29—he was defeated for speaker of the house.
At age 31—he was defeated for elector.
At age 34—he was defeated for Congress.
At age 37—he was elected to Congress.
At age 39—he was defeated for Congress.
At age 46—he was defeated for the Senate.
At age 47—he was defeated for vice president.
At age 49—he was defeated for the Senate.
At age 51—he was elected president of the United States.

Who was this man who refused to quit? This is the record of Abraham Lincoln. His willingness to endure his troubles won him the presidency of the United States.

Unjustly cast into prison, John Bunyan wrote *Pilgrim's Progress* from behind prison bars.

In his old age, Sir Walter Scott penned some of his most famous classics to pay off a half-million-dollar debt for which he was not legally responsible.

Almost totally deaf and his heart burdened with deep sorrow, Beethoven composed his soul-stirring symphonies. Handel and Mozart, both approaching death, gave us their most memorable works.

Martin Luther, hiding in the castle of Wartburg from the enemies who sought to take his life, translated the Bible into language that the humblest peasant could understand.

Blind Fanny Crosby left us hymns full of comfort and inspiration. Helen Keller, out of her blindness, said, "As I walk about my chamber with unsteady feet, my unconquerable soul soars skyward on the wings of an eagle."

What did they all have in common? They endured. They refused to quit! Whatever your troubles of life may be, determine in your heart that you will endure and that God will see you through.

5. *Leave the Rest to God.*

The Bible says, "Trust in the Lord with all thine heart; and lean not unto thine own understanding. In all thy ways acknowledge him, and he shall direct thy paths" (Proverbs 3:5-6). This passage reminds us that we cannot trust our own wisdom in solving the troubles of life. Rather, there must come a point at which we totally entrust ourselves to the wisdom and sovereignty of God. A sovereign is someone who has the power to do as he wills. While this concept may seem frightful to some, it ought to be a tremendous encouragement to all of us who know the Lord because He is our Sovereign King. He is all-powerful, all-knowing, all-loving, and all-wise. He will never do anything to harm us, and He will always do everything He can to help us. That is why we need to turn to Him to meet our deepest need.

The real answers of life are not found in the advice columns of the newspapers or in the talkshows on radio and television. The real answers to the troubles of life are found in the Word of God. They are composed of the principles of truth which are expressed in Scripture. As we learn these truths, meditate upon, and obey them daily in our living, we can learn to face any trouble, knowing that God is on our side.

There is no problem that God cannot solve. He loves you more than you could ever love yourself, and He understands you better than you could ever understand yourself. He knows what you need, when you need it, and why you need it. When those truths sink into our hearts, we are brought to the calm assurance that we can trust God completely. His promises will never fail.

2

Where Is God When We Need Him Most?

I have in my hand a letter I received not long ago. It says, "Dear Pastor Lee, I am very discouraged and downhearted at this time. I'm a middle-aged man who is in good health. Because of problems in my field of work, I've been unemployed for many months now. I can get no unemployment compensation. My wife has been sick for a long time, and it is evident she will never work again. I need a job. I want a job that will support us, but it's just not there. Often I think of suicide, but I believe that is wrong. I pray and I try, but nothing seems to happen. Where is God, Pastor? I've been a Christian for forty years, but I see no light at the end of my tunnel. Pastor, where is God when I need Him the most?"

I have to admit that is a pretty good question. It is one we all ask ourselves sooner or later. No matter how exciting your Christian walk may be now or may have been in the past, most of us come to those difficult moments where we do not know for sure which way to turn. When we are sick or lonely or unemployed these feelings of inadequacy come over us like a dark shadow of despair which seems to reach into every crevice of our being. It asks us the haunting question: "Where is God in all this?"

Things can seem to go wrong even when we are doing everything we can to live right. You don't have to be living in deliberate sin, shaking your fist in the face of God, for something to go wrong. The truth is that bad things do happen to good people. If you haven't yet experienced this for yourself, and in time you will, you surely know someone else who has. Real problems are a part of the reality of life. No one is immune to them. They come upon all of us sooner or later.

"But where is God in the middle of my problems?" people often ask. The answer to that is implied in the question itself. He is right where He said He would be—in the middle of your problems. He is never totally absent from our troubles. He is right there ready to help us handle them. That is why the Apostle Paul wrote that He "comforts us *in* all our troubles" (2 Corinthians 1:4, NIV [italics added]). He does not necessarily always keep us *from* trouble.

Lucy in the "Peanuts" comic strip was complaining about her problems. Charlie Brown tried to comfort her by saying, "Lucy, into life a little rain must fall. Besides, life will always have its ups and downs." To this Lucy replied, "But Charlie Brown, I don't want any ups and downs! All I want is ups and ups and ups!" Most of us want just the "ups" of life, but unfortunately we cannot isolate one truth about life, such as God's blessings, from another truth, such as God's justice. Every attribute of God works in perfect harmony with every other attribute. We cannot select one and avoid the other any more than we can choose one scripture and neglect others.

Some time ago, I was visited by a dear lady who told me that she felt God had abandoned her. Here is the way she expressed it, "No matter how hard I pray," she said, "God just doesn't answer me."

"What kind of answer are you expecting?" I asked.

"One that says yes to what I feel I need, of course," she replied abruptly.

"Well, my understanding is that God doesn't always say yes," I suggested. "Sometimes He tells us no for our own good."

"But that's not what I want to hear," she stated.

"I know it may not be what you *want* to hear," I answered, "but it just may be what you *need* to hear!"

Nowhere does God promise to always give us all that we want. In fact, the Scripture warns us that if we ask for something with the wrong motive, we can be sure that we won't get it. How many times have you prayed selfishly for something that, if God had given it to you, it would have ruined you? Remember, God is too wise to help us destroy ourselves with selfish desires.

FINDING GOD'S DIRECTION

If you really want to find God's answers to your troubles, turn to His Word. The Bible is filled with principles for living, and in it we find the answers to the questions that so often trouble our souls. Seeking God is not some vague mystical experience. Rather, it is a deliberate search for truth in His revealed Word.

God is always there in our darkest hours. Even when we think all is going wrong, He is still at work in us. We simply need to learn to see His hand at work in our lives. Consider these thoughts when you seem to be wondering where God is in your situation.

1. When Your Request Is Wrong, God Is Denying You.

James 4:3 says, "Ye ask, and receive not, because ye ask amiss." To "ask amiss" means to ask with the wrong motives. When your motive for asking is not right, God will not grant your requests. He has not deserted you. He is still there, but He is denying your request for your own good. We cannot expect God to contradict His own wisdom and give us something that is not good for us simply because we demand it.

God is too wise to be fooled by our clever devices and our petty insistence that we get our own way. God is omniscient, or all-knowing. He knows all about us. Our past, as well as our future, is ever present before the mind of God. How could a loving God who knows everything that ever will be answer yes to our prayers if He knows that answer will ultimately hurt us?

A classic example of this kind of request is found in 1 Kings 19:1-4. Elijah the prophet was God's spokesman. He had called down the fire of God on the altar on Mount Carmel. He had slain the prophets of Baal and called down judgment on the royal family of Israel. But when wicked Queen Jezebel determined to kill him, he fled for his life. He escaped into the wilderness and took shelter under a juniper tree. There, in total exhaustion, he begged God to take his life. But it was a prayer God refused to answer.

Elijah didn't really want to die. If that had been the case, he could just as well have stayed in town; Jezebel would have been glad to accommodate him. Elijah was simply looking for an easy way out of his troubles. He wanted to pull the ejection cord and catapult out the escape hatch of life. But God said no for his own good.

We are all often guilty of the same kind of selfish requests. We want God to bail us out of our troubles, when He wants to use those troubles to mold and shape our lives. In reality, He is often protecting us from our own selfishness and greed. When He refuses to answer our prayers that are prompted by wrong motives, He is actually proving that He is there when we need Him most to say no for our own good.

2. When Your Timing Is Wrong, God Is Delaying You.

In Ecclesiastes 3:1, we read: "To every thing there is a season, and a time to every purpose under the heaven." Timing is crucial to almost everything in life. This is especially true in athletics. It does not matter how much physical ability an athlete has, he will not be a winner if he cannot achieve the proper timing. There have been many baseball players, for example, who had the strength to hit home runs but could not time the swing of their bat to meet the ball properly, and they failed to make it in baseball.

This principle is often true in our daily lives. Even when we desire something within the will of God for ourselves, we must be willing to wait for His timing to bring it to pass. God never promised to answer our prayers on our timetable. There is not one guarantee in Scripture that He will always give us what we want *when* we want it. Don't ever think that you can just snap your fingers and God will jump right then and answer your request. If He did that, you would be God and He would be your servant. It just doesn't work that way.

Unfortunately, many people think that God exists simply to take care of their needs. They treat Him as though He were a puppet on the end of a string. When they pull the string, they expect Him to get moving. I remember hearing someone say, "I've got the faith, He's got the promises, so He has to answer me." That kind of mentality treats God like a heavenly vending machine. Some people think all they have to do is stick in a prayer, pull the promise knob, and out pops a miracle.

We live in an instantaneous age. We want everything right now. That is why we have fast food and instant coffee. Our generation knows little or nothing about delayed gratification. There was a time when people had to wait a long time to be able to afford something they wanted. Now we just lay down a credit card and take it home today.

When we turn to God in prayer, we expect the same results. Unfortunately, that is not how God works. He moves on His schedule, not ours. He is our Father and we are His children. We had better not forget how that relationship works. We don't set the agenda. He does. The sooner we realize that all of God's blessings aren't sent by Federal Express, the better we will be able to appreciate and accept His timing.

And remember, God's timing is always crucial to our ultimate well-being. God is the One who made time. He knows us best and always operates on schedule. When we are in a holding pattern, it does not mean that God is not there, but that He is delaying the answer for our own good. Sometimes you may find yourself in a divine time delay. Don't give up at those times. Trust in the truth that God will answer in time, on time, when the time is right.

3. When Your Course Is Wrong, God Is Directing You.

When we get off course in life, God lovingly, yet firmly, directs us back on the proper path. For some of us, this happens frequently. For others, this is an occasional experience. But for all of us, it is a necessary process in order to keep us in line with His will. When things are going well, most of us pay little attention to the priorities of our lives. But when the bottom falls out, God can get our attention in a hurry. In times of trouble we are usually quick to re-examine ourselves and seek His direction.

Jonah was a prophet of God who got off the right course. God had commanded him to go east to Nineveh, the Assyrian capital, to preach to the enemies of Israel. Instead, he fled in the opposite direction. He went down to the Mediterranean seacoast town of Joppa and took a ship headed west to Tarshish. Exhausted, he fell sound asleep in the ship, only to be awakened by a violent storm. The Bible declares that God sent the storm deliberately because Jonah was running away from God's will. In desperation, and perhaps because of self-inflicted guilt, Jonah told the mariners to throw him overboard to appease the wrath of God.

I have met a lot of people in my lifetime who were just like Jonah. They were moving in a direction opposite to God's will for their lives, and He sent a storm along to get their attention. But some, instead of repenting and changing direction, wanted to end it all by a self-destructive act. That is never the right answer to your problems. God is greater than that. He has plans and purposes for you that are far more grand in their design than to simply leave you on the trash heap of life.

At the moment of Jonah's desperation, the Bible says, "The LORD had prepared a great fish." Jonah wasn't swallowed by accident, but by divine purpose. There inside that uniquely prepared vehicle of God's grace, Jonah cried out to God in prayer. The Bible says, "*Then* Jonah prayed." He had not prayed when he decided to run away. Nor had he prayed when he first entered the ship and fell asleep. But now, *in* the depth of his troubles, he called out to God, and God redirected his course.

Often you and I are a lot like Jonah. We know what God wants us to do, but we are unwilling to do it. In our rebellion, we devise our clever plans to exclude God from our lives and run off in our own direction. When we think we have escaped His notice, God sends the storms to get our attention. Why? Because He knows that trouble will cause us to re-examine our priorities and put our lives back on course with His will and purpose.

When the difficulties of life come your way, don't give up on God. He hasn't forsaken you. Many times He is right there in all the troubles trying to get your attention. Turn to Him, seek His face, and follow His direction for your living. As you do, you will experience the assurance of His presence, and the peace of His purpose will finally be accomplished in your life.

4. When Your Life Is Wrong, God Is Disciplining You.

You and I cannot sin and get away with it. God always holds us accountable for our actions. He is our heavenly Father, and like any good father, He disciplines His children. That does not mean He enjoys disciplining us, but He does so because He knows it is ultimately good for us.

My father was a strong disciplinarian. He did it the old-fashioned way by turning me over his knee and spanking me. I clearly remember that when he spanked me, he would always say, "Son, this hurts me more than it does you." At times I wanted to suggest to him that we trade places if it hurt him so much!

But I never could understand or appreciate what he meant by that remark until I became a father myself. Then when my own children would misbehave and I had to discipline them for their wrongdoing, it often broke my heart to have to give them the "rod of correction." I loved my children, and my heart ached for them. Yet, I knew they needed to be disciplined in order to change their direction in life.

When God disciplines us, I believe He does so with a broken heart. He gets no pleasure out of the process, but love compels Him to do it for our sakes. Yet, through the whole process He knows He is risking our displeasure. When I discipline my children, I am laying my reputation on the line with them. I am risking their anger. They may turn against me through the process, but I am compelled to do what is right for their ultimate good. God operates the same way. He knows that we may rebel against Him in our innermost being, but He risks disciplining us because He loves us. He is willing to sacrifice our opinion of Him for our own benefit.

When we are under God's discipline, He is there correcting us. He has not forsaken us, nor has He abandoned us. The Bible reminds us, "No chastening for the present seemeth to be joyous, but grievous: nevertheless afterward it yieldeth the peaceable fruit of righteousness" (Hebrews 12:11). No matter what you are going through, God is in control of the process, and afterwards it will be worth it all.

5. Through It All, God Is Developing You.
We are all in a process of spiritual development. We are progressing in our walk with God. The Bible calls this process sanctification. It means that we are gradually and progressively being conformed to the image of Christ. In Philippians 1:6, the Apostle Paul put it this way: "Being confident of this very thing, that he which hath begun a good work in you will perform it until the day of Jesus Christ." If God has started a work in your life, He will complete it and bring it to fruition.

Many have the idea that they have to become perfect overnight. The process of sanctification is a slow one. Do not try to heal yourself before you call the doctor. Come to Jesus and He will help you with your problems. So many try to save themselves before they come to the Savior. They try to clean up before they come. You might as well try to get full before you eat. You might as well say, "I will never get in the water until I know how to swim;" or, "I will never touch a piano until I know how to play."

None of us have attained perfection. We are all pilgrims journeying through this world on the road of life. We have not yet arrived at our celestial destination, but we are on our way. Thus, our path may be filled with many obstacles and pitfalls. But through it all, the Savior guides us. No matter what process of God's grace you find operative in your life at this time, He is there and He is at work.

In Romans 5:3, the Apostle Paul urges us to "glory in tribulations [troubles], knowing that tribulation worketh patience." The word *glory* in the original Greek means to "rejoice." So in this sense we are to rejoice in our troubles because we know that God is at work in our lives producing His qualities of patience and endurance.

What the word *patience* describes here is not an attitude of simply waiting for something to happen, but the ability to endure under a tremendous load. And the term *tribulation* comes from the Greek word meaning to "squash" or "smash." In New Testament times, the Romans commonly executed their victims by piling heavy stones upon them until they died. What the Apostle Paul tells us is that we can endure under the heavy load of life because God will never put any more pressure on us than we can bear. Therefore, we can rejoice despite our pressures because God is greater than all our problems.

I can recall many times early in my ministry when I would visit elderly saints who had known the Lord for many years. "Isn't God good?" one of them would say, despite a terminal illness or a long period of loneliness. I would think, "How can you have the courage to talk about God's goodness right in the middle of your suffering?" But what I had yet to realize was that they had learned that God's grace was greater than all their troubles. They knew that in spite of all the problems of life, God was with them. This is one of the great lessons of life we all must learn. God is at work even in our greatest difficulties. When we wonder where He is, He is right there, molding us into the image of His Son.

You may feel that God has forsaken you for the moment, but He has not! He has promised never to leave you nor forsake you. In His temporary silence, He is still speaking to the ears of your soul. Even now, His denials, delays, and redirections are all part of His answers to your prayers.

3

Don't Dodge the Fire

Trouble is something everybody has and nobody seems to want. But the trouble with trouble is not the trouble itself but the way we handle it. One young man loses his girlfriend and jumps off a bridge, committing suicide. Another young man loses his girlfriend, writes a song about it, and makes a million dollars! The difference is in the way you treat the problems of life.

In the third chapter of Daniel, we read the story of three Hebrew boys, Shadrach, Meshach, and Abednego. They had been taken captive to Babylon as teenagers along with another young man by the name of Daniel. While in Babylon, the four of them were placed in a training school for three years to prepare them for government service under the king of Babylon. It was during this time that they had refused to eat the meat or drink the wine which the king had provided for them because they felt it was in violation of their beliefs and convictions. Having taken a stand for righteousness, they had already come under criticism from some of the Babylonian officials. However, God had blessed them, and they were the most outstanding students in their graduating class. By the time we get to the third chapter of Daniel, Daniel himself has risen to the position of prime minister to the king. Apparently he has been sent away on official business, since his name is absent from the story in this chapter. The king had ordered a golden statue to be erected. And he planned for all of his people to bow down and worship this image. Perhaps he knew Daniel would never comply, so out of his high regard for him, he may have sent him away.

When the day came for the celebration and worship of the idol, the plan was simple. When the musicians played, according to the king's command, all the nation would bow before the golden idol. All went well as the music loudly sounded. Suddenly, all of the nation went to its knees—all the nation that is except three young Jews. You can guess who they were. Shadrach, Meshach, and Abednego!

Nebuchadnezzar was infuriated by their refusal to worship the idol, but he gave them another chance to bow before the image. When they politely refused to do so, he commanded that they be thrown into a burning fiery furnace which had been heated seven times hotter than ever before.

Talk about trouble! It can't get much worse than this! Surely it's true that all of us get into a mess sooner or later in our lives. But few of us will ever have to face the kind of trouble these young men faced on that day. They had taken a stand for their beliefs and convictions, and now they were being called upon to pay for it. It is one thing to claim to believe something, and it is an entirely different matter to be willing to die for it if necessary. These three young men had taken such a stand. They had faced the king of the greatest nation in the world and told him that they would not bow to his demands regardless of the consequences. Yet, in the midst of their troubles, God delivered them.

REQUISITES FOR DELIVERANCE

You don't have to be in the kind of trouble these three young Hebrew teenagers found themselves in, to appreciate the power of God's deliverance. But whatever your difficulties are, it is good to know that there is always deliverance available from God. If you are struggling right now with some great problem in your life, let me remind you that it is not likely that it is as severe as what these three men faced. And the same God who delivered them can deliver you as well.

Shadrach, Meshach, and Abednego were convinced that God was in control of their lives. At their moment of greatest need they were willing to trust themselves to His sovereign will. That is why they were able to face Nebuchadnezzar and say:

> Our God whom we serve is able to deliver us from the burning fiery furnace, and he will deliver us out of thine hand, O king. But if not, be it known unto thee, O king, that we will not serve thy gods, nor worship the golden image which thou hast set up. (Daniel 3:17-18)

On the one hand, they were expressing their faith and confidence in God's power to deliver them. But on the other hand, they were not presuming upon His will to deliver them. In other words, their attitude was one of perfect balance and submission to the will of God. They were saying that they believed that God had the power to deliver them if He chose to do so, but even if He did not so choose, they would still serve Him. That is the kind of attitude which reveals an individual's confidence in the power and purposes of God. It is a kind of confidence which most people know little about today. We tend to want to manipulate the will of God and to convince God that He should do it our way.

If you were to ask the average person on the street, "Who do you think is running the world?" most of them would give some kind of political response. They would refer to the president of the United States or the Russians or some other political figure. The tragedy is that many politicians do not think that God is in control. They seldom use the name of God unless it is used in vain. In the business world, the average person does not believe that God is in control. Rarely do businesses begin the day with a word of prayer and request for God's blessing and guidance upon that business. While there are always exceptions, the tragedy is that most people in the influential positions in our nation are not at all convinced that God can help them. One of our national leaders recently said that as a nation we control our own destiny. I am not sure that this line of reasoning is fully true. While we certainly have a responsibility for our national affairs, we cannot overlook the fact that God still rules in the affairs of men.

Interestingly, the Book of Daniel opens with a story of the Babylonian invasion of Judah. In that invasion the Babylonians were totally successful and a number of the children of Israel were deported into captivity, including Daniel and his three friends. But in that opening chapter, the prophet makes the statement, "And the Lord gave Jehoiakim, king of Judah, into his [Nebuchadnezzar's] hand" (Daniel 1:2). The scripture makes it clear that Nebuchadnezzar was only successful as far as God allowed him to succeed. While his army may have been militarily superior, it was not the only key to his victory. These young men understood that they were not in Babylon by chance. God had put them there. He was in control of the situation from the very beginning.

The Bible tells us that God knows what is going to happen before it happens. It is that knowledge that is the basis of all predictive prophecy in Scripture. God can tell the future because He controls the future. He knew from the very beginning that the people of

Judah would be conquered by the Babylonians. He knew that they would be taken into captivity. Many times He had predicted the captivity in advance. And He had also predicted His eventual deliverance of His people and their return to the Promised Land. Shadrach, Meshach, and Abednego knew those promises. They understood that their captivity was for a specific purpose in order to fulfill the will of God. But even in their moments of desperation, they would not turn against the God whom they knew to be in control of the whole world.

God knew what kind of persecution His children were facing and what He would have to do to deliver them out of it. At this point the text says:

> And these three men, Shadrach, Meshach, and Abednego, fell down bound into the midst of the fiery furnace. And Nebuchadnezzar the king was astonished, and rose up in haste and spake, and said unto his counselors, Did not we cast three men bound into the midst of the fire? They answered and said unto the king, True, O king. He answered and said, Lo, I see four men loose, walking in the midst of the fire, and they have no hurt; and the form of the fourth is like the Son of God. (Daniel 3:23-25)

The fiery furnace, the intensity of the heat, and the anger of Nebuchadnezzar were all human efforts to thwart the will of God. But He overcame them all! At the moment of His children's greatest need, He sent His Son to deliver them from the fire. In so doing, God gives us a beautiful picture of His working in our lives. He does not always choose to keep us from the fire, but often brings about our deliverance while we are in the fire itself.

If God could deliver these young men from a fiery furnace, it should seem evident He can deliver us from whatever trouble we find ourselves in. He is still in control of this world. Satan may do all he can to disrupt the process, but God is still in control. He can even use the wrath of men to praise Him. That is exactly what God did in this situation. Nebuchadnezzar had responded in anger and had made a decision that even went against his own rational senses. He knew these young men were of the highest possible intellect and ability, yet he chose to try to destroy them anyway. But his angry decision was reversed by the power of God.

The sooner we understand that God is the One who has final authority over all, the better off we will be. We can avoid wasting a lot of energy worrying about things that are already under His control. As believers, we know that God is working all things together for our good (Romans 8:28). While God is not the source of our troubles, He can use those troubles and overrule them to produce good results in our lives. That means no matter what difficulties life throws at us, God can use them for good. I am convinced that even when we get out of His will and make serious mistakes, God can overrule our failures and problems to bring about His will in our lives. He may use these difficulties to teach us great lessons and to bring us to a point of repentance, but ultimately, He can also use these difficulties to produce a wonderful result that only He could bring to pass. It is only when we understand the sovereign control of God that we can really trust Him with the everyday details of our lives.

Someone may say, "What if I get into trouble, and God doesn't come through?" Whoever said God has to come through the way we determine, anyway? If I have the confidence that God truly knows best for my life and that He has the power to overrule anything for my own good, then I must believe that He has already properly prepared to come through on my behalf. If, on the other hand, I mean that God must meet my needs in a way that I have predetermined, then I am going to be disappointed. We cannot judge God on a performance basis. If something succeeds in our fleshly, materialistic eyes, we tend to say that God was in it. The truth is that He may not have been in it at all. It may simply be a work of human effort and nothing more. On the other hand, when God appears to be inactive, the truth is that He may well be accomplishing a greater purpose than we could ever have imagined. The mature believer understands that and is willing to say, "I trust you, Lord, no matter what the circumstances may be."

If there was ever a person who had a right to give up on God, it was certainly Job. He lost everything he had, including his children, and then he lost his health as well. In his most desperate moment, his wife abandoned him and his three friends condemned him. Yet Job remained confident in the sovereign purposes of God. In the face of great personal tragedy he said, "Though he slay me, yet will I trust in him" (Job 13:15). Despite his circumstances, Job's faith remained firm in God.

REVELATIONS IN THE MIDST OF THE FIRE

As God works in our lives, He often reveals His will and purposes to us in the very circumstances in which we are struggling. He wants us to understand that He has not given up on us. He also makes it clear that His sovereign power is still at work in our lives no matter what those circumstances may be.

Consider once again King Nebuchadnezzar. Imagine the great confrontation which was about to take place between this human king and the sovereign God. Nebuchadnezzar was the leader of the greatest nation on the face of the earth at that time. He was an absolute autocrat whose very word was law. In his pride, he had decided to build a huge image overlaid with pure gold. The ninety-foot structure was built on the great plain outside the city where it could be seen for many miles. When the image was completed Nebuchadnezzar assembled all the pomp that Babylon could provide to make a great display of his authority. A band of musical instruments, mostly imported from Greece, was on hand to play and all of the officials and dignitaries of the empire were there—except Daniel. Perhaps Nebuchadnezzar thought that the other three would not take a stand without him. But he could not have been more wrong. The same spiritual qualities which Daniel possessed were also a reality in the lives of these three young men. When they took their stand against the king, they were taking their stand for God. I am convinced that when we are willing to do that, God will not overlook our needs.

These young men were men of conviction and maturity. They were not demanding that God deliver them. They were not making any ridiculous promises based on their own merit or even on their own faith. They were fully prepared to die for what they believed in, even though they understood that God had the power to deliver them if He chose to do so. But even if He chose otherwise, they wanted Nebuchadnezzar to know that they would not succumb to the pressure which he had placed on them. I do not know what they thought as they listened to the decree of judgment pronounced against them. I am not certain how they may have felt as the soldiers carried them up the outside steps to the top of that domed furnace. But every indication of the text would seem to tell us that they faced their punishment with absolute confidence in the power of God.

The Bible tells us that Nebuchadnezzar's soldiers tied them up in their own stockings and threw them into the fire through the opening in the top of the furnace. The fire was so intense that the heat and smoke overcame the soldiers and burned them alive as they tried to flee. In the meantime, the three Hebrews landed in the middle of the fire, where they should have been instantly destroyed. Instead, not a hair on their heads was even singed. God had come to reveal His faithfulness to them.

The Bible tells us that Nebuchadnezzar was totally astonished when he realized that the fire had not destroyed the three young men. He apparently ran to a side entrance to the furnace where he could see into the fire itself and observed that they were walking around unhurt in the midst of the fire. What's more, he saw a fourth person with them in the furnace.

While God did not choose to deliver them *from* the fire, He did choose to deliver them *in* the fire. He wanted to show His power to all of the people who were assembled at the great event. Therefore, God allowed them to be thrown into the furnace. There are so many times in our lives that we want to tell God how to solve our problems. We want to make sure that He is not going to allow us to be thrown into the furnace, so to speak. We claim that we believe in His deliverance, but we want Him to deliver us before we face any trouble. In contrast, the Scripture clearly tells us that, more often than not, God will deliver us *in* our troubles rather than *from* our troubles. This concept is clearly stated in 2 Corinthians 1:4, where the Apostle Paul says that God "comforteth us in all our tribulation, that we may be able to comfort them which are in any trouble." God allowed these young men to stay in the furnace just long enough for them to realize the greatness of His deliverance. He also allowed them to stay in long enough for the Babylonians to realize it as well. I know that it is never fun to go through the furnace of persecution and suffering, but when you do you can be reassured that God is with you. Problems knock away our pride, they cause us to lose our self-dependence, and more than anything else, they tend to bring us closer to God. When everything is going well for us we tend not to need God nearly so much as when everything is going wrong.

As a pastor I have watched many people over the years who have developed a self-sufficient attitude when life was going their way. But when the bottom fell out or they found themselves flat on their back, it was a totally different story. That's when they began to cry out to God to meet their needs. Suddenly those who had little time for God found themselves spending much time with God. I am not suggesting that God is heartless in the manner in which He deals with us. I do not believe that He wants to inflict suffering on us in order to get us to love Him or trust Him. Rather, I am convinced that the sufferings and difficulties of life are a part of life itself. They are going to come our way whether God uses them in our life or not. The difference for the Christian is that he understands that God does use those experiences for good, and not for evil. The believer knows that no matter what has gone wrong on the surface of circumstances, God is still at work in the depth of his life.

Not only did the Hebrew children receive their revelation of deliverance in the furnace, but they also received a revelation of the Deliverer. It has been debated by commentators whether the fourth figure was an angel or whether it was Christ Himself. I personally believe that it must have been Christ. Notice that when Nebuchadnezzar called to them to come out of the furnace they did not respond immediately. Most of us would have been glad to go running out of the furnace, but they seemed content to stay in there because of who was in there with them. The king had to beg them to come out of the furnace. I am convinced that they were not so much excited about being in the furnace as they were excited about who was in the furnace with them.

I would rather be in a fiery furnace with Christ than in a place of luxury without Him. I would rather be in trouble with Jesus than appear to have my life together and not have Him in my life at all. While He is always present in the believer's life, the truth is that we are never closer to Him than we are in times of trouble. It is then that we plead with Him not to leave us or forsake us. It is then that we call upon Him with a heart of fervency. It is then that we desperately reach out to Him for help and guidance and direction. And the wonderful truth of Scripture is that it is also then that He stands by us and delivers us to His glory and honor.

THE RESULTS OF THE FIERY FURNACE

The results of the suffering of these three Hebrews were incredible. First, these men made an indelible impression upon Nebuchadnezzar himself. This impression may well have led to the king's subsequent conversion, which is recorded in Daniel 3:28-29. When Shadrach, Meshach, and Abednego came out of the fiery furnace, the Bible says, they were not burned nor was there even the smell of fire or smoke upon them. Nebuchadnezzar was so stunned that he immediately blessed the God of Shadrach, Meshach, and Abednego and gave testimony to His power to deliver. Second, the king made a decree that no one could speak anything amiss against God because of His power to deliver. And third, he promoted Shadrach, Meshach, and Abednego to greater authority and responsibility in the province of Babylon.

Greater results could not have come from a more catastrophic beginning. For a few moments, it must have seemed that the heavens were silent and that God had not chosen to deliver His children. But when He did deliver them, He did it with such great power that everyone was convinced that He was indeed God. This is the key that we must learn to understand in our own lives. We cannot put God on our timetable nor can we demand that He meet our needs in relation to our demands. While we can claim His promises and trust Him to meet our needs, at the same time we need to understand that He knows better what we really need in our lives. God's perspective is one that is eternal. He sees your life from beginning to end and He knows what will best benefit you in the long run.

When you get to a place in your life where you are in the middle of trouble and you feel that you are all alone, remember that God is still there. He is ever present in our lives and He is constantly at work on our behalf. The Bible promises us, "Being confident of this very thing, that he which hath begun a good work in you will perform it until the day of Jesus Christ" (Philippians 1:6). When God saved you and brought you into a personal relationship with Himself, He began a work in your life. But that work did not end at salvation. Therefore, you can rest assured that the God who loved you enough to save you loves you enough to continue His work in your life. No matter what problems you may face, God is still in control and God is still at work. With that in mind, you can, if you will, turn life's troublesome fires into triumphant faith.

4

When Saints Get Sick

Almost no one likes to be sick! Americans proved that last year as they consumed over twenty thousand tons of aspirins in their efforts to feel better. No matter how successful you may be in other areas, when you are sick it is difficult to enjoy life at all. Therefore, the desire for physical healing is one of the strongest desires human beings can have. When we are not well, we crave wellness. When we are healthy, we hope to continue in good health. But when sickness comes, it is not without significance in the life of the believer.

Sickness is a topic that was dealt with constantly in the New Testament. There were many occasions on which Jesus healed the sick during His earthly ministry. There were also times when the early apostles healed people of physical illness. But just as plainly there were times recorded in Scripture when even great saints of God *did not* receive physical healing.

One of those whom God did not choose to heal is recorded in 2 Corinthians 12:7-10. In this passage the Apostle Paul pours out his heart to the Corinthian believers. He acknowledges that he has been suffering from a "thorn in the flesh," which he does not define specifically. He then explains that he has asked the Lord three times to remove this illness from him and has discovered that God's purposes are to be fulfilled by allowing the illness to remain. Notice how he describes his personal trauma over this illness and how he accepts the grace of God as sufficient to sustain him in his weakness.

> And lest I should be exalted above measure through the abundance of the revelations, there was given to me a thorn in the flesh, the messenger of Satan to buffet me, lest I should be exalted above measure. For this thing I besought the Lord thrice, that it might depart from me. And he said unto me, My grace is sufficient for thee: for my strength is

made perfect in weakness. Most gladly therefore will I rather glory in my infirmities, that the power of Christ may rest upon me. Therefore I take pleasure in infirmities, in reproaches, in necessities, in persecutions, in distresses for Christ's sake: for when I am weak, then am I strong.

The depth of truth expressed by Paul in this one passage, when truly understood, is more than adequate to help us face the problem of physical illness. There is little doubt that the "thorn in the flesh" to which Paul refers here was a physical illness. He also notes that it was being used by Satan to "buffet" him, meaning that Satan was attempting to use that sickness to discourage him and literally beat down his spirit. Yet through it all, those of us who have studied the life of Paul realize that God used this illness to produce genuine humility and an unbelievable level of spiritual maturity in his life. God's answer to Paul was to point him to His sufficient grace, which could enable him not only to endure the suffering but to use it for God's glory.

What was Paul's reaction to all of this? Instead of becoming bitter because God would not heal him, he was at peace because of his recognition that God was using his illness for His own greater purposes. Paul's response was that he would most gladly glory in his infirmities. Thus, he could say that he could experience gladness in all of the difficulties of his life, whether they involved physical infirmities or were the result of reproach and persecution. He understood that in his personal weaknesses, the power of God was manifested to make him strong.

In Paul we find the perfect and balanced response to the problem of physical suffering. The apostle makes it clear that he has personally suffered because of these infirmities of the flesh. He does not take the attitude that these things really do not bother him at all. Rather, he makes it clear that he was deeply distressed by his physical weaknesses. But, at the same time, he realized that God was at work in his life in spite of these circumstances, and that He would bring about a greater work as a result of them. Therefore, Paul was able to accept that physical suffering has a purpose in the life of the believer. Suffering is not a meaningless experience had by meaningless and insignificant individuals. Rather, even physical suffering can have a divine purpose in the life of the believer. Once we understand that, we are able to accept the process by which God has chosen to work in our lives.

A BALANCED APPROACH

In Christian circles today there are three basic approaches to dealing with the problem of physical illness. Each of these contains elements of truth; but when isolated from one another, they lack a balanced approach to the total problem of physical illness. Sickness is certainly not something that any of us desire, but it is something that most of us will experience. When it comes, you need to understand why you are suffering, what you are suffering, and what the significance of all of it really is in your life.

1. The Sin Approach.

There is one group of believers who are convinced that people are suffering physically because of sin in their lives. They are quick to point out that sickness is a consequence of the Fall of man into sin. In other words, with our sin nature come the inevitable results of that nature—sickness and death. Therefore, they conclude that whenever someone is suffering physically that person must be under the judgment of God because of sin in his or her life. This was the approach taken by Job's three friends who supposedly came to comfort him in all of his distress and anxiety. Job had lost his children, his possessions, and finally his health. But when his friends arrived, they began to rebuke him for hiding some unknown sin. Because he was suffering physically, they assumed that he must have committed some terrible sin of which he was unwilling to repent. When Job protested his innocence, they did not believe him and continued their criticism. In many ways they were not unlike a lot of misinformed Christians today. When someone has suffered from an illness or an accident, they automatically assume that he or she must have done something wrong to deserve it. That is a terribly judgmental way to live.

2. The Faith Approach.

Next is a group of Christians who believe that no matter what sickness you may be experiencing, God wants to heal you if you will only have enough faith to let Him do it. They are convinced that all sickness is a violation of the will of God. They generally base this conclusion on the belief that sickness is a result of sin and, therefore, God wants to remove it from our lives. They emphasize the importance of exercising faith in the power and promises of God, but if you come away from one of their services without being healed, you will likely be told that it is because you did not have enough faith.

Thus, they leave the person who remains sick in a state of frustration and disappointment at being unable to generate sufficient faith. The major problem with the "just muster up enough faith" approach is that it simply doesn't work!

3. *The Sovereignty Approach.*

There is yet a final group of Christians who are convinced that God is sovereign over the experiences of our lives and that if He has chosen to allow us to suffer from sickness, there really isn't anything that we can do about it. While they properly recognize the authority of God over the life of the believer, they almost fatalistically resign themselves to the fact that God probably does not want to heal them and there really isn't any hope.

Now I realize, of course, that each of these approaches can be taken to an extreme. There are many well-meaning Christians who lean toward each of these views. And they do so in genuine faith and sincerity. However, when each approach is isolated from the others, I am convinced that it only represents an element of truth. Each is but one facet of the total picture. The three approaches are like three sides of a diamond. Someone who only looks at one side at a time will never see the fullness of that diamond. The same is true with these perspectives of the question of human sickness and divine healing.

Physical sickness is a terrible thing to have to experience. It is true that there is a definite sense in which that sickness is ultimately a consequence of the sinful nature we inherit from Adam and Eve. But that does not mean that the individual who is ill has necessarily committed a specific sin in his or her own life which has brought about this illness. Certainly God can send sickness into our lives as a judgment for our sin, but that does not mean that all sickness is a result of the judgment of God.

On another hand, it is true that the "prayer of faith shall save the sick" (James 5:15). There are many times that God answers our prayers with a positive and complete healing. But that does not mean that He is obligated to do that in every situation. Nor does the lack of healing imply that God is against us. For example, Joni Eareckson Tada is one of the finest Christian women in our country today. Yet she is a quadriplegic who is confined to a wheelchair. It is not likely that she will ever be healed of her paralysis in this lifetime. She has accepted that condition with such grace and sincerity that God has used her to speak from her wheelchair in a manner that has undoubtedly been far more significant and effective than she could have ever had under more normal circumstances.

Then there is also the truth that God is sovereign in the events of our lives and that there are times that He does not choose to heal us. But that does not mean that we should not pray for healing. You and I do not know what His ultimate will may be in our situation. Therefore, we have every reason to appeal to Him in faith for healing.

CAUSES OF SICKNESS

We need to understand that there are a number of causes of physical sickness. The experience of illness is not always brought about for the same reasons; it is, therefore, important for us to understand why we are sick if we are to understand the purpose in that sickness. Let's look now at some of those causes.

1. Sickness Results from Aging.
Whether we like to think about it or not, the older we get the closer we come to death. Our bodies are in the process of aging every single day. We may try to camouflage that process, or cover it up, but it is still going on in our bodies. We can dye our hair, buy a wig, get a face-lift, or tuck our tummy, but the truth is we are still getting older. I once heard an elderly man say, "I can see with my bifocals, my dentures work just fine, I can live with my arthritis, but I sure do miss my mind." While that may have been said in jest, it still represents the reality that the aging process is an ongoing process within us.

It does not matter how healthy you may be at the moment. One day illness will catch up with you and you will eventually die. The Bible says very clearly, "It is appointed unto men once to die" (Hebrews 9:27). Unless Christ returns in our lifetime, we all have an appointment with death. You may not like thinking about it, but it is an ever-encroaching reality that must be faced. Most of us are like comedian Woody Allen, who said, "I don't mind the thought of dying so much; I just don't want to be there when it happens." But ultimately we will.

One of the greatest men who ever lived was the prophet Elisha. He was the understudy to the prophet Elijah. When Elijah departed to Heaven, the Bible says, a double portion of his spirit fell upon Elisha. As God's new prophet, Elisha was used of God to accomplish incredible miracles. On one occasion he healed Naaman of his leprosy, and on another occasion he raised a young boy from the dead. There can be no doubt that Elisha worked miracles by the power of God. Nevertheless, the Bible says, "Now Elisha was fallen sick of his sickness whereof he died" (2 Kings 13:14). It is highly unlikely that he died because of the judgment of God against a particular sin in his life. Rather, he died as a result of old age. Even Lazarus, whom Jesus raised from the dead, eventually died again. For the vast majority of people, death comes as a result of sickness due to aging.

2. Sickness Can Result from Sin.

The Apostle Paul also understood this truth when he said, "For this cause many are weak and sickly among you, and many sleep" (1 Corinthians 11:30). He was writing to the Corinthian believers about various problems of sin and disobedience in their lives. "For this cause" refers to the sin which had caused many of them to suffer physical illness and had even caused the premature death of some.

There can be no doubt that sin causes sickness. The tragic consequences of a sinful lifestyle often bring about serious illness and even premature death. The alcoholic who drinks himself into an early grave is certainly a prime example. The excessive smoker who destroys his own respiratory system is another example. Dr. Linus Pauling, a Nobel Prize-winning chemist, has observed that every cigarette reduces a person's life expectancy by fourteen minutes. That means that every pack of cigarettes takes 4.8 hours off your life. The excessive eater faces similar consequences. Many Christians who are strongly opposed to smoking and drinking are often just as guilty of excessive overeating, which can also damage one's physical body. The drug addict is certainly another example of someone who is being destroyed physically and mentally because of abusive habits.

The real tragedy of the sickness resulting from sinful habits and practices is that it destroys a person physically, mentally, and spiritually. You cannot abuse your body physically and expect God to simply reverse the destructive process that you have brought about by your abuse. When that abuse takes the form of substance abuse, it often affects the abuser mentally as well. Undoubtedly, the most serious consequence of all is the spiritual damage that a life of self-indulgence produces in an individual. It is not my purpose to specify one form of abuse as necessarily more serious than another. Rather, I am concerned that you understand that your body is the temple of the Holy Spirit of God (see 1 Corinthians 6:19-20). Therefore, it does make a difference what you do with your body and what you put into your body, because your body belongs to God. You and I cannot permanently forestall the aging process in our lives, but we certainly have an obligation not to speed it up.

3. Sickness Can Come from Satan.

In the story of Job we certainly see the fact that Satan put his hand against Job to cause both calamity and physical illness in his life. While God set a limit on the extent of Satan's ability to inflict this illness on Job, He nevertheless allowed Satan to do it. The Bible says, "Satan went forth from the presence of the Lord and smote Job with sore boils" (Job 2:7). Job was suffering, not because of sin in his own personal life, but because Satan had afflicted him. Again, that does not mean that all sickness is a direct result of Satan's activity. But this passage makes it clear that in some cases it certainly is. In Luke 13:11-13, we read the story of a woman who cried out to Jesus and asked Him to cast out the devil within her, and when He did, she was made well physically. Acts 10:38 refers to the healing ministry of Jesus and states that He healed those who were "oppressed of the devil." Even the Apostle Paul referred to his physical suffering as the act of Satan "to buffet me," referring to the fact that Satan was using that sickness to discourage him and wear him down.

4. Sickness Is Sometimes Allowed by God.

So, we see that sickness was allowed by God in the lives of both Job and Paul in order to accomplish His greater purpose. In the case of Job, God allowed Satan to put his hand against Job. But He also set a limit on what He would allow Satan to do and demanded that he not take Job's life. This truth brings great reassurance to us that if we are suffering as a believer, we can rest assured that God will not allow us to suffer beyond the limit that He has set. If you are suffering the consequences of sin in your life, you need to repent of that sin and turn away from it. But if you are suffering for a reason other than that, you can be assured that God in His sovereignty will not allow you to suffer beyond the point that He has set. The experiences of Job were actually designed by God as a lesson to Satan himself. Most of us will never be put in that position. But in Job's case, God understood that he was such a righteous man that even his personal and physical suffering would not cause him to lose his confidence in Him.

In the case of the Apostle Paul, God used his suffering to display

His glory. In so doing, Paul believed that he was actually sharing in the "sufferings of Christ" (2 Corinthians 1:5). For Paul, this was a cause for rejoicing. He was more than willing to allow God to accomplish His purposes in his life, even if it meant personal physical suffering.

THE SOLUTION TO SICKNESS

As we have seen, there are many reasons why people are sick. In some cases, their sickness is a direct result of a sinful lifestyle. But in other cases, it is merely a result of the aging process. For some, sickness is an attack of Satan. But in every case God sets sovereign limits on that suffering and overrules it for His own good purposes. If you are presently suffering from physical illness in your life, let me suggest the following steps for dealing with that sickness.

1. *Confess and Forsake Known Sin.*

Examine your heart and make sure you're not suffering because of deliberate sin in your life. If you are, confess that sin to God and forsake it. If you are ill because of a destructive habit that is destroying your physical body, you may not be able to undo all of the damage that has been done, but the sooner you quit, the better. Without making a complete break from that habit, you may never know the kind of health that you could have known had you quit.

You can continue to go through the routine of life pretending that your illness is not all that serious. But chances are that it will eventually take you. I can think of nothing more tragic than for a person to die prematurely because of a sinful habit that he or she knew was harmful but refused to give up. The psalmist put it like this, "Before I was afflicted I went astray: but now have I kept thy word" (Psalm 119:67). He acknowledged that his sinful lifestyle had led him astray and resulted in physical illness. But he had now come to a point of physical repentance and had returned to the Lord and was keeping His commandments. The longer you indulge in sinful habits, the more you will accelerate the process of sickness and death in your own body. The sooner you turn away from those habits, the more quickly you can hope to return to health.

2. *Pray in Faith for Your Healing.*

I believe that Scripture clearly teaches that we can come to God by faith and claim physical healing. I do not believe that we can demand it of God in every situation. But I am convinced that we can come boldly before the throne of grace and call upon God for healing.

One of the great promises in the Word of God is found in 1 John 5:14-15, which says, "And this is the confidence that we have in him, that, if we ask any thing according to his will, he heareth us: and if we know that he hear us, whatsoever we ask, we know that we have the petitions that we desired of him." This is a response of confidence in the goodness of God. There are many times in our lives that God responds with physical healing and a restoration of health. As the aging process continues, we cannot expect this to go on forever, this side of Heaven, but we can have the confidence that God does hear our prayers and delights in healing us.

The key to the balanced approach to this issue is understanding the importance of the phrase "according to his will." It is vitally important that we understand that healing is conditioned upon the will and purposes of God. Therefore, we must understand that there are multiple facets to this truth. When sickness results from sinful practices, that sickness may continue to have ongoing consequences in our lives even after we have repented. The drug addict who stops taking drugs cannot expect to be instantly cured of all of the consequences of drug abuse. But with repentance comes the cessation of that habit, which would have caused even greater damage if it had persisted. Another facet of truth is that when God answers the prayer of faith, He does so within the context of His will. The Bible does not tell us this to dampen our faith, but to balance it. I am convinced that God wants us to come to Him in faith and ask for His miraculous intervention on our behalf. But He does not guarantee healing based upon the degree of our faith. The healing response of God is conditioned both upon our faith and upon His will.

3. Trust in God to Do That Which Is Best.

There is a vast difference between trusting the sovereignty of God and fatalistically resigning oneself to sickness without any hope of change. For example, if you have been told that you have cancer, you can either resign yourself to the consequences and sit there and die or you can take every possible medical procedure to help cure the cancer and pray in faith asking God to heal you. I believe the latter option is the correct one.

All of us have seen many who have received their healing through prayer and medicine working hand in hand. With that in mind, the essence of the prayer of the believer ought to be:

Dear Lord, I know that You love me more than I love myself. I believe that Your purposes for my life are greater than my own could ever be. Therefore, I believe You will answer my prayer in the greatest way possible. I am asking You to heal me of this sickness. And I am trusting You to do what is best in my life.

When you pray like that, you will have come to a point of spiritual maturity where you are able to trust the sovereign purposes of God, while at the same time believing Him to move miraculously in your behalf. Your petition can be made in bold confidence, but also in the attitude of honest acceptance of God's ultimate will as best. Then you can rest in the calm assurance that Romans 8:28 is true, "And we know that all things work together for good to them that love God, to them who are called according to his purpose."

PART TWO

THE TRANSFORMATION

There hath not failed one word of all his good promise.

—1 KINGS 8:56

5

How to Master Your Mind

The mind is a marvelous thing. It operates like a personalized computer, filled with millions of bits of information. Virtually every action we commit is triggered by our mind. The Bible says, "As [a man] thinketh in his heart, so is he" (Proverbs 23:7). Everything that we think on can potentially affect our behavior for good or evil. That is why the mind is so crucial to proper behavior. A person who dwells on negative things will become negative and pessimistic. A person who focuses his or her attention on rotten thoughts will begin to do rotten things. By contrast, if we fill our minds with good and wholesome things, we will begin doing good things.

Recent psychological studies have shown the interrelation between thinking and behavior. We do what we think about, and what we think about, we do. If we are willing to let God cleanse our mind and fill it with wholesome thoughts, the results will be apparent in every area of life. But if we are unwilling to submit our thought-life to Him, we will continue to be shackled by guilt and by powerful, destructive habits. Temptation will overwhelm us because we are not armed against it. So, before looking more closely at these serious problems in the life of the believer, let's see what God's Word has to say about handling thoughts and mastering the mind.

The Apostle Paul put it this way:

> I beseech you therefore, brethren, by the mercies of God, that ye present your bodies a living sacrifice, holy, acceptable unto God, which is your reasonable service. And be not conformed to this world: but be ye transformed by the renewing of your mind, that ye may prove what is that good, and acceptable, and perfect, will of God. (Romans 12:1-2)

This familiar text is at once both profound and simple. The keys to Christian living are to present your body and renew your mind.

"But how do I do it?" you ask. Let's take a look at the marvelous truth in this passage.

The phrase "present your bodies" means that believers are to *yield* their bodies to Christ. The word *present* is a technical term in Greek meaning "to present for sacrifice." The believer is to dedicate himself to God in a deliberate and intentional manner, just as one would dedicate a sacrifice to God. In fact, Paul goes on to say that such an act of dedication is our "reasonable service."

The word *reasonable* (Greek, *logikos*) means "rational" or "logical." Thus, the only logical thing for believers to do is to present or dedicate themselves to the service of God. Therefore, the use of our bodies is characterized by conscious, intelligent, and consecrated devotion to the service of God.

Before you can mature in your walk with God, you must face the fact that your body belongs to God. Christ died for your sins and His blood has redeemed you from the clutches of Satan. Therefore, it does matter what you do with your body, because it is now not your own—it is God's.

The second aspect of this text refers to the "renewing of your mind." This is the process by which we are transformed from the world and into the image of Christ. The negative command "be not conformed" literally means "do not be formed or molded" to this world. The Phillips translation, "Don't let the world around you squeeze you into its own mold," is exactly correct.

The term *transformed* (Greek, *metamorphousthe*) comes from the same root words as *metamorphosis*, meaning an inward change that results in an outward transformation. When the sluggish old caterpillar goes through metamorphosis, it is transformed into the beautiful brightly colored butterfly. It has been changed.

This renewing of the mind is directly related to the new birth, which brings regeneration to the soul. When we are born again, we begin to think differently because we have had our spiritual sight illuminated by God. Therefore, the moral quality of our reason and activity is dramatically transformed by the power of God.

"This is fine," you say, "but how can I experience it?"

WRONG THOUGHTS

In this day of confusion and turmoil, people want to know how to find inner peace and strength. They are searching for a reality upon which to build their lives. In counseling with others, I have observed four basic thought patterns which I see as the major ones that are adversely affecting people today.

1. Thoughts of Immorality.

This may seem like a wide category, but it really is not. Almost every area of our society is permeated with immorality. Newspapers, magazines, movies, and television programs are saturated with an emphasis on the immoral. Temptation virtually leaps off the page into the mind. The battle for the mind and the subsequent battle for the body are being waged within every one of us.

Time and time again, I am asked, "Pastor, how can I keep my mind clean in a dirty world?" This question is being asked by good people who really care about their families and their relationship to God. The temptation to get caught up in immoral behavior is not something which affects only dirty-minded people. It can affect us all.

Jesus said that if we lust after someone in our hearts, we are as guilty of adultery as if we had committed it (see Matthew 5:28). Obviously, the act itself is more serious in its consequences than is the thought. But actions begin as thoughts in the mind. That is why the attitudes and intentions of the heart are viewed so seriously by God. If we can learn to deny thoughts of lust, we can control our actions toward the opposite sex.

The Bible makes it clear that thoughts of temptation are one of the realities of life. They are going to come into your mind as long as you are living on planet earth in a physical body of human flesh. But the ultimate problem is not in the temptation, but in yielding to it. D. L. Moody said it like this, "You can't keep a bird from flying over your head, but you sure can keep it from nesting in your hair!"

Some will object, arguing that they are free adults who can do what they want to do without doing wrong. I have heard people insist that they could read pornographic magazines, attend certain R-rated movies, or watch questionable cable television channels without being enticed into sin. Horsefeathers! That may sound acceptable to some, but it is nothing more than playing with fire.

Remember that sin is a process that begins in the mind. The entertainment of sinful thoughts in the mind feeds sinful attitudes in the heart and leads to sinful action and behavior in our lives. As someone once wrote:

> Sow a thought, reap an act;
> Sow an act, reap a habit;
> Sow a habit, reap a character;
> Sow a character, reap a destiny.

I think of David, the mighty warrior-king of Israel, who accidentally saw a woman bathing herself as he walked on the roof of his palace. The Bible says that David "saw a woman washing herself; and the woman was very beautiful to look upon, and David sent and inquired after the woman" (2 Samuel 11:2-3).

Notice the progression of David's sin. First, he saw her, then he gazed upon her, and finally he sought her out. Had he dealt with this sinful progression at any point, he could have stopped the process. Instead, he actually fostered the process by continuing to look. His curiosity and passion were aroused. He sent to find out her identity. This implicated others in his sinful desire. Eventually he spoke with her and clearly revealed his interest and intentions. Immorality begins in the mind. It is a thought long before it is an action.

2. Thoughts of Trouble

Some of us battle with negative and destructive thoughts in our minds. We imagine trouble even when trouble doesn't exist. When we let our minds become filled with all sorts of negative thinking, we become pessimistic about everything in life. If the kids are late coming home, we imagine that they have all been in an accident or that they have been up to no good. If the boss was grouchy at work that day, we toss and turn all night thinking about the possibility of being fired in the morning.

Our Lord dealt with this problem when He said, "Take therefore no thought for the morrow: for the morrow shall take thought for the things of itself" (Matthew 6:34). To "take thought" means to "worry" or "be anxious." Therefore, Jesus was telling His disciples not to worry about tomorrow because God would take care of them.

We often fill our minds with worry about food, drink, clothes, job, security, and the future. Our Lord reminds us that He will care for all these things and that we need not bother ourselves with worrying about them. If we cannot trust Him to meet our needs day by day, we will never be able to enjoy each new day. That is why He added the statement, "Sufficient unto the day is the evil thereof" (Matthew 6:34). By this, He meant that each day has enough trouble of its own without spoiling it by worrying about tomorrow.

The English word *worry* comes from an Anglo-Saxon term meaning "to strangle." When you worry, you strangle yourself. You strangle your spirit, mind, and soul with the anxieties of life. Worry keeps us from enjoying the blessings we have. It takes us beyond our immediate cares and overburdens us with the cares of a day which has not yet arrived.

Worry is an unrighteous imagination. It means taking on God's responsibility for the sovereign care of the world. It involves taking your life out of God's hands and putting it under your own control. Ultimately, worry is nothing more or less than doubting God. It is an affront to His love and care for us because it is an admission that we are not sure He really loves us.

3. *Thoughts of Criticism.*

Some people would never criticize anyone directly, but they are filled with criticism in their hearts. Criticism is often a reflection of bitterness within the soul. Every time I see someone criticizing someone else, I wonder what is wrong in that person's own life that is feeding that critical spirit.

I recall hearing a story about a father trying to get some work done while his small son kept insisting that they play together. After a while the father thought, *I've got to find something for my boy to do so I can get back to my work.* He picked up a magazine and thumbed through it until he found a picture of the world. Then he carefully tore out the picture and cut it into several pieces.

I'll make a puzzle out of this to keep him busy, the father thought. Handing the pieces to the boy, he announced, "Here, put this picture of the world back together, and when you are through I'll stop everything and play with you the rest of the day."

The dad thought the boy would never be able to fit all the pieces together. So the little fellow began to work, taking the pieces and taping them together. In just a few minutes he was finished and returned to his father. "How could you be finished already?" the dad asked.

"It was easy," the boy said. "On the back of the world was a picture of a man. When I got the man together right, the world was right too!"

The reason many people complain that their world is not right is because they are not right. Only when your heart is changed will your criticism subside. A critical, fault-finding spirit will destroy your life and your relationships with others. It sours everything about you and drives others away.

4. Thoughts of Torment.

Sometimes our minds are bombarded with thoughts of torment. These are disturbing thoughts that seem to come upon us unconsciously. We are tormented by past failures or by future worries. The emotional torment of the mind is a terrible thing to experience. It robs us of joy and perpetuates fear and anxiety in every area of life.

I remember talking once to a man who was troubled by deep anxieties, but could not specifically pinpoint what they were. He lost sleep nearly every night worrying about worrying. This is especially difficult for Christians who know they are not supposed to worry. Such a state of mind can actually drive someone to the edge of insanity.

No matter how simple or how complex your troubles may seem to be, God has an answer to your problems. He is the God of love and peace, who fills our minds with those positive qualities which can help us overcome wrong thoughts, attitudes, and actions.

RENEWING YOUR MIND

I have found four simple steps to be very helpful in my own life. These steps have enabled me to keep my mind freshly focused on the things of God. I think you, too, will find that they will help keep your mind under the control of the Holy Spirit.

1. Commit Your Mind to the Son of God.

God has a wonderful plan for every aspect of your life. That plan includes the provision of His perfect peace to keep your mind sound and stable. The prophet Isaiah put it like this, "Thou wilt keep him in perfect peace, whose mind is stayed on thee" (Isaiah 26:3). The mind that is committed to God is "stayed" (resting) upon Him.

If you are struggling with thoughts of temptation or torment, commit your mind afresh to God. Determine to let Him have total control to keep your mind from the bombardment of wrong thoughts. But let's not forget we have a part in it too. We must remain alert ourselves to guard our minds from the garbage of ideas that Satan will send our way. If we don't, they can ever so quickly overcome us.

Recently I heard a story on the radio about a seventy-year-old man who lived on the streets of Chattanooga, Tennessee. He was discovered by a city worker one day under a pile of trash in the city dump, just before it was to be taken to be burned in the incinerator. After rescuing him, the worker asked how he got there. The man said, "All I remember is that I went to sleep in a pile of trash and the next thing I knew I woke up in the dump!" Likewise, we cannot afford to sleep for one minute and let evil thoughts dirty our minds.

A clean mind comes in two ways. First, we must clear out all the wrong thinking, and second, we must fill our minds with the truth of God. The same God who saved your soul also saved your mind. You belong to Him now. So, let Him have control.

Just as we need to cleanse our bodies with soap and water, so we need regularly to cleanse our minds in the Word of God with a fresh commitment to Jesus Christ. There is nothing more refreshing than a clean, clear mind.

Have you ever noticed how good it feels when you first come out of the shower with your skin so clean that it actually squeaks as you rub your hand across it. Fresh! Pure! Cleansed! In just the same way, when our minds have been washed in repentance and committed to thoughts that are pleasing to our Lord, we can know the blessing of having our minds fresh, pure, "squeaky clean."

2. Feed Your Mind on the Word of God.

The psalmist said, "Thy word have I hid in my heart, that I might not sin against thee" (Psalm 119:11). When we feed on the Word of God, we can expect to grow into spiritual maturity. Life operates on a simple principle: Whatever I feed is going to grow and whatever I starve is going to die.

If you want to overcome bad thoughts, stop feeding them into your mind. Stay away from those things which lead you away from God. Fill your mind with those things that will help you to grow in your relationship to God.

Our Lord described His followers as those who "hunger and thirst after righteousness" (Matthew 5:6). The more you learn to hunger for His Word, the more you will be filled with His truth. Only then will you be truly satisfied within your soul.

3. Fill Your Mind with the Things of God.

It's a fact—all of us are going to fill our minds with something. Although many are accused of being "empty-headed," no one is actually without something constantly in his or her mind.

The Apostle Paul said, "Finally, brethren, whatsoever things are true . . . honest . . . just . . . pure . . . lovely . . . of good report; if there be any virtue, and if there be any praise, think on these things" (Philippians 4:8). Notice the imperative command is "to think," "to focus one's attention" on the good things of God. Things that are virtuous and praiseworthy alone are worthy of the attention of the believer. When you fill your mind with good things, you will be amazed at the good things that will come to your life.

William James, the famous American psychologist, developed what he called the "as if" theory. It merely states that if you think and act "as if" conditions are one way, eventually they will become that way in your life. I don't totally agree with him on this idea, but I do agree that what we fill our minds with is what we have a strong tendency to become. Perhaps that is what the Holy Spirit meant when He moved upon Paul to say, "Let this mind be in you, which was also in Christ Jesus" (Philippians 2:5). To think on Christ is to move closer to becoming like Him.

4. Focus Your Mind on the Will of God.

The ultimate goal of the Christian life is to glorify God by doing His will. That means finding His will according to His Word and doing it with all your heart. The whole purpose of renewing our minds is that we "may prove what is that good, and acceptable, and perfect, will of God" (Romans 12:2).

God has a plan for your life which encompasses every detail of your life. As you seek to live for Him, He will reveal the specific details of that plan to you. The will (Greek, *thelēma*) of God is that which God has decreed for you. The verb *"that you may prove"* is an expression of purpose. It means that if you live according to God's purpose you will prove it to be good, acceptable, and perfect.

There are several aspects of God's will for our lives which are clearly stated in Scripture. He wills for us to repent of our sins and receive Christ by faith in our hearts. He wills for us to grow in His Word and to be a witness of His salvation. He wills for us to be involved with other believers through His Church. Beyond this, the specific details of His will are normally worked out one step at a time as we serve Him.

It does not matter so much *where* God wants you in His will, but *that* He wants you in His will. Wherever He leads you, what really matters is that you allow Him to lead you one step at a time.

The Bible promises that when we stop worrying and start praying, "the peace of God . . . shall keep [our] hearts and minds through Christ Jesus" (Philippians 4:7). Being kept (literally, "guarded") by God's peace brings security and stability to our innermost being. So keep your mind filled with God's truth and focused on His direction, and you will find yourself being kept each day in His perfect peace.

6

Say Goodbye to Guilt

Some of the most difficult thoughts to control stem from a troubled conscience. Guilt is a form of self-judgment and self-condemnation that we often impose upon ourselves. It produces anxiety, inferiority, fear, and worry. Guilt is a major factor in psychological and emotional problems. If unresolved, it can lead to such self-destructive acts as suicide.

In Psalm 32, we read the words of a brokenhearted man who is struggling with the problem of guilt. In these verses, we read the confession of David as he faced the sin in his own life.

> Blessed is he whose transgression is forgiven, whose sin is covered. Blessed is the man unto whom the Lord imputeth not iniquity, and in whose spirit there is no guile. When I kept silence, my bones waxed old through my roaring all the day long. For day and night thy hand was heavy upon me: my moisture is turned into the drought of summer. (Psalm 32:1-4)

David was one of the greatest men in all of Scripture. But despite his successes, he had just suffered a tragic defeat that involved a triple transgression. He had committed adultery with Bathsheba, arranged for the murder of her husband, Uriah, and had lived a lie before the people of Israel. Though initially he seemed to get away with his sin, David confessed that the hand of God was against him day and night. Because he was a man of God, he could not sin and get away with it in his own conscience. He was deeply disturbed by the reality of guilt, and it took its toll on him mentally, emotionally, and physically. He felt as though he were losing his strength and that he was about to die.

If you have ever felt guilt like that, you can begin to understand the terrible inner pain that David felt. Guilt can take away your sleep, ruin your life, and destroy your relationships with others. Many times I have wondered why a certain individual suddenly seemed to look so terrible. Normally healthy men and women who had no apparent physical problems seemed old and worn before their time. Often, I would discover that they were burdened down with terrible guilt inside and it was beginning to show in their physical appearance. Guilt can take its toll in many different ways.

If you are struggling with the guilt of some past failure in your life, I want to point you to some principles of truth that I believe can help you. No one on earth can undo the wrong that was done in the past. You cannot go back and relive that moment in your life. The mistake was made, the sin was committed, and the guilt is an automatic consequence of it. But the guilt that God gives you is not intended to destroy you. It is the spiritual and psychological reaction that He uses to draw us unto Himself. Though it is a consequence of our sin, it is not a consequence with which we must live for the rest of our lives. The same Savior who died for our sins also died for our guilt and wants to set us free from it. But if you do not let Him set you free, you will experience depression produced by guilt. Your conscience will become bound by that guilt, and you will find yourself unable to enjoy the blessings of life.

SOURCES OF GUILT

1. *Others: Imposed Guilt.*

People are experts at putting others on guilt trips. They can actually manipulate others through guilt. Psychologists call this *manipulative guilt*. In other words, people make you feel so guilty that they can get you to do whatever they want. For example, Johnny comes to the dinner table and Mother orders him to eat his spinach. Johnny, like most little boys, hates spinach. He doesn't want to eat it. So mother begins to tell him about the little children who are starving all over the world. While he may think, "What does my eating spinach have to do with starving children all over the world?" he will assume that Mother must be right, and because he feels guilty, he will eat the spinach anyway. Mother has manipulated him by using guilt.

Teenagers are experts at using manipulative guilt. For example, a teenager will say, "Dad, Billy down the street got a brand-new car from his dad for graduation. I wish I had a dad like that!" That is manipulative guilt. It is the same tactic which people use with each other when they imply, "If you really loved me, you would do this . . ." These kinds of guilt-manipulating tactics are provoked by selfishness on the part of those who use them. They are not expressions of genuine guilt, but are rather, socially or psychologically imposed guilt.

2. Satan: Condemning Guilt.

The Bible calls Satan the "accuser of the brethren" (Revelation 12:10). This is Satan's greatest tactic to get us to give up on our relationship with God. He uses the trick of accusation to turn us to self-condemnation. In essence, he condemns our conscience when we make a mistake and implies that we have no hope of ever making it right in our spiritual lives again.

You need to remember that the Bible calls Satan a liar and the father of all lies. Every time that he attempts to condemn you or put you on a guilt trip, you have to determine not to listen to his lies. Now it may well be true that you have made a mistake and are guilty as a result of that mistake. But the guilt that comes from God is not intended to destroy you, but rather to draw you closer to Him. Satan uses guilt in a totally destructive manner by attempting to get us in such a state of self-condemnation that we are of no real value in serving God at all. That kind of guilt manipulation is not from God.

3. God: Gracious Guilt.

The guilt that God sends into our lives is an expression of His grace toward us. He cannot sit back and merely allow us to continue in sin until we destroy ourselves. Therefore, He begins to convict us through His Holy Spirit that we should turn away from sin. When we refuse to do so, and persist in our sins, He then allows that guilt to grow. This is the kind of guilt that David experienced. It is as though God were saying, "Listen, I know that you have sinned, and that sin is causing a separation between us. But I want you to repent of it and return to Me." That is what real guilt is all about. True guilt comes from God through our conscience as we are being convicted by the Holy Spirit who dwells within us. That guilt is designed to drive us back into a right relationship with God.

As strange as it may sound, you can actually become excited about being guilty. When you are convicted by the Spirit of God, it is obvious that you are a child of God. When the Holy Spirit within us is so sensitive that He reacts to all sin in our lives by producing the kind of guilt that will cause us to repent, then we can rest assured that God is in control of our lives.

Unfortunately, there are those whose consciences have been seared with sin. They have sinned so many times and suppressed the guilt that results from such sin to the point that their consciences are dulled towards sin. Like it or not, we live in such a society today. Many people have had their consciences seared by a lifetime of deliberate and rebellious sin. Only when you are convicted about the guilt of your sin will you do what is necessary to resolve that guilt and confess that sin to God.

I am convinced that God did not intend for you to carry the burden of guilt for the rest of your life. All of us have failed in one way or another, and we all stand guilty before God. While our guilty conscience condemns us, the Bible reminds us that God is greater than our hurts and that He will defend us on the merits of the blood of Jesus Christ which has been shed for us. Thus He gives us the gift of gracious guilt to awaken us to our need for repentance and to turn us back to Him.

IMPROPER RESPONSES TO GUILT

How you respond to guilt determines what it can do to you. If you allow yourself to become so overwhelmed by guilt that you are driven to self-despair and even self-destruction, then it is obvious that you have responded improperly. On the other hand, if you merely sublimate that guilt into the unconscious depths of your mind and thereby sear your conscience, you are also making a choice which is headed toward self-destruction. There are three improper ways to respond to guilt.

1. Refuse It.

Some people just try to block guilt out of their minds. They refuse to feel guilty about anything. They have suppressed that guilt and seared their consciences to the point that they can continue sinning and not ever really be deeply convicted about it. This is certainly the case of mass murderers, serial rapists, pathological liars, and others who engage in persistent criminal behavior. Those who refuse to face sin in their lives have the attitude that they have never been guilty because they have never been wrong. They are like the basketball player who charges against his opponent, knocks him down flat, and stands there shocked that the referee has called a foul. When people react that way, they refuse to accept guilt. We find that attitude in Adam when he blamed his sin on Eve. And we also find that attitude in Cain when he refused to take responsibility for murdering his brother Abel.

After Adam and Eve's sin, God had apparently made it clear that they could approach Him with a blood sacrifice. The Bible tells us that Abel was a "keeper of sheep" and that Cain was a "tiller of the ground" (Genesis 4:2). In time, Abel brought a lamb to God for sacrifice while Cain attempted to bring the fruit of the ground. The Scriptures tell us that God accepted the blood sacrifice of Abel but not the vegetable sacrifice of Cain. A reasonable inference is that this was because the latter represented an offering of self-works.

When God would not accept his offering, Cain became angry with God and eventually took it out on his brother. Even in his anger, God gave him an opportunity to correct the problem. He told Cain, "If thou doest well, shalt thou not be accepted?" (Genesis 4:7). The Hebrew text of this Old Testament passage even implies that the option of an appropriate sin offering was at hand by stating that "sin lieth at the door" and Cain refused to give it.

The audacity of Cain's rebellion was incredible. He refused to acknowledge his own failure, rejected the opportunity to resolve the problem, and turned around and killed his brother out of anger and hostility. It is no wonder that God dealt so severely with Cain in holding him accountable for the murder of his brother. Even under the pronouncement of his condemnation, Cain asked that the sentence not be too severe, rather than confessing his sin and throwing himself on the mercy of God. He is a perfect picture of a person who has refused to face up to the issue of sin and guilt in his life.

2. Abuse It.

There are also those people who seem to be the opposite of those who refuse to face guilt. These are the people who are so overwrought with guilt that they condemn themselves for everything that ever went wrong in life. They have the "I did it" mentality. They feel that everything that has gone wrong is their fault. I used to have a little puppy like that. One day he tore a bedspread and I had to scold him. From then on, every time I walked into the house he would put his tail between his legs, bend his head down, and crouch on the floor. I guess it was his way of trying to say that he was sorry for tearing the bedspread when he was a puppy. I tried to explain to him that I had forgiven him and that all was forgotten, but he never seemed to get the point. Some people are like that as well! They seem to go through life feeling sorry for themselves and blaming themselves for everything that goes wrong. Unfortunately, they never come to experience the wonderful cleansing and forgiveness which God has made available to them.

This is the mentality of abusive guilt. I am convinced that many people almost enjoy abusing themselves with guilt because they feel that in some way it will help atone for the wrong that they have done. But I remind you that there is nothing that you could ever do to pay for the sins in your life. This is why Jesus Christ died for those sins.

3. Excuse It.

There is another category of people who are willing to acknowledge that they have sinned, but then try to excuse their sin as though they are not responsible for it. Several years ago I dealt with a man who had committed an act of cold-blooded murder. As he described to me the details of that murder, he began to ask about the consequences of what he had done. As we talked together, I did not sense any remorse or guilt in him at all. So I interrupted him with the question, "How do you handle the guilt of this murder?"

The man looked at me and actually said, "Oh, I don't feel guilty. It was God's time for him to go anyway. God just used me as an instrument to bring about His will." I asked him to leave my office, fearing he might think my time had come.

This man had so rationalized his guilt that he could acknowledge the crime that he had committed and then excuse the whole thing by blaming it on God. Over the years, I have heard more people use this tactic than any other in trying to avoid the problem of guilt. I have listened to husbands who have blamed all of their problems on their wives and wives who have blamed all of their problems on their husbands. I have listened to young people explain to me that their parents made them run away from home. I have heard people blame things on God, the Devil, and the church, but in every one of these cases they never came to grips with their own problems. Excusing your sin and its guilt will never resolve the problem.

GETTING RID OF GUILT

Freedom from guilt is not something that we can merely develop within ourselves. It is not something that we can resolve by suppressing it into our subsconscious minds or blaming it on someone else.

Rather, guilt is something that must be acknowledged, the mistake that produced it must be confessed, and our lives must become transformed by the grace of God's forgiveness. David understood this as he expressed his own inner turmoil in Psalm 32; the turning point came when he finally said, "I acknowledged my sin unto thee, and mine iniquity have I not hid" (Psalm 32:5). He confessed his sin, and it was then that he experienced God's forgiveness for that sin. By the time that he finished the psalm, he was able to "be glad in the Lord and rejoice" (Psalm 32:11). David had experienced the tremendous blessing of God's forgiveness and the cleansing that it can bring to the heart of the individual transgressor. He knew what it was to fail, but he also knew what it was to be forgiven.

The key to getting rid of guilt is to recognize that only God can take it away and cleanse your conscience. When we understand that we have not only sinned against individuals, but against God Himself, then we will begin to understand why it is so important that we have God's forgiveness. I am convinced that David fully recognized this. He did not try to blame his sin on Bathsheba, or on his circumstances, or on the fact that Nathan the prophet had confronted him. He was accepting the full responsibility for his sin and confessing it to God. In so doing, he was able to admit his need and find God's solution.

In his prayer of confession, David said, "Mine iniquity have I not hid . . . I will confess my transgressions unto the Lord" (Psalm 32:5). David recognized that his guilt was the conviction of the Spirit of God at work in his soul. He accepted the truth of that conviction and acknowledged his sin to God. As a result, he could say, "Thou forgavest the iniquity of my sin."

It is one thing to understand intellectually that God is willing to forgive your sins, but it is another matter to accept His forgiveness. Many times our own conscience so condemns us that we think that by remaining in a state of morbid contrition we are somehow atoning for the sin that we have committed. Unfortunately, such an attitude is contrary to all that the Bible teaches. The Scripture makes it clear that the only atonement for sin is the blood of Jesus Christ. He alone can cleanse and He alone can forgive.

An army chaplain told the story of reaching a young man just before he died on the battlefield in Vietnam. It was evident as he held the boy's hand that he had been mortally wounded and these were the last moments of his life, so the chaplain tried to console him the best he knew how. "Son," he said, "is there anything I can do for you?" "No," the young soldier replied as the memories of his life passed before his eyes. "Sir, what I need now is someone who can 'undo' some things for me." That's what Jesus Christ is all about: He can undo the errors of our past. It is our responsibility to accept that forgiveness by faith and to believe that the whole matter has been settled at the Cross.

One of the most amazing features of David's confession in Psalm 32 is the triumphal manner in which the psalm ends. First, he acknowledged his security in God's forgiveness by saying, "Thou art my hiding place; thou shalt preserve me from trouble; thou shalt compass me about with songs of deliverance" (v. 7). David understood that God was the source of his security and his deliverance. Second, he also understood that the mercy of the Lord was cause for rejoicing. He announced, "Be glad in the Lord, and rejoice, ye righteous: and shout for joy, all ye that are upright in heart" (v. 11). What a triumphal ending to a psalm of confession and a prayer for forgiveness! David recognized that having repented of sins, he had every right to rejoice in the freedom of forgiveness.

If you have been struggling with the weight of guilt upon your soul to the point that you can hardly sleep at night or barely make it through the day, rest assured that God's forgiveness is available to you. You may have felt as though your heart would burst or your mind would crack because of guilt. You need not struggle any longer. God's grace is so great and His forgiveness is so full that He offers you complete pardon if you will accept the Cross as sufficient payment for your sins. Like David, you have every right to be glad in the Lord, rejoice, and shout for joy. The New Testament puts it this way, "If we confess our sins, he is faithful and just to forgive us our sins, and to cleanse us from all unrighteousness" (1 John 1:9). When you acknowledge your mistake, confess it to God, and repent of it, your soul is cleansed and the weight and guilt of that sin is gone forever. God's forgiveness is an everlasting forgiveness. When He forgives, He forgets! So why don't you?

7

You Can Handle Your Habits

Not long ago, as I was driving to the office one morning, I tuned in a religious talk show on the radio. On this particular day, a counselor was taking calls from listeners. I'll admit I hadn't paid too much attention, knowing that I would do my own share of counseling that day, until I heard one man's voice. You could tell he was weeping on the other end of the line, as he said, "Sir, I'm being destroyed. My life is absolutely being devastated. You see, it's something I've gotten involved with. Up until now, I've been able to hide it from most everyone else, but it's about to cost me everything I've ever wanted or worked for. My problem is, I'm hooked on cocaine. It's got me so bad, I can't live a day or rest a night without thinking about it. At first, I thought it was just a habit, but now it's more than that. Now it's my life, and I'm about to lose my mind because of it."

As I heard this poor man, my heart went out to him. I was reminded that he is not alone, for I am convinced that there are countless others who are in the grip of some destructive habit they can't seem to shake. It has become ingrained into their lifestyle, and Satan is using it as a stronghold to wreck their happiness and all that God intended for them to have. I honestly believe it can happen to anyone. When it does, it can become so much a part of people's lives that it sears their consciences and destroys their sensitivity to its wrongness. They convince themselves that they are trapped and there is no way out, so they'll just have to learn to live with it. Of course, that is simply not true.

Destructive habits in people's lives may vary greatly from one person to another. Some are hooked on drugs, while others are addicted to alcohol. Some, like this poor man, are enslaved to cocaine, while others are living in illicit sexual sins. Sometimes these destructive habits involve such socially accepted practices as gossiping, boasting, or just downright pride. No matter what the problem, the end result is still the same. A habitual sin has a hold on your life and it won't seem to let you go. Instead of your having the habit—the habit has you!

The Book of Hebrews tells us to "lay aside every weight, and the sin which doth so easily beset us" (Hebrews 12:1). In the context of the verse, the writer is using the illustration of one who is running a race. Wanting to make the fastest time possible, the runner lays aside anything which might slow him down in the race. Just as it would be ridiculous for us to run a race carrying a concrete block on our shoulders, it is equally ridiculous for us to attempt to run the race of the Christian life bogged down by a destructive habit.

Whether anyone else knows about that sin is not the real issue. You know about it, and it is destroying you. That means that you are the only one who can ultimately deal with it effectively. If you want to live a victorious Christian life, you must face the fact that Satan has a grip on your life. If you have been regenerated by the Spirit of God, then God lives within you. Your life is not the domain of Satan any longer. You belong to God and have been indwelt by His Spirit. But even as a believer, you can still struggle against both the flesh and the powers of spiritual wickedness (see Ephesians 6:12).

Realize what Satan is doing to you. Once you committed your life to Christ, Satan lost his control over you. You have been snatched from the gates of Hell and delivered into the Kingdom of Heaven. But now, Satan may be trying to do all that he can to destroy your testimony, negate your faith, and wreck your mind. He will come bringing his temptation, attacking you at your weakest point. Once you give in to that temptation to sin, it will return again and again. As you continue to succumb, that sin becomes a habit in your life. In time, that habit becomes your lifestyle itself. Then is when Satan comes along and begins to accuse your soul. "How can you claim to be a born-again Christian and live like this?" he begins to ask. "You are no better than those who have never been saved," he suggests. "In fact, perhaps you have never been saved in the first place!"

Once you begin thinking like that, you become almost worthless from a spiritual standpoint. A Christian who is filled with doubt and confusion because of a sinful habit in his life will never be able to put forth the spiritual effort and energy to serve God effectively. D. L. Moody once said, "I have never known God to use a discouraged person." That is true, no matter what the cause of discouragement may be. But it is especially true when we are discouraged because we are being defeated by habitual sins.

When you became a Christian, God entered your soul. He adopted you as His child and made you an heir of the Kingdom of Jesus Christ. But despite all that God has done for us, He does not eradicate our fleshly nature this side of Heaven. That means that you and I still have the potential of committing sin and that sin has the potential of becoming a habit in our lives.

There are two types of habitual sin. The first is unconscious sin, such as gossiping. I am convinced that most people who struggle with this sin do not deliberately intend to malign others. They do it unconsciously and yet maliciously. When one struggles with unconscious sin, he or she must be confronted deliberately in order to bring the conscious mind to bear upon the sinful habit.

Second, there are deliberate sins which we consciously commit. These are usually related to fleshly urges within us, like drinking, drugs, or adultery. In order to overcome physically related sins, one must learn to deny the flesh. When someone is trapped in such a sin, that person's body will become accustomed to experiencing that sinful desire. Though a very difficult battle may ensue, we will see later how believers can learn to overcome sins of the flesh.

The ultimate tragedy of habitual sin is that it leaves the participant in bondage. It is as though Satan were wrapping you up like a mummy. The first few loops of sin seem harmless enough, but they are just the first steps. In time, Satan has wrapped up your entire life in bondage to him. You begin to feel trapped and incapable of throwing off that bondage. It is at such a point that many people stop trying to deal with their sin at all. They simply rationalize to themselves that this is the way life is and there is nothing they can do about it. Tragically, they resign themselves to a life of bondage to some damaging habit.

REASONS PEOPLE REMAIN IN BONDAGE

As a pastor, I have often questioned why people allow themselves to remain in bondage to sin once they see its awful consequences in their lives. One would think that they would want to do whatever they could to throw it off. But like a great yoke of bondage, that sin seems to have weighted them down. They have so capitulated to it that they have lost all hope of deliverance. In counseling with people, I have found that there are basically four reasons why they remain in bondage to sin.

1. They Lack Understanding.

Many Christians simply don't understand that they don't have to put up with such bondage in their lives. They do not seem to understand that Satan does not have an automatic hold on their lives. Now that you belong to God, the potential for victory is within your grasp. The Bible says, "Whatsoever is born of God overcometh the world: and this is the victory that overcometh the world, even our faith" (1 John 5:4-5). Christ has already won the victory over Satan, sin, and temptation. The Scriptures tell us that in Him we are "more than conquerors" (Romans 8:37). All of the resources of Jesus Christ are available to His children in order to overcome the Evil One. When Jesus died on Calvary, He put our sins to death. All of the wrath of God against those sins was poured out at that time. When our Lord arose from the dead, He arose triumphant over those sins. The victory has already been won!

2. They Don't Realize That the Victory Is within Them.

You don't have to depend upon a pastor, priest, or rabbi in order to get the victory over a habit controlling your life. If you know Christ as your Savior, and He dwells within you, then the potential for victory is already within you. The Bible says, "Greater is he that is in you, than he that is in the world" (1 John 4:4).

When you became a child of God, you became a child of the King. The victory you need has already been settled at Calvary. The Holy Spirit who indwells you can empower you to overcome any temptation that you face in life. You have all the resources within you that are necessary to overcome any sinful habit. Imagine that you are living in England and go into a local bank for a loan. You walk in and ask for a loan of one thousand dollars. If you are willing to put up enough collateral, they just might loan you the money. But what a difference it would make if Prince Charles himself were to walk into that same bank and ask to borrow a thousand dollars. Because he is royalty, they would instantly make any arrangements necessary to lend him the money. Christian friend, could I remind you that you too are a child of the King? You don't have to go through life like a spiritual beggar.

Unfortunately, that is what most of us do. We keep begging God for the things that He has already promised to give us. We tend to approach Him with a timidity that implies, "Lord, you really don't want to do this for me, do you?" By contrast, the Bible assures that God wants to answer our prayers and meet our needs in order to show Himself powerful on our behalf. If you want to overcome some habitual sin, you need to realize that the power of God dwells within your innermost being and that you have within you already all the resources necessary in order to do it.

3. They Lack Confidence in Their Own Spiritual Nature.

Whenever sin enters our lives, it draws our attention away from Christ and His indwelling Spirit. This causes a lack of spiritual self-esteem. We get down on ourselves and begin condemning ourselves as viciously as Satan would condemn us. While it is important for us to be convicted of our sin, we must also not allow that conviction to sentence us to a life of self-condemnation. The Bible promises, "There is therefore now no condemnation to them which are in Christ Jesus, who walk not after the flesh, but after the Spirit" (Romans 8:1). Once the Spirit of God takes control of your life and you are able to resist the Devil and deny the flesh, you should feel freedom and release because your sin has been paid for by Jesus Christ. However, as long as there remains habitual sin in your life, it will rob you of the freedom of spirit which God has intended for you to experience. You will remain in a feeling of self-condemnation instead of realizing confidence in your own spiritual nature.

Satan delights to cause us to view ourselves inadequately even though we are in Christ Jesus. That is why many people lack spiritual self-confidence. I'm not talking about the kind of self-confidence we drum up on our own. I personally do not place total confidence in Richard Lee. But I can place that kind of confidence in Jesus Christ who lives within me. I have the assurance of His Spirit who indwells my heart. Therefore the spiritual confidence that fills our hearts is produced by the Spirit of God Himself.

I believe that many people remain in bondage to sin because they have no real confidence in themselves or in God at all. They have allowed a habit to take root in their hearts, and they think they can't get rid of it. Tragically, they believe this lie of Satan and are robbed of the delivering power that is literally within them.

4. They Don't Want to Give It Up.

I realize this is a strong indictment to make, but I am convinced that there are those who never overcome temptation or break habitual sins because they simply do not want to. They have given in to this sin for so long, and enjoy it so much, that they will not make the kind of commitment that is necessary to break with it and give it up. They harbor that habit because it feeds the desires of their flesh. Often they will even excuse themselves by saying, "The Devil made me do it," when in reality the Devil cannot make you sin. He can certainly tempt you and try every trick in the book to get you to stumble and fall, but he cannot make you commit the act itself. That is a decision that you make, and it is an option that you must learn to reject.

HOW CAN I FIND DELIVERANCE?

Despite the serious hold habitual sin has on some lives, so much that some actually desire to stay beneath its power, there are those who seek deliverance. Many times I have spent long hours in prayer with people whose hearts were broken over problems with habits that gripped their lives. They have come seeking a direction, and it has been my privilege to share with them principles that help them to be set free.

I think the first thing that a person must do in successfully handling a habit is to *recognize the need to change*. Most of us will never even try to change unless we feel we have a serious need to. Who likes the bother of changing his or her way of living? Who wants to go through the effort if it's not absolutely necessary? Not many of us. We all normally like to live as we have been living until we find there is a serious problem in our lifestyle.

Understand this: Habitual sin is a serious problem! It is not only a problem that can wreck your family, social, and personal life, but it will also ultimately destroy your relationship with your heavenly Father. God cannot tolerate sin. It is against His nature. Never forget that God is a holy God and that anything evil we hold in our lives, sinful habits included, separates us from God. You might be convinced to treat sin lightly, but make no mistake—it is deadly. David said, "If I regard iniquity in my heart, the Lord will not hear me" (Psalm 66:18). The word *"regard"* (Hebrew, *rā'â*, literally, "see") means "to approve." Simply stated, if we give our approval to our sinful habits, God will not have fellowship with us. Therefore, the need for change is evident.

Second, we should *confess our sinful habits to the Lord*. Confession is in reality the recognition of one's sin to another. When we genuinely confess our sins we are agreeing with God that they are wrong. It's not only saying we are sorry for our mistake, but it is also seeing that sin as God sees it.

Repentance (Greek, *metanoia*) is a change of attitude that leads to a change of action. Genuine repentance results from true conviction of sin in which we see it the way God sees it and we learn to hate it in the way He hates it. When that happens, the habit, which at one time seemed to bring such satisfaction into our lives, is now repugnant to us and holds nothing that we desire.

A number of years ago, during my first pastorate, there was an elderly lady in the church who invited our family to her house for an evening meal. Of course, having just started my ministry there, and knowing that the lady was a longtime member, I made every effort to assure her that we could go. The night came, and after arriving at the house we sat down for the meal. I could not believe what I saw. Sitting in the middle of the table was a large bowl of collard greens. Now if you don't know what collard greens are, don't feel alone. They are something like turnip greens, but oh, so much stronger in their taste. On each side of the big bowl were plates of biscuits. Suddenly it occurred to me that this *was* the meal. The only meal. Needless to say, my fears were true.

Being the polite pastor I am, I stomached down the first plate, and our hostess quickly filled it up again. "Oh, Pastor," she said, "I'm glad you like it so much. Here's another plateful." By that time I was just about as green as her collard greens! After I suffered through the final helping, she kindly sent a plate home with me. You know what was in it, don't you? You guessed it—more collards! I hate to admit it, but somehow on the way home, I accidentally dropped the plate and spilled my prize. They tell me that for six weeks after that, our neighborhood had the sickest dogs in town. I understood exactly how those dogs felt. I was so ill the next day that even now the thought of collard greens makes me sick.

What has that got to do with sin? Well, if we ever understand what sin is, and how sickening it is to God, even the very thought of it will sicken us too. We will quickly confess and repent of it because we will hate it in the same way God hates it.

Next, *make your thoughts captive unto Christ*. One of the most powerful statements in Scripture regarding overcoming habitual sin is found in 2 Corinthians 10:4-5:

> For the weapons of our warfare are not carnal, but mighty through God to the pulling down of strong holds; casting down imaginations,

and every high thing that exalteth itself against the knowledge of God, and bringing into captivity every thought to the obedience of Christ.

This passage clearly states that our war against the flesh begins in the mind. That is why our weapons for conquest are spiritual and not material. The "strong holds" of which this passage speaks are those areas in which Satan has become entrenched in our lives. In describing this conflict, Paul tells us that they can only be cast down by "bringing into captivity" every thought in obedience to Christ. We are literally to capture our thoughts and focus them upon our obedient servitude to the Lord Jesus.

As a young man I was faced with many moral decisions, as we all are. Often the areas of my decisions would seem to be rather gray. Perhaps I desired to do a particular deed or attend a particular function but realized that, although it would violate none of the acceptable values of our society, I still questioned it in my heart. How was I to determine what was right or wrong for me? Well, one day as I was discussing it with my mother, she said to me, "Richard, if you can picture Jesus doing what you are about to do, then do it. If not, then don't!" From that day on, I've tried to live by that rule.

Can you picture Jesus participating in your habit? If not, you need to bring your mind into captivity to that thought and each time you are tempted, say to yourself, "Would Jesus do this? If not, I won't!" Then each time you deny the habit, God will strengthen you to pull down that stronghold that has its grip on your life.

Finally, you must be willing to *resist the Devil*. The Bible urges us, "Submit yourselves therefore to God. Resist the devil, and he will flee from you" (James 4:7). *Resist* is a defensive term. It means that we are to stand against our enemy, the Devil. Remember, we are in a war, and you can never be neutral with your enemy.

Notice also that this verse tells us that if we resist Satan he will flee from us. Think of that! We have power over him through Christ. If that is true, which it is, then Satan is not our problem with sinful habits. We are the problem. That is why if you are giving in to those things which are destroying your life, you must decide the issue. The decision is up to you. If you are willing to do what is necessary, the power of God within you will enable you to overcome them. Everything you need for complete and final victory is available through Jesus Christ. Take Him at His word, put His power into action in your life, and you will be set free.

8

Dare to Tackle Temptation

From the day we are born until we leave this physical world, we have a constant companion called temptation. Whether or not we sense its presence, temptation is always there stalking us like a lion stalking his prey. No matter how long you have walked with God, temptation is always a potential danger in your life.

But I have good news for you. God understands the pressure of our temptations and He has made provision for our escape. The Bible says, "There hath no temptation taken you but such as is common to man: but God is faithful, who will not suffer you to be tempted above that ye are able; but will with the temptation also make a way to escape, that ye may be able to bear it" (1 Corinthians 10:13).

Isn't that a marvelous thought! God knows us so well that He not only knows us personally, but He knows all the trials and struggles we are going to face in life. That is why He gave us His Word to help us understand the temptations we would face and to help us gain the victory over them.

I recall counseling with a man in his mid-fifties once. He admitted a particularly difficult sin in his life and said, "Pastor, will this temptation ever go away?"

"Not this side of Heaven," I replied.

"Do you mean that I'm always going to have to fight this in order to defeat it?" he asked.

"Yes," I said, "in all likelihood, you will always have to deny its claim on your life."

Not all temptation works like that. Sometimes it is little more than a fleeting glance or thought. Other times, the temptation is lodged deep within our own depravity. Still other times it is a reflection of our own personal weakness. Whatever the case, God can help us overcome it.

The word *tempt* (Greek, *peirazō*) has a twofold meaning in the New Testament. In a positive sense, it means "to test," "try," or "prove." In a negative sense, it means "to ensnare" or "lead astray." Thus, while the Devil attempts to ensnare us through temptation, God often uses such trials to prove and strengthen our faith in Him.

WHAT IS TEMPTATION?

If temptation is something I am going to face all my life, then I had better understand what it is and how it works. Only in so doing can I ever hope to control it and defeat it. Thus we must begin by discovering where temptation comes from and clearly defining it in our minds.

Many people blame temptation on God. They act as though their enticement to sin comes from Him. I have actually had people ask me, "Why did God tempt me to sin?" or "Why did God bring this temptation into my life?"

The Bible clearly tells us that God is not the author of sin. In James 1:13 we read, "Let no man say when he is tempted, I am tempted of God: for God cannot be tempted with evil, neither tempteth he any man."

This scripture makes it clear that God is not the creator of temptation. He is not the source of our enticement to do wrong. To the contrary, He wants to live with us in perfect peace and harmony. God loves us and wants the very best for us. While He may allow us to be tempted, He is not the source of that temptation.

There are really two major sources of temptation. One is internal and the other is external. Internal temptation is described in James 1:14, "Every man is tempted, when he is drawn away of his own lust, and enticed." Sometimes our struggle with temptation is an internal battle that we just desire to blame on someone other than ourselves.

Psychologists call this "projection." Often we are projecting upon others the blame for problems that we really make for ourselves. Edwin Sabin says it this way in the poem "Myself":

> An enemy I had whose face
>   I stoutly strove to know,
> For hard he dogged my steps, unseen,
>   Wherever I might go.

> My plans he balked, my aims he foiled,
>   He blocked my onward way.
> When for some lofty goal I toiled,
>   He grimly said me nay.
>
> "Come forth!" I cried, "Lay bare thy guise!
>   Thy features I would see,"
> But always to my straining eyes
>   He dwelt in mystery.
>
> One night I seized and held him fast,
>   The veil from him did draw,
> I gazed upon his face at last . . .
>   And lo! Myself I saw.

But other times the conflict is external, and we are tempted by Satan himself. When God created Adam and Eve, He placed them in the Garden of Eden. There, it was heaven on earth, full of the love and protection of Almighty God. But when Satan entered the scene in the form of the serpent, he tempted Adam and Eve by telling them if they ate of the forbidden fruit they would be as gods themselves. They yielded to that temptation and humankind has had to suffer the consequences ever since. In all that took place in the Garden, one thing was clear: Satan was the author of temptation. He still is, and he has used it since that day to try to destroy the children of God.

With that in mind, let us think about what temptation really is. After all, if we are going to overcome it we must be able to identify it. It's difficult to win a war without understanding the nature of your enemy's weapon. Temptation is Satan's *attempt* to get you to commit an act of sin. Notice I said, "attempt." The whole aim and purpose of temptation is to cause you to violate God's laws and principles. Just as it is the nature of a bird to fly, a dog to bark, it is the nature of Satan to try to get you to sin.

Think of the predicament Satan is in with regard to your life. If you have committed your life to Christ, he has lost your soul. He once had you twisted around his finger, and now you have escaped his dominating control. You found a better way and took it. You discovered the avenue of escape which led to Christ and through repentance and faith you fled to Him. Now your life belongs to God, and Satan has lost you forever.

Unfortunately, this does not mean that Satan has given up on you.

Now that he has lost you, he is likely to do all he can to neutralize your faith and testimony by bombarding you with temptation. The only thing he can do to you now is to try to trip you up. He was the ruler of your life until you came to Christ by faith. Now Christ is your Lord and Satan is rejected. God has entered your life, and that makes all the difference. He has regenerated your heart and filled your life with His Holy Spirit. All hope of damning your soul has been lost and Satan knows it!

You and I are free in Christ. We have been redeemed by His blood and released from the bondage and shackles of sin. The condemnation of guilt has been cancelled, and we have been set free. We have been granted pardon, and we have been given a brand-new life in Christ.

Satan's only remaining tactic is to target your weakness and try to tempt you to sin. In so doing, he hopes to bring guilt and defeat into your life so that you will stop trying to be a witness for Christ.

Remember that temptation itself is not sin. Yielding to temptation is the sin. Don't let Satan put you on a guilt trip because thoughts of temptation enter your mind. Jesus Himself was tempted without sinning. Temptation is a real, and often daily, experience that every believer must learn how to handle. But temptation itself is not a sin. It is the lure that Satan uses to try to get us to sin.

Temptation is the enticement to sin. It may be triggered by external stimuli, but it comes to fruition in our own minds. It is our own lusts and desires that drive us toward sinning. Therefore, we must learn to deal with and control these desires if we are going to overcome temptation.

WHERE DOES THE BATTLE BEGIN?

Temptation may be triggered by a physical urge or desire, but it is essentially a mental process. The Bible describes the threefold nature of temptation as (1) "the lust of the flesh," (2) "the lust of the eyes," (3) "the pride of life" (1 John 2:16). This description makes it clear that the physical and mental aspects of temptation are closely interrelated.

1. The Body.

The *"lust of the flesh"* is the desire for physical gratification. This can lead to such sinful indulgences as overeating, excessive drinking, or illicit sex. As long as we live inside a physical body, we are going to be tempted to sin with that body and to sin against that body. In reality, the body is the believer's major spiritual battleground. That is why the Apostle Paul urged his readers to present their bodies as a "living sacrifice" to God (Romans 12:1).

The body is where the battle begins. It cries out for satisfaction and indulgence. But giving heed to that cry often drives people to destruction. The alcoholic who keeps on drinking is headed to an early grave. The drug addict who keeps popping pills or smoking dope is slowly but surely destroying himself. The adulterer or adulteress who continually pursues an illicit relationship is gambling with life itself.

We live in a society of instant gratification. It is very difficult for most of us to wait patiently for anything. We want it all, and we want it now! When we can't afford our desires, we just charge it up on a credit card. Ours is a society that has seen it all and done it all. Yet, most people are still restlessly unhappy. They keep frantically searching for peace, only to have it elude them at every turn. They keep trying to find happiness in thrills that leave them cold and empty inside.

The body is a wonderful machine when it is properly cared for and used. God has designed us so that every aspect of the human anatomy functions to the fullest potential for our physical wellbeing. The tragedy is that some people spend a lifetime, often a short one, destroying what He has made.

2. The Mind.

Temptation really begins to ferment in the mind. It may germinate from the physical, but it comes to full fruition in one's mind. Rarely do people jump into sin spontaneously. Most of the time, people fall into sin because they spent a great deal of time thinking about it.

Once your mind focuses and dwells upon a particular temptation, you are in real danger of going all the way. You start trying to talk yourself out of it. You may even argue and debate with yourself. But it is difficult to talk oneself out of a desire with an argument.

The mind is the gate through which everything enters our lives. That is why we are warned in Scripture to "guard" our minds and to "think" on those things which will strengthen us spiritually (Philippians 4:7-8). This is especially true today, when Satan has so infiltrated our society that our world is filled with pictures, movies, magazines, and television programs which can quickly and easily lead us astray from the very things we believe.

The Bible reminds us, "As [a man] thinketh in his heart, so is he" (Proverbs 23:7). The mind is like a computer. It can be programmed with spiritual truth or with evil thoughts. The choice is really up to you. You can choose to think on good, wholesome, positive, and virtuous things or you can fill your mind with sinful thoughts.

The other two aspects of temptation are the "lust of the eyes" and the "pride of life," both of which involve the mind. It is in our minds that we talk to ourselves, and in some cases, even argue with ourselves.

A study by a noted psychologist recently stated that the average American speaks between 150 and 200 words a minute. I think the 150 is a Georgian and 200 is a New Yorker! That study also indicated that we think 1300 words a minute in our minds. That means that you can think faster than you can verbalize those thoughts into words. That is why we must learn to discipline our minds to focus on the things of God.

The ultimate problem with temptation is that it will always hit you at the weakest point of your strongest desire. It is not necessarily the desires themselves that are wrong, but the temptation to fulfill those desires in a wrong way. The desire for food is not a reason to gorge oneself. The desire for sexual fulfillment is not an excuse for sexual permissiveness. God has ordained that sexual satisfaction come from the bond of marriage. But Satan often tempts people to fulfill their desires in some other manner outside that bond.

You may desire praise, admiration, success, education, acceptance, or a thousand different things. The desire may vary, but the pattern is always the same. Temptation always hits your strongest desire at your weakest point. Therefore, you must be honest with yourself by identifying and acknowledging that desire so that you can guard against it when temptation comes.

HOW CAN I OVERCOME TEMPTATION?

It is not enough to know what temptation is, where it comes from, and how it works. If you ever hope to conquer it, you must begin to take specific and forceful steps of action to confront and deny it.

1. *Expect it.*

No matter how spiritual you may think you are, temptation can easily come when you least expect it. When you think your life is all it ought to be you are in greater danger of falling than when you know you're in trouble. That is why the Bible reminds us, "Wherefore let him that thinketh he standeth take heed lest he fall" (1 Corinthians 10:12).

The method, mode, and nature of temptation may change, but it is still temptation. For example, you may not be as easily tempted by the sins of the flesh as you once were, but you may be more susceptible than ever to the sins of pride, arrogance, and self-righteousness. Don't overestimate yourself and underestimate temptation. Be prepared to deal with it at every turn. The Bible tells us that our Lord was "in all points tempted just as we are" (Hebrews 4:15). If He faced temptation, you and I can be certain that we will face it, too.

2. Don't Panic.

You don't have to fear temptation. Just because it comes into your life doesn't mean you have to be defeated by it. Some people panic in advance. "If I'm tempted like that I know I'll give in," they rationalize to themselves. Let me set you at ease. You probably will be tempted, but you don't have to give in to it. The Bible promises, "greater is he that is in you, than he that is in the world" (1 John 4:4).

The apostle's words to the church at Corinth say the same thing. He makes two promises that are essential to overcoming temptation. First, he wrote, "There hath no temptation taken you but such as is common to man" (1 Corinthians 10:13). That means that you are not alone in your struggle with temptation. You are not the only one being tempted. Such temptation is common to human experience. Second, Paul said, "But God is faithful, who will not suffer you to be tempted above that ye are able." To rephrase that promise in modern English, he said that God will not allow us to be tempted beyond the point of our ability to resist.

If you find yourself giving in to temptation, perhaps you need to face the fact that you are the problem, not the temptation. "But you just wouldn't believe what I have to face every day," someone will object.

May I remind you that God has said your temptation is common to all human beings and that others have learned to resist it. Second, may I remind you again that God said you can endure it because He has set a limit on it. Finally, remember there is always a "way to escape" if you will only take it!

3. Identify It.

Learn to identify the kind of temptation with which you are faced. Are you jealous by nature? Then identify your jealousy as a weakness which is prone to temptation. Do you tend to lose your temper easily? Then identify anger as a potential area of temptation.

Your area of temptation could be lust, frustration, depression, self-pity, or any one of a hundred things. Whatever it is, face up to it and plan to deal with it. Search the Word of God and see what He has to say about it. Then tackle it head on.

Several years ago I visited a lady in the hospital who was a hypochondriac. She was always "sick" from some psychosomatic illness. She was constantly in and out of the hospital. When I asked the doctor what was wrong, he would just say, "Oh, nothing really, it's all in her head!"

I even recall visiting her at home one time when she had hundreds of pills strewn on a table. She was reading feverishly in a large black book, which I assumed was the Bible. To my dismay, I discovered it was the *Home Medical Guide*, and she was doctoring herself according to all the symptoms she thought she had. That can be dangerous as well as foolish. But that is how some people deal with temptation. They try a little of this and some of that and hope it will go away. That simply doesn't work. But if you are willing to be honest with yourself, God will show you precisely your area of weakness.

4. Deny It.

Ultimately the matter of overcoming temptation comes down to a decision. You must decide in your heart that you will resist temptation by the power of God. You may have yielded to it in the past, but now you determine never again to do so. Usually the people who don't overcome temptation don't really want to overcome it.

I once heard a story about a woman who was a compulsive spender. She had just bought another new dress when her husband demanded to know why she had done so.

"Well, I guess the Devil made me do it," she suggested.

"Why do you say that?" he asked.

"When I put it on, I could hear this voice telling me how good I looked in it and that I ought to buy it," she added.

"If you thought it was the Devil," her husband responded, "why didn't you say 'get behind me, Satan'?"

"I did," she said with a twinkle, "but he said it looked good from back there, too!"

Most of us are just like her. We have already made up our minds that we want something regardless of the consequences. That decision can be disastrous.

5. Prepare for It.

Since we already know that temptation comes to all of us, we need to learn to be ready for it. We tell our teenagers that if someone ever offers them drugs, or tempts them to do wrong, "Just say no!" But we seldom make the same preparation ourselves. What will you say if someone asks you to bend the law in a business deal? What will you say if you are ever approached by a prostitute? What will you do if the opportunity comes to "get even" with your worst enemy? Will you "just say no"?

I believe that many Christians fall into temptation because they think it could never happen to them. Therefore, they are not prepared to deal with it when it does come. Think ahead. You don't have to go out looking for trouble. It will usually find you soon enough. But you had better be prepared to say no when it comes.

6. Deal with It.

Some time ago I visited the U.S. Naval Air Base in Pensacola, Florida, where I was privileged to see an F-18 fighter plane. I was fascinated as the pilot showed me around it. It was specially equipped to detect enemy aircraft up to one hundred miles away. It was a magnificent machine. "Many of its details are classified information," said the pilot. "But I can tell you this much; no enemy can ever take this airplane by surprise!"

You and I, as God's children, have the same kind of detection device. The Holy Spirit dwells within us, and He enables us to develop the sensitivity to detect temptation before it ensnares us. He convicts us of the difference between sin and righteousness and urges us to deal drastically with sin before it deals with us.

"What if you really did spot the enemy at one hundred miles?" I asked the pilot.

"When the plane got within fifty miles, we would fire a missile and destroy it instantly!" he answered confidently.

That is exactly what you need to do when you recognize temptation coming your way. Identify it and deal with it immediately. The best method is to get away from the source of temptation and stay away from it.

There were once two young boys who cut through a cow pasture on their way to school. Unfortunately, there was an old bull in the pasture who became angry because they had invaded his turf. He suddenly charged toward the boys, snorting and stomping as he came. As the boys turned to run, one turned to the other and said, "We need to stop and pray about this."

But the other boy said, "I've got a better idea. Let's run and pray!"

That is the best advice one could ever heed in regard to temptation. Don't stand around thinking about it. Run and pray!

PART THREE

FOUR AGAINST FAITH

[Abraham] staggered not at the promise of God through unbelief; but was strong in faith, giving glory to God; and being fully persuaded that, what he had promised, he was able also to perform.

—ROMANS 4:20-21

9

The Way Out of Worry

Dealing with destructive habits and specific acts of sin is only part of the process of "renewing" that is to be going on in our minds as we offer ourselves to God. Another aspect of this process focuses on the positive qualities that God wants to develop in our lives. According to His Word, the natural result ("fruit") of His Spirit's work within us is "love, joy, peace, longsuffering, gentleness, goodness, faith, meekness, temperance" (Galatians 5:22-23).

Yet, most of us find our lives at times characterized by one or more of these less admirable attitudes: worry, fear, anger, and bitterness. We are going to look at each of these in depth, but let me say at the outset that there are not really four problems here, but only one. Worry, fear, anger, and bitterness creep into our lives when we let faith slip away—when we do not really believe that God will keep His promises to us.

Worry is a terrible way to live, but millions of people are choosing to live that way every day. Worry is practically an epidemic in our affluent society. Every year Americans spend millions of dollars on tranquilizers, attempting to conquer worry.

Yet, worry is a choice. Nobody forces you to worry. I doubt your husband or wife woke you up this morning and said, "Honey, please wake up and start worrying." Your boss at work didn't say, "If you want to keep your job, you've got to learn to worry." Neither did the teacher at school say, "Class, for your homework today, go home and worry." It all sounds ridiculous, doesn't it? But it proves the point. Worry is not something someone else forces upon us. It is something that we choose to do ourselves.

I am convinced that God never intended for us to live with anxiety and all the nervous conflict it produces. In the Sermon on the Mount, Jesus told His disciples how to overcome the problem of worry. He said,

But seek ye first the kingdom of God, and his righteousness; and all these things shall be added unto you. Take therefore no thought for the morrow: for the morrow shall take thought for the things of itself. Sufficient unto the day is the evil thereof. (Matthew 6:33-34)

Our Lord understood how to handle the pressures of life. He realized that life was more than meat and drink and the material things of this world. He also understood that those things were not wrong in and of themselves, but that much of the worry that people exerted was in relation to those things. It is for that reason that He told His disciples to seek first "the kingdom of God" and those things would be added unto them.

1. *Learn to Live One Day at a Time.*

By telling His disciples not to worry about tomorrow, Jesus was trying to help them understand the importance of living for today. None of us has a guarantee of tomorrow; therefore, we must learn to appreciate what we have today. That is not to say that we cannot plan ahead for the future, for such planning is certainly wise. But what our Lord was trying to help us to see in this passage is that we have no certain knowledge about tomorrow, so we might as well stop worrying about it.

Think about it. Most of our worries are about the future. We focus on the fear of what might happen in the next few days, or next week, or next year. If we are not careful, we can become consumed with worrying about our job, our family, our health, our finances, or whatever. Once you shift your focus from the present to the future, you will fail to do what you ought to do today in order to guarantee a better future. It is today that really counts in your life.

The great thinker Thomas Carlyle said, "Our main business is not to see what lies dimly in the future, but to do what lies clearly at hand."

All the worry in the world is not going to change tomorrow. There is no way that worry is going to assure us a better tomorrow. Worrying about education, marriage, occupation, or even retirement does not make any of those matters come more easily. In fact, most worriers destroy the present by becoming consumed over the past or the future.

When the children of Israel were passing through the wilderness of Sinai, God fed them manna from Heaven one day at a time. Every night God rained manna on the children of Israel and in the morning they collected it and ate it. The Hebrew word for manna (mân) literally means "what is it?" The Hebrews were never sure what it was they were eating. All they knew is that it came from God to meet their daily needs.

On one occasion they attempted to save enough manna overnight to last them for several days. But when they woke up in the morning, the manna they had kept was rotten. It was as though God were trying to teach them to trust Him one day at a time.

Whenever someone is going through a great difficulty, someone else will inevitably say, "You will have to take it one day at a time." While that is the best advice you could ever give, it is the kind of advice most of us don't want to hear. We would rather be able to figure out the whole solution to the entire situation ahead of time. But the truth is that you and I cannot live more than one day at a time. Therefore, we need to take life one day at a time and enjoy it as it is given.

This same truth is communicated by the psalmist when he says, "This is the day which the Lord hath made; we will rejoice and be glad in it" (Psalm 118:24). Notice his emphasis on *this day*. He tells us we are to rejoice right now.

Not when you finish school.
Not when you find a new job.
Not when the boss gives you a raise.
Not when all the bills are paid.
Not when you get that dream house or car.
Not when your kids finally grow up.
Not when you save enough money to retire.

No, not then—but now. THIS IS THE DAY. Rejoice, and be glad in it!

2. Learn to Do One Thing at a Time.

How often we get our lives into trouble when we scatter our minds in a hundred different directions. The Bible reminds us of this as it talks about a double-minded man being unstable in all of his ways (James 1:8). The Apostle Paul had this singularity of purpose in mind when he said, "This one thing I do" (Philippians 3:13). Once he discovered God's plan and purpose for his life, he became totally committed to fulfill that one goal. Therefore, he said that he would press on to the mark that God had set for him. He became so single-minded in focusing all of his activity toward accomplishing that purpose that he was able to achieve a tremendous amount for God in one lifetime.

When all of our activities center around the most significant thing to which God has called us, everything that we do will contribute to the fulfillment of that purpose. And I believe that God has a unique and specific purpose for the life of every believer. While your life may include many facets of serving the Lord, and while you may have been gifted with a number of qualities and abilities, there is ultimately one thing God wants you to do. He wants to bring your life into conformity with the image of His Son; He wants to make you so much like Christ that you become a reflection of His glory.

When I was a young student away at school, I roomed with several other guys. We had just about everything you could imagine in our room. And I do mean everything! We thought it was neat to see just how much junk we could put in one dorm room. Every night when we were supposed to be studying, we would close the door and do things like turn on both the radio and the stereo, get out the Monopoly game, and dribble a little basketball. Have you ever tried to study algebra while listening to the stereo and the radio, playing Monopoly, and dribbling the basketball? The grades I sent home at the end of the first quarter taught me a great lesson. That lesson was that you cannot do several things at the same time and do any of them effectively. We must live life one day at a time and do things one thing at a time; then God will help us achieve perfect peace of mind.

3. *Give God the Best of Your Time.*

When our Lord told His disciples to seek first the Kingdom of God and His righteousness, He was urging them to give the work of the Kingdom of God first place in their lives. Our tendency today is to spend most of our time and energy concentrating on the comforts and desires of our flesh and to neglect the things of God. It is no wonder that we are filled with worry and anxiety when God is on the back burner of our lives. On most of our priority lists, God would be lucky to come in number ten. Yet our Lord reminds us that He must be number one if we are going to live life successfully.

I believe a good definition of worry is this: Worry is *the distance between you and God.* Whenever worry and anxiety begin to take over our lives, we are really acknowledging that God is not in control. When we are close to Him, we will be able to express a greater confidence in God. But when we have fallen away from Him, our anxiety will always increase. There is a real sense in which God is ever present in our lives. The theologian Francis Schaeffer called Him "The God Who Is There." By this, he meant that God is always present and with us. He is not the absent God. He is the ever-present One who will never leave us. The more we realize His presence and the closer we draw to Him, the smaller the gap of worry becomes. When we are convinced that we are not alone in the struggles of life, but are assured that God is there, we can learn to trust Him for anything no matter what our outward circumstances may be. The closer we come to God, the more we will sense His care, His strength, and His resources to meet our needs.

Why is it important to give God the best of our time? The answer to that really lies in the area of our priorities. We always give the best time to those people and things that we love the most. As Jesus spoke to His disciples, He was trying to help them understand that the things of this world are not the most important things in life. Your relationship with God is the most important thing you have.

When you fell in love with the guy or girl who was to become your life's partner, you wanted to spend as much time with that person as you possibly could. Every time you were unable to see each other, you were probably disappointed. No matter how much time you had together, it was never enough. I remember when I first fell in love with my wife, Judy. I wanted to be with her *all the time*. The same ought to be true with our relationship with God. If we really love Him, we will want to spend time with Him.

When Christ is *the obsession of our hearts*, we will give Him the best of our time. We will take time to pray, read His Word, and seek His face. When we fully understand His importance in our lives, it will not be difficult for us to put Him in His proper place of priority.

4. Trust God the Rest of the Time.

In teaching His disciples to overcome the problem of worry, Jesus reminded them that God had clothed the grass which would soon fade away. If He has that much concern about the grass, Jesus asked, "Shall he not much more clothe you?" (Matthew 6:30). He went on to explain that your heavenly Father knows what you have need of and delights to meet those needs. If we are really under the care of God, we have nothing to worry about at all. If the Divine Being who rules this world really lives within our hearts, then He can give us the inner peace and calm that will enable us to face any of the storms of life. If God can keep the universe going, and He lives within your life, He can certainly keep you going as well.

When I was a boy, we used to sing a hymn that said, "Many things about tomorrow / I don't seem to understand; / But I know who holds tomorrow, / And I know who holds my hand."* It was a beautiful reminder that Christ is in control of our lives. He not only knows the future, but He also controls the future. Therefore, worrying about the problems of life is a most futile effort. Once I've cast my care upon Him, there is no reason to worry about anything. When we become filled with anxiety we are really saying to the Lord that we do not trust Him to meet our needs. If you are struggling with the problem of worry today, turn your anxieties over to Him by faith. Trust in His love and His goodness to meet your needs. He will not let you down. We who know the Lord have every reason not to worry.

There are no easy answers to the problems of life. Each problem must be faced directly and confidently knowing that the power of God is on our side. The real antidote to worry is spiritual maturity, which leads to true freedom from worry's bondage. No one matures overnight. Don't be discouraged if you are not yet what you wish to be, for it is only as you continue to grow in your walk with Christ that you will become all that God intends for you to be. As you learn to trust Him in all the troubled times of life, you will progress into a deeper relationship with Him than you have ever known before. It is in this context that the Bible promises that the "peace of God" will be with us and that He will keep us by literally standing guard over our hearts and minds (Philippians 4:7).

I once heard the story of a man who was carrying a heavy load on his back as he walked down a lonely country road. A farmer drove by in his truck and offered to give him a ride. The man accepted the offer and climbed into the back of the truck. As the farmer drove down the road, he looked into the rearview mirror and saw the man sitting in the back of the truck, with the burden still on his shoulders. Finally the farmer pulled over to the side of the road, rolled

---

* Ira F. Stanphill, "I Know Who Holds Tomorrow." Copyright © 1950 by Singspiration Music/ASCAP. Renewed 1978. All rights reserved. Used by permission of the Benson Company, Inc., Nashville, TN.

down the window, and shouted, "Mister, if I'm carrying you, why are you still carrying that load?"

As foolish as it may sound, that is exactly what we do when we who know the Lord cares for us continue to fill our own minds with care and worry. The Bible tells us that our lives are in the hands of God. But by the way we live we act like the man who sat in the truck carrying his own burden. If God can carry you through the problems of life, then you need to lay down the burden and trust Him all the way.

10

Facts about Fear

The first step to overcoming fear is to admit that you have it. There is not a single person I have ever known who has not experienced fear at some time in his or her life. It is certainly not a sin to admit, "God, I am afraid." The Bible is filled with examples of men and women who faced fearful circumstances and learned to overcome their fears by the power of God.

I have read several books recently on the subject of fear, written from a Christian perspective. They have dealt with a multitude of topics, such as "Conquering Fear" and "Winning over Fear." Most of these books have as their premise the concept that if one knows Christ as his personal Savior, he really has no reason to fear anyone at any time. While that sounds nice, it just doesn't work that easily.

Life is filled with all sorts of fears. Some are serious, while others may seem trivial. A partial list would include:

Hydrophobia—the fear of water
Mysophobia—the fear of dirt
Acrophobia—the fear of high places
Hematophobia—the fear of blood
Necrophobia—the fear of the dead
Algophobia—the fear of pain
Photophobia—the fear of light
Nyctophobia—the fear of night
Claustrophobia—the fear of confined places
Xenophobia—the fear of strangers
Triskaidekaphobia—the fear of the number 13

I have even discovered a kind of phobia that I did not realize existed. It is burglaphobia, or the fear of having burglars enter your home. I recall hearing a humorous story once about a couple who were awakened in the middle of the night by a burglar. The wife said to her husband, "Wake up, John, there's a burglar downstairs." The man rolled out of bed, took his pistol, and apprehended the burglar before he could get out through the window. Pulling him back into the room, the man said to the startled burglar, "Sir, before I telephone the police I want to take you upstairs to meet my wife. She has lain awake all night for the past twenty years waiting for you to come!"

Fear is a common emotion. It affects nearly every one of us. In the fourth chapter of Mark, Jesus dealt with the issue of fear. He and His disciples had entered a boat and were crossing the Sea of Galilee. As they were crossing the water, a storm suddenly arose and a tempest began to rage. The rain beat upon them and the waves began to lash into the boat. Fearing that they might sink, the disciples panicked and awakened the Lord, who was asleep in the hinder part of the boat. The Bible says,

> And they woke him and said to him, Teacher do you not care if we perish? And he awoke and rebuked the wind, and said to the sea, "Peace! Be still!" And the wind ceased, and there was a great calm. (Mark 4:38-39, RSV)

It is easy to understand their fears. Storms come off the Mediterranean Sea rather quickly and flow inland, sweeping unexpectedly over the Sea of Galilee. The disciples were literally taken by surprise and caught out in the middle of the lake. Not only can we sympathize, but we can also empathize with their fears. Yet, it was out of this incident that our Lord taught His disciples to overcome their fears.

1. The Certainty that Storms and Fears Will Come.

As long as you are living on this planet, you are going to experience storms, difficulty, and trouble in life. There are many people who will try to tell you that Christians never have any real problems or troubles. They want to imply that when you receive Jesus Christ as your Savior, your life is going to be problem-free from that point on. Unfortunately, that is just not true. Most of the people who make such statements have not walked with the Lord very long themselves, or else they are simply blind to the realities of life.

Difficulty and trouble are a part of our lives. While some tribulations come as the direct result of our disobedience, as in the case of the prophet Jonah, this is not the only cause of difficulty. There have always been wonderful servants of God who have suffered greatly in this life and have done nothing disobedient to bring that suffering upon themselves. In fact, our Lord Himself warned us in John 16:33, "In the world ye shall have tribulation." *Tribulation* (Greek, *thlipsis*) means "affliction." This affliction may be brought on by any one of a number of things. As we mature in our walk with God, we will learn that there are always going to be tough times in life, and opportunities to fear, no matter how close we are to Him.

Life has variety. Not every day is a sunny day. Some days are filled with sunshine, to be sure, but others are filled with rain. Life itself is not one long mountaintop experience. Some days we are up and other days we are down.

I like what one man said about his father, whom he admired very much. His father was a man of great character and dependability. The man wrote a poem about his father and remembered him in this way:

> Whether the weather be good,
> Or whether the weather be not,
> Whether the weather be cold,
> Or whether the weather be hot,
> Whatever the weather,
> He weathered the weather,
> Whether he liked it or not.*

What this man was saying about his father was that he had developed the kind of character that was necessary to face the storms of life, no matter what they were or when they came. I realize that this is not a popular concept. There are those who would prefer to believe that life is one fantastic experience after another. But I must honestly tell you that that is not how life is for most people. While every believer has the right to expect good things from God, we must also recognize that we are still living in a vulnerable body of human flesh. We are subject to disease, difficulty, and death.

Despite the difficulties of life and the reality of tribulation that each of us must face, our Lord also said, "Be of good cheer; I have overcome the world" (John 16:33). Here is the delicate balance of

---

* From *Pepper 'N Salt* by Vance Havner, copyright © MCMLXVI by Fleming H. Revell Company. Used by permission of Fleming H. Revell Company.

truth in Scripture regarding the concept of fear. On the one hand, the Bible tells us that trouble is a reality of life. On the other hand, the Scripture reminds us that God can overcome the greatest fears. Therefore, our faith is not in believing that the troubles will never come, but in believing that God can overcome the troubles.

2. The Source of Fear Is No Secret.

The Bible tells us that Jesus responded to the disciples' appeal for help in a twofold manner. First, "he awoke and rebuked the wind, and said to the sea, 'Peace! Be still!'" (Mark 4:39, RSV). The scripture goes on to say that the wind ceased and was followed by a great calm. Christ had displayed His incredible power over nature. Second, He asked the disciples, "Why are you afraid? Have you no faith?" (Mark 4:40, RSV). Now He was attacking the source of their fear, for fear is caused by a lack of faith.

It must have amazed Jesus that His disciples were so fearful. Had they not seen Him give sight to the blind and hearing to the deaf? Had they not been there when He caused the lame to walk? Did they not realize that He was with them in the boat? It is no wonder that our Lord questioned their unbelief!

On another occasion recorded in Scripture (Matthew 14:22-33), Jesus walked across the Sea of Galilee toward His disciples who were in a small boat. Startled by the figure approaching them, the disciples thought it to be a spirit of some sort. But when Jesus spoke to them, Peter realized who He was. Peter called to Him and said, "Lord, if it be thou, bid me come unto thee on the water" (v. 28). And the Lord replied, "Come." Then the Bible tells us that Peter got out of the boat and walked on the water toward Jesus. All was well until Peter began to reason how he was walking on water. Suddenly fear overtook him and he began to sink. The Lord reached out His hand, caught him up, and placed him in the boat. Then He said, "O thou of little faith, wherefore didst thou doubt?" (v. 31). Again, the issue becomes one of faith versus fear. As soon as Peter took his eyes off the Lord and focused on his circumstances, he began to sink. In the same manner, you and I must focus our faith on the Savior in order to overcome our fears. As you put your eyes on Christ, faith increases, and when it does, fear flees.

3. The Solution to Fear Is Faith.

In dealing with His disciples, our Lord made it clear that faith and fear cannot mix. As we have more faith, we will have less fear.

Somebody once put it like this: Fear knocked at the door of my heart, and when I sent faith to answer the door, no one was there!

"How can I have that kind of faith?" you may ask. Let me suggest several steps based upon Mark 4:35-41.

First: Trust in the promises of God. Jesus had told His disciples that they would "pass over to the other side." He had given them His promise on the matter and had gone to sleep entrusting them with the details. When the storm arose, however, they became frightened and turned to wake Him in order to get His help. I am convinced that the disciples would have made it to the other side, whether they had awakened Jesus or not. I base that observation on His promise to them that they would go to the other side.

In the allegory *Pilgrim's Progress*, John Bunyan told of the soul's pilgrimage through this life. In one scene, two characters, Christian and Hopeful, were tired of traveling down the rough road and chose to journey across By-path Meadow instead. There they were captured by Giant Despair and thrown into Doubting Castle.

For days they were held captive in Doubting Castle. Finally, Christian could stand no more and cried out, "What a fool am I, thus to lie in a stinking dungeon, when I may as well walk at liberty! I have a key in my bosom, called Promise, that will, I am persuaded, open any lock in Doubting Castle."

Christian reached into his coat and pulled from it the key called Promise. He thrust it into the lock, gave it a turn, and opened the door. Thus Christian and his friend Hopeful were set free to travel again on the King's Highway.

In our humanity it is easy to become imprisoned by fear and despair. But we need not remain there. Trust in the key called Promise, and as you do, your fears will diminish; your despair, no matter how large a giant it seems to be, will flee; and your faith will be set free.

The disciples had forgotten that although Christ was asleep in the boat, He was still Lord of the universe. He still had everything under control, for they had His promise of that.

Second: Realize that God is with you. Before the storm, during the storm, and following the storm, Christ stayed with His disciples in the boat. He never left them on their own. When they needed Him, He was there.

In thinking of the three Hebrew children, Shadrach, Meshach, and Abednego, we are reminded once again of how they were thrown into the fiery furnace of King Nebuchadnezzar. They refused to bow down to the king's idol, and he had commanded that anyone who refused to do so would be cast into the furnace. "Our God is able to deliver us," they announced. But they also made it clear that even if God chose not to deliver them and allowed them to be destroyed, they would not turn against Him. Nebuchadnezzar threw them into the furnace, all right, but God was with them in the fire and delivered them unharmed.

Most Bible commentators believe that the fourth person who appeared in the furnace with the three Hebrew children was Christ Himself. It is interesting to observe that not only did He stand by them in the midst of their troubles, but He even led them on a walk around the fiery furnace. If I had been one of them, I probably would have said, "Let's get out of here right now!" But our Lord just kept walking around, leading them through the fire. That is the way that God always works. He meets us at the point of our troubles and leads us through the troubles and out into a brand-new experience of freedom in Him. In the midst of our greatest difficulties, He is there!

Third: Develop courage and confidence in God. Courage isn't not having fear. Courage is acting in the face of fear. There really was no question about whether or not Christ loved the disciples. He had proved that to them over and over again. In time, He would prove it in the ultimate degree by giving His life for them on the Cross. The real issue at stake was whether or not they had the courage to place their confidence in Him. The question "Carest thou not that we perish?" (Mark 4:38) was an expression of their uncertainty and lack of faith.

What they failed to understand is that it is impossible to have one foot upon faith and the other upon fear. But why should they have feared? Christ had never failed them before. He would not fail them now. And why should we fear? He has never failed us either. Perhaps that is the only thing that He cannot do. He cannot fail! It isn't within His possibility. With that in mind, courage should swell within us; and when fear comes, we should hold that fact as a shield against it.

Fourth: Place your final confidence in the power of God. The Bible tells us that when our Lord awoke and rebuked the storm, the disciples wondered at His power. The scene is almost too awesome for us to imagine. Here they are, in a state of panic because of the storm. The Savior is sound asleep in the boat, and they wake Him up, calling upon Him for help. He stands up, rebukes the storm—and there is an instant calm across the Sea of Galilee. The very problem to which the disciples requested a solution has been resolved. But now they stand face to face with the One whose personal power is greater than that of nature itself. The Bible says that they "feared exceedingly" and said to one another, "What manner of man is this, that even the wind and the sea obey Him?" (Mark 4:41).

I'll tell you what manner of man He is—He is God! He is not just a figure of history like Napoleon. Nor just a great philosopher like Socrates. Nor was He merely a religious leader like Gandhi. He was God incarnate in human flesh! That is why we can rely upon Him to meet our needs. Not mere man—but God!

So, fear is an emotion we all experience. It is not something that we can merely wish away. Real problems cause real fears, but when they come, we need to turn our attention to the Savior—for He alone can still the storm and calm the fear in you and me.

The next time you face your fears, think on these things:

- When your moments of trouble come, Christ Himself is in the boat with you.

- God cannot fail, and He has promised to meet your needs.

- Fear can only overtake you if you take your eyes off the Lord Jesus.

- God has given you the key of promise; use it to release yourself from the prison of fear.

- Courage is *not* not having fear. Courage is acting in the face of fear.

11

Answers to Anger

Anger is one of life's most destructive emotions. It can ruin a friendship, destroy a marriage, or split a home. It can cause you to say things and do things that you may regret for the rest of your life. Anger is so powerful that it can erupt like an explosion and leave the irreparable damage of shattered lives strewn over the pavement of life. If left unchecked, it will not only destroy your relationships with others, but it will ultimately destroy you.

Let me ask you: Are you a hothead? Do you have trouble with anger? Are you the kind of person who gets mad at the drop of a hat and will even be glad to furnish the hat?

Or perhaps you are one of those who always seem to remain cool on the outside while hot on the inside with anger. Some people are experts in hiding their anger like that. They always try to give the impression that nothing bothers them. They have their act together. Everyone else can blow up, but not these people. They are not going to let anybody ever see their temper. They keep their anger all inside for a while; but because they really never admit it and come to terms with it, their anger eats them alive from the inside out.

Notice what the Bible says about anger in Ephesians 4:26-27, "Be ye angry and sin not: let not the sun go down upon your wrath: Neither give place to the devil." Anger is a natural impulse which can be used for good or for evil.

When it takes the form of righteous indignation, it can cause us to stand up against sin, evil, and injustice. But when it takes the form of vindictive vengeance, it can destroy all that is good.

Anger can also provide Satan with a place to work in our lives. Therefore, the Scriptures warn us not to "give place to the devil." Once you allow him to gain a foothold in your life, he will try to take over completely. He will sour your disposition and breed conflict with everyone in your path.

Perhaps you are already in serious trouble because of anger in your life. Your home is in trouble. Your friendships are about to blow apart. Your words and attitudes reveal a bitter spirit within. You know it, and so does everyone else. Somehow you have become angry. Your heart is filled with bitterness, contempt, malice, and hatred. If something does not happen soon to reverse this process, you will go beyond the point of no return.

You are probably wondering if there is any hope for you. I can tell you with great confidence, "Yes, there is!" God can help you resolve this problem no matter how great it seems to be. He can help you learn how to control your anger. He can give you victory over this powerful force within you.

CAUSES OF ANGER

Let's begin by looking at the three basic causes of anger. Each of these causes feeds the problem of anger in our lives. Left out of control and unchecked by the power of the Holy Spirit, they can ultimately destroy us.

1. Fear.

Many times we get angry because of fear. Something happens that frightens us. All of a sudden we are fearful, but after we calm down, we become angry. Have you ever had a close call that frightened you? Perhaps you were driving down the highway minding your own business when someone pulled out in front of you and ran you off the road. You slammed on the brakes and skidded to a stop. At first you were frightened out of your skin. Then you calmed down, got hold of yourself, and blew up!

Your initial reaction was to thank God that you were not seriously hurt. But then you got red in the face, started thinking about what happened, and said something like, "Where did that guy get his driver's license?" You were afraid and then your fear turned to anger.

Perhaps you have gone to bed at night hoping for a peaceful night's sleep. Suddenly, at 2:00 A.M., your telephone rings, shattering your sleep. Startled, you leap out of bed and start running to the phone. As you race through the dark you just know something terrible must have happened. Is it my family? Who died? Who in the world would be calling me at this hour? You grab the phone and pick it up just in time to hear someone hang up on the other end! You become so upset with the caller that you can't go back to sleep. There goes another night, and your fear turns to anger.

2. *Frustration.*

Another cause of anger is frustration. It may not be as stunning as fear, but it feeds anger nevertheless. Have you ever been frustrated because you couldn't pay your bills? Perhaps you tried to clean house in preparation for company and became frustrated because the kids kept messing it up. Dads get frustrated at work, moms at home, and teenagers at school. Frustration is a part of life. When we don't handle it right, it can lead to anger.

Perhaps you have studied long hours as a high-school or college student, only to fail an exam. The normal human tendency is to become frustrated and want to blow up at the teacher. You may have taken piano lessons and practiced diligently, only to perform miserably. Your frustration turns to anger and you would like to break the piano in half!

Remember the frustrations of Moses as he tried to lead the children of Israel? The Bible tells us that Moses was the meekest man that ever lived. He led the children of Israel out of Egypt in the great Exodus to the Promised Land. He miraculously led them across the Red Sea on dry ground and then through the wilderness of Sinai. Despite all of his patience, he finally lost his cool in the wilderness of Zin. We read about it in Numbers chapter twenty.

There we see that even though the people of Israel had seen God miraculously provide for their needs time and time again, they began to blame Moses because they had run out of water. It's an old tactic: When all else fails, blame the preacher!

The people began to "chide him," which means they began yelling and screaming at him. Moses tried to remain calm through it all. He went to the Lord to ask Him what to do. God told him to take his rod, gather the people together, and *speak* unto the rock and it would give forth water (Numbers 20:8). But in his frustration Moses became angry and *smote* the rock twice instead. Moses had had all he could take. He had had enough of their bickering, complaining, and screaming. In essence, he was saying, "If you want water, get it yourself."

As Moses hit the rock, water gushed out for all the people to drink. But Moses had openly disobeyed God by striking the rock, and because of that one act of anger, provoked by frustration, Moses was denied entrance into the Promised Land.

Frustration means to be provoked out of control. When Moses was provoked out of control, he lost his temper and with it he lost some of his leadership. The tragedy with anger is that it can do irreparable damage.

3. Hurt.

Another cause of anger is hurt. Sometimes we blow up because we have been deeply hurt. We may be hurt by something someone says or by some thoughtless thing someone does. People may not even mean to hurt us, but they do.

Perhaps someone has let you down. Your disappointment turns to hurt, and then anger. It can be almost anything: a broken promise, an unfaithful partner, a forgotten anniversary. Whatever may have happened, you hurt for a while. You cried all you could cry. You grieved all you could grieve. Then you thought, *How could they do this to me? To me, of all people. I love them. Just look at all I did for them.* Then you internalized the hurt, and the hurt became anger, and anger turned to revenge. You began thinking, *I'm going to get even. I'm going to show them how much they hurt me. They are going to get what is coming to them.* Before you knew it, your emotions were out of control.

That kind of thinking, I'm sorry to say, is not that unusual. It is a problem almost all of us have to deal with from time to time. It's a part of our makeup as individuals. Everyone has the psychological capacity for anger. The biblical term for anger means "any natural impulse." In the Greek language of the original New Testament it conveys the idea of *energy*. Anger is a form of human energy which may be used for good or evil. Anger may make one person become a murderer and cause another person to defend himself against a murderer. Whichever response we choose, anger, like any form of energy, must be released.

ATTEMPTS TO CONTROL ANGER

There are several ways in which people most commonly try to deal with anger. Usually, these don't work. They only complicate the situation all the more. In time, these futile attempts prove to make the problem even worse.

1. Nurse It.

We have already mentioned briefly those who try to hide their anger. They say to themselves, "I'm really angry, but nobody's going to know it." They bundle it up inside themselves. They fume within, but never let anyone know how they really feel. Instead, they start boiling like a pressure cooker about to blow its lid!

People who suppress their anger either destroy themselves emotionally or spew it out belatedly. Day and night their anger brews and churns inside. It eats them up like acid.

The Apostle Paul said, "Let not the sun go down upon your wrath." What he meant was, "Don't keep it within you." Don't internalize it. Anger is an emotional force. It needs to be released, or it will destroy you from within. Suppressed anger can lead to an emotional breakdown.

One of my favorite old-time television programs was "Amos and Andy." In one episode, Amos saw Andy walking down the street with an overcoat on in the summertime. There was a large bulge sticking out of the overcoat. Amos asked him what was under his coat, and Andy proceeded to tell him about his frustration with a certain man who always thumped him on his chest while he talked to him. "I'm going to fix him," Andy announced. "I've got two sticks of dynamite strapped to my chest. When he thumps me this time, I'm going to blow his hand off!" What Andy forgot was that he would also blow his own heart out in the process.

That is how internalized anger works. It destroys us from within ourselves. You may think that hiding your anger is the "Christian" thing to do, but it isn't. It is only a temporary solution with long-term consequences.

2. Disperse It.

These are the people who go off like the atom bomb every chance they get. They don't even try to internalize their feelings. They are just waiting for the opportunity to explode. They love it. To them, everything is a battlefield: their home, their job, their friends. No one dares to get close to them.

Something goes wrong, and boom! They just start screaming. They explode frequently and violently with a verbal barrage of shouting, cursing, threatening, and condemning. Sometimes they say terrible things they will regret for a lifetime.

The Bible says: "Let no corrupt communication proceed out of your mouth, but that which is good to the use of edifying, that it may minister grace unto the hearers. And grieve not the holy Spirit of God, whereby ye are sealed unto the day of redemption" (Ephesians 4:29-30). The term *corrupt* means "rotten" or "unfit" in the original Greek. *Edify* means "build up." Therefore, the Apostle Paul is literally saying, "Don't use your mouth to say rotten things that cut people down; use it to build them up." By your positive conversation you "minister grace" to all who hear you.

The most serious problem with angry responses is that they "grieve" the Holy Spirit. God does not want to listen to all our negativism and hostility. We can grieve Him just as a child grieves its parents. When a child falls into sin, the parent's heart is grieved. That is the same thing we do to God when we grieve His Spirit by our anger.

Some will always try to excuse themselves by saying, "That's the way I was raised" or "It just runs in our family." But anger is not genetic. It is a learned behavioral response. You learned how to display it, and you can learn how to control it. Anger has nothing to do with being Irish, Spanish, Italian, or anything else. It has to do with how you handle pressure. If you don't master it, it will master you.

3. Rehearse It.

These are the people who give their anger out a spoonful at a time, day after day. They never seem to tire of talking about it. It seems they are always upset about something. They are mad at the family, people at work, and everybody at church. Nobody can please them. They are perennial grouches. Something is wrong with everybody but them.

How do people get like this? Most of the time it comes from years of stockpiling their bitterness. Their feelings have rotted until everything they see is rotten. They are like the fellow whose hat was lined with garlic: He thought everybody stunk but him! Sometimes we are the last ones to see ourselves as we really are.

Those who constantly want to talk about their frustrations make everyone around them miserable. They themselves live a miserable existence and continue releasing just enough bitterness every day to make everyone else miserable, too.

I once heard a humorous story about a lady who was bitten by her own dog. When she went to the doctor, he told her that she had a severe case of rabies and only had a short time to live. Instead of being upset, she took out a pencil and paper and began writing. "Is that your will you are writing?" the doctor asked. "No," she replied, "It's a list of all the people I want to bite!"

The tragedy is that the world is full of people just like that. They want to bite you with their anger, their frustration, their hurt, and their misery. They virtually go through life looking for someone to latch onto and bite with their hatred. Such people are living miserable, pessimistic, negative lives.

CURE FOR ANGER

What can we really do about anger? Since it is an emotional response that can become a sinful action, it is important that we learn how to cure it. Anger is a problem that is common to all of us, although it affects some more than others. At the same time, we dare not excuse it, or simply hope that it will go away. We must discipline ourselves to deal with it.

1. Reverse It.

The same passage of Scripture that warns us against the problems of anger tells us what to do about it. Ephesians 4:32 states, "And be ye kind one to another, tenderhearted, forgiving one another, even as God for Christ's sake hath forgiven you."

The person who has a problem with anger has a deeper problem with unforgiveness. It's that unforgiving spirit that keeps feeding anger. It calls out for revenge. It is that attitude which says, "I'm not going to forgive you because you deserve my anger."

Do you remember what Jesus said as He hung on the cross? "Father, forgive them; for they know not what they do" (Luke 23:34). You need to let God forgive you before you can really forgive anyone else. Anger cries out, "I'll never forgive you." But the Cross of Christ cries out, "Father, forgive them."

It is only in the Cross that we can find true reconciliation with God and man. We who have been forgiven must learn how to forgive. The real problem with anger is not your temper; it is your unforgiving spirit.

2. Redirect It.

In order to fully correct the problem of anger we must learn to take positive steps to redirect our relationships. *First*, you need to ask God to forgive you for the sin of anger. *Second*, you need to ask those you have offended to forgive you for your anger. *Third,* you need to forgive yourself.

Once you have taken these steps, you will be able to concentrate on rebuilding your relationships with others. You will never grow to maturity in your Christian life until you learn how to deal with anger. Only then will you be able to respond with kindness, tenderheartedness, and forgiveness in every situation in life.

The writer of Proverbs put it this way: "He that is slow to anger is better than the mighty; and he that ruleth his spirit than he that taketh a city" (Proverbs 16:32).

The opposite of anger is love. It is often the missing ingredient in our lives. A popular song once said, "What the world needs now is love." Not only does the world need love, but so do a lot of Christians. Love is the essential dynamic that makes life worth living. It is the ultimate expression of our concern for one another. Those who really know how to love can overcome the problem of anger.

The process works like this: Anger is the problem; forgiveness is the cure; and love is the result. Once we learn how to forgive those who hurt us and wrong us, we can learn how to love them. Usually, we are hurt the most by those we love the most. It is a tragedy when people spend the rest of their lives hating the person they really love.

Are you angry with someone? Why don't you settle it right now? Don't let the sun go down on your wrath. Deal with it today. The sooner you do, the happier you will be. God loved you so much that He forgave your sins. The least you could do is to forgive those who have sinned against you.

12

The Cure for a Bitter Spirit

Bitterness is a destructive power which can drain your life of joy. In Luke 15 we see the problem of bitterness in the life of the older brother in the story of the Prodigal Son. When the Prodigal Son returned to his father's house, he was received in forgiveness and restored to his rightful position of sonship. The father ordered that the best robe be placed upon his shoulders, that a ring be put on his hand and shoes on his feet, and that a banquet be held in his honor. He announced to one and all, "This my son was dead, and is alive again; he was lost, and is found" (Luke 15:24).

The whole story of the father's restoration of the Prodigal Son is one of the most beautiful in all of Scripture. It certainly expresses the love of God for the sinner as well as the fallen saint. He is a Father of mercy who delights to call His children back to Himself. But there is another side to this story that is often forgotten. It is the story of the elder brother. The Bible tells us that as the family began to celebrate the Prodigal's return, an elder brother was at work in the field. Hearing the noise of the celebration, he came to the house and discovered that his brother had returned home. He was in shock. He could not believe what was happening. After all, he was the one who had been there all these months with his father. He was the one who remained faithful when his younger brother had deserted them. And now his despicable brother, who had caused all of this grief, had returned home, and his father had thrown a party. The Bible says that "he was angry, and would not go in" (Luke 15:28).

When we think about, it does seem rather unfair. Here this elder son had been faithful to work in the fields day after day, sweating to earn the income while his younger brother had been away in a far country wasting his inheritance on harlots and wild living. But look who is getting the party! The elder son's heart began to boil with bitterness toward his younger brother.

The father, seeing what was happening, came out to the elder brother and questioned his attitude. The conversation must have gone something like this:

"Father, what do you mean, asking me why I'm upset? Don't you remember when my brother left, I was the one who stayed faithful? And now just look at what it's gotten me!"

The father responded, "But, Son, don't you understand, your brother was lost, and now he is found. We thought he was dead, but now he's come home—he's alive."

"I don't care," said the elder brother. "I'll bet if I had blown the family income like my spoiled little brother did, you and everybody else would have just written me off."

His anger was not merely a reflection of sibling rivalry. Rather, it was the reflection of everything that was wrong in his life. He had become bitter toward his brother, and that bitter spirit had warped and twisted his own understanding until he was more concerned about his own feelings than the fact that his repentant brother's life had been saved.

One of the great tragedies of a bitter spirit is that it corrupts all that is within us, and we in turn vent its poison on all of those who are about us. Many times, even the most bitter men and women do not realize that it is tearing their lives apart. They have few friends, their own family members don't want to be around them, their marriages fall apart, and they continually criticize and blame everyone else for their problems. "What's wrong with these people?" they will often ask. "Why don't they just accept me as I am?" they will say. Life seems so wrong, but even if they try their best, they cannot figure out why. All the time, bitterness is eating their life away.

Perhaps someone who is reading this chapter today is vexed with a bitter spirit. You may say, "Well, how can I know if I have a bitter spirit?" I believe if we take a moment to give a closer examination of the problem of the elder brother, perhaps you can discover in your life whether or not you are gripped by bitterness.

RESPONSES OF A BITTER SPIRIT

The elder brother's attitude is typical of those who live their lives centered on self more than on others. Our Lord used this story to speak to the people of Israel about their attitudes toward those who had wandered from the commandments of God. The self-centered attitude that asks "What's in it for me?" is also quite prevalent in the lives of Christians today. Sometimes it seems to ooze out all over. So it was with the elder brother; this attitude can be clearly detected in his response to the situation.

First, it is evident that he was *angry at the joy of others*. Before he ever got to the house as he came in from the field, he heard laughter and celebration and it made him angry because he was not part of it.

There are people in this world who cannot seem to bear the thought of others being happy without them. When they get together with their friends, or at work every day at the office, or even in the fellowship of the church, if they are not at the center of attention, if they are not the ones everyone else is looking to, they build up such a bitter and jealous spirit that they become livid with anger.

Have you ever observed others smiling, laughing, and enjoying the pleasure of their family or friends, and said within your heart, "I despise them for that!" Perhaps you have even felt that no one deserves to have such joy. If that has been your attitude, then you must face the fact that more than likely it is spawned by bitterness.

The second mistaken response from the elder brother was *he isolated himself from the fellowship of others*. The Bible tells us he refused to enter into the house and join in the celebration. In essence he was saying, "If they are going to have their fun, let them have it without me!" He stood outside the door, sulking and feeling sorry for himself, no doubt thinking that his refusal to join in their joy would somehow prove some kind of point. But when he isolated himself from his family and friends, he only made his problem worse.

Perhaps you are a father or a husband and you feel that your family does not treat you with the respect and appreciation you deserve. Or you may be a wife or mother and you think that all your loved ones want you around for is for what they can get out of you. They simply refuse to give you the kind of love and attention that you feel you have earned. Those feelings are not uncommon! All too often we become so self-centered in our thinking that we withdraw from those who care most about us and isolate ourselves in a self-imposed cavern of our own emotions. And as long as we remain isolated in our own little world of self-pity, we will inwardly continue to conduct our daily pity party and never resolve the inward bitterness that is ruining our relationships with those who really love us most.

Over the years of my ministry I have dealt with countless people who have almost wrecked their lives in this trap of bitterness. Let me share with you a letter from a lady who wrote to me from Oklahoma.

> Dear Dr. Lee,
>
> Recently I heard you speak about the problem of bitterness. As you spoke, I began to see that I have a bad case of bitterness in my heart against my husband.
>
> Several years ago he hurt me about as bad as I felt I could ever be hurt. I don't want to go into the details about how he wronged me, but later he became broken about it and asked for my forgiveness. Although my husband and I are both Christians, I'll admit I found it hard to forgive him, but I said I would and believe I meant it when I said it.
>
> What I thought was that after a while if I tried to forget the pain it would go away, but somehow that never happened. Oh, I don't ever bring it up to him. I promised him I wouldn't. Now he goes on with his life, smiling as though nothing ever happened. I guess it never crosses his mind. But I never live a day without it churning down inside me.
>
> Now let me tell you what is happening. Every time my husband comes in the door, I want to run and hide. He hugs me and kisses me, and I just want to run away. The only way I know how to keep from wrecking my home by "letting it out" is to keep away from him as much as possible. But as you can imagine, that in itself is destroying our relationship. I guess I am bitter. But what am I going to do?
>
> Sincerely,
> Nancy

When I read Nancy's letter, I wanted to share with her some of the things I'll share with you later on in this chapter. Believe me, I also hurt for her. Here she was, trying her best to do what she could do to handle her bitterness, not really understanding what was going on inside her; but by turning to isolating herself from her husband, she was destroying the very thing she was trying her best to save.

Unfortunately, the world is filled with emotional isolationists, some carrying it to the extreme. And it is not limited only to adults like Nancy. Often teenagers find themselves embittered against others and literally imprison themselves in their own rooms. There they remain, in a self-imposed fortress of bitterness and rebellion. In some cases, they will not come out for anything other than a meal. When

The Cure for a Bitter Spirit

this kind of thing happens, it is tragic because it prohibits effective communication in resolving family problems.

I am convinced that most family conflicts and marital difficulties could be resolved if we could settle the problem of bitterness. The real tragedy is that one bitter experience often leads to another. Couples who become divorced because of their conflicts with one another often even become embittered against the idea of marriage itself. Others become bitter toward their friends because they feel rejected now that they are divorced. No matter what anyone does to attempt to resolve this situation, it seems that the bitterness continues to spread into every area of life.

If you have been hurt by someone else, it is important for you to get that resolved as quickly as possible. We cannot judge why certain people have had certain difficulties or failures in their lives. We can only extend to them the love and forgiveness that God offers to all who will come to Him. There are many people in life that I may never fully understand, but that does not keep me from loving them with the love of Christ.

If you've been hurt by some serious experience in life, please don't let yourself become bitter over it. In an ultimate sense, bitterness is *harbored hurt*. You may not be able to help the fact that you were hurt by someone else. But you do not have to become bitter toward them, nor do you have to remain bitter for the rest of your life. If you find yourself wanting to avoid someone else, chances are pretty strong that you are suffering from a bitter spirit.

We also notice another thing about the elder brother: *He was critical of the blessings of others.* Apparently the younger son had been gone for some time. He had left home decisively and had not sent any word of his destination. For all practical purposes the family assumed that they would never see him again. That is why the father described his condition as being dead. When he returned home his father said, "For this my son was dead, and is alive again" (Luke 15:24). In the father's mind, he had received his son alive again and nothing could have been more thrilling.

The question that remains is, why was the elder brother so critical of his brother's return? We could try to blame his attitude on many things, but the real answer is that the elder brother was selfish. He was so wrapped up in himself and his relationship to his father that he became totally self-centered. Notice his selfish attitude. The Bible records that he spoke accusingly to his father, saying, "I never disobeyed your command; yet you never gave *me* a kid, that I might make merry with *my* friends" (Luke 15:29, RSV [italics added]). Everything the elder brother expressed was a statement of his own selfish viewpoint in life. While it is true that there was no excuse for his brother's behavior, there was also no excuse for his own.

Not only was the elder brother self-centered, but he was also self-righteous. His insistence that he had never transgressed his father's commandments is highly unlikely. While he may have been an ideal son in many ways, he certainly was not perfect. Remember, our Lord was using this story as an illustration to His own people. They had certainly transgressed the commandments of God on numerous occasions, and yet they prided themselves on their righteousness. On that basis, we can conclude that the elder brother was making an empty assertion. He had undoubtedly violated his father's laws at times, though he certainly had not transgressed them as severely as the younger brother had done. The problem is not in the issues of righteousness, but in the attitude of the elder brother. The Prodigal Son had done wrong and he had paid for it dearly. The father was not overlooking the wrong that was done. Rather, he was rejoicing at the return of his son. The elder brother refused to enter into the rejoicing because of his own self-centeredness, which was expressed in his self-righteous assertion that he had never transgressed his father's commandments. As he continued to explain that a banquet had never been thrown in his honor he was expressing his selfishness. A person with a bitter spirit is always filled with selfish pride.

Notice that there is a cycle of criticism in the attitude of the elder brother. First of all he began by criticizing his younger brother for wasting his inheritance. But then he turned to criticizing his father for holding the party in his brother's honor. Here we see a cycle in the expression of a bitter spirit. The one who is bitter begins by criticizing one person and usually ends up criticizing someone else. In the same manner, I am convinced that those whose hearts are filled with bitterness against another are ultimately bitter against God.

When we criticize and complain, we are really saying to God that He has not done an adequate job in meeting our needs. Our pride tells us we know what is best. Inevitably the isolationism and bitterness is turned against God Himself. The problem is that such an attitude never draws us closer to God, and only pushes us further away from Him. When I think of God's great love in allowing the curse of our sin to be placed upon His own Son, I wonder how anyone could ever be bitter against Him.

THE RESULTS OF BITTERNESS

When bitterness is allowed to remain, it will result in the destruction of those elements of life that are essential for maintaining our balance and joy.

1. It Destroys Your Perspective.

Bitterness clouds our spiritual vision. It causes us to become blinded to the reality of life itself. Once you become bitter and proud, you don't see things clearly and your entire spiritual perspective is blurred. But that's the way it always is with pride. It causes people to think more highly of themselves than they ought.

I remember reading about the American humorist Will Rogers. As the story goes, one day a young woman came to him and said she was worried about having too much pride. "Why?" he asked. She said, "Well, every morning when I look into the mirror I think about how beautiful I am." Will Rogers looked at her and said, "I'm sorry to tell you this, young lady, but that's not pride, that's a mistake!" Bitterness and pride will always lead to a wrong perspective of self and others.

When the father responded to the elder brother he said, "Son, thou art ever with me, and all that I have is thine" (v. 31). He was reminding his elder son that the celebration for his brother's return had cost him nothing. The father was also reminding the elder son that he had not forgotten his faithfulness and devotion to him. He was trying to help his son see that the extension of forgiveness to his brother was not intended in any way at all to be a rejection of him. The father had the right perspective on the situation, but the elder brother did not. His perspective was clouded by bitterness.

2. It Destroys Your Usefulness.

As long as you have a bitter spirit you are useless in serving God. There is almost no way that you can be involved in a positive ministry to others because of the bitter attitude within your own soul. Once we allow ourselves to get in that condition we will drive people away from us more than we will be able to point them to the Savior.

Let me remind you that there is nothing more important than being used by God. There is nothing more wonderful or more fulfilling than to know that God is working through your life to touch the lives of others. By contrast, there is nothing that will destroy your spirit any more than to know you are no longer being used of God.

I am convinced that you were born into the family of God for a specific purpose. That is why you were created, and that is why you were born again. But once you become bitter, your usefulness greatly diminishes.

I often think of King Saul in the Old Testament as an example of one who developed a bitter spirit. The Bible tells us that Saul was tall and handsome and a man whom the people selected to be their leader. But something tragic happened in Saul's life. We read that he was envious of David because of David's success against the Philistines, and in particular against Goliath. As a result, Saul became angry and embittered toward David. In his state of bitterness, he began to isolate himself from his advisors. He developed a critical and bitter spirit and even turned against his own son Jonathan. On more than one occasion he actually attempted to kill David.

The real tragedy is that David was the one person who could have delivered Saul from the Philistines, but Saul drove David into the wilderness, where he became a fugitive. In the meantime, the Philistines mounted a major assault against Saul. In the battle, Jonathan was killed and Saul severely wounded. Saul then took his own life. The sad truth is that Saul died more from his own bitterness than he did from his defeat in battle.

THE REMEDY FOR BITTERNESS

As we examine the story of the Prodigal Son and the father's dealing with the elder brother, we find the solution to the problem of bitterness. There is no problem which comes into our lives for which God does not have a solution. And the solution to the problem is stated very clearly in these verses.

1. *He Reminded Him of Who He Was.*

When the father said to the elder brother, "Son, thou art ever with me," he was reminding him of his position within the family. It does not matter how bitterly you may have turned your heart from God, if you are a true believer God is still living within you. He has promised that He will never leave or forsake you and He will keep that promise. You are His child, and through His grace and keeping power you forever will be. When you remember who you are and that you really belong to the Father, you will realize that there is no excuse for being bitter.

2. He Reminded Him of What He Had.

The father reminded the elder brother, "All that I have is thine." While the Prodigal Son had been restored with a banquet of celebration, the fact remained that he had blown his inheritance. The father had to remind the elder brother that his inheritance was still due him. As I read this, I am reminded that all too often we forget the inheritance that we have in Christ. We start feeling sorry for ourselves because of some little insignificant problem that has occurred in our lives, and we get our attention off the fact that we are His heirs. There is no reason to go around feeling sorry for yourself. All that God has given to Christ, He has made available to you as His joint heir. As children of God we have far more than the rich and famous.

3. He Reminded Him of What He Needed to Be Doing.

The father reminded the elder son that his brother had been lost and was now found. He further reminded him that there was appropriate need for rejoicing and reconciliation. In essence, the father was explaining to his son that his bitterness was destroying his relationship with him as well as with his brother. The appeal of the father was the appeal of mercy versus self-righteousness. It was the request of grace versus judgment.

It has always caught my attention that there is no conclusion to this story in Scripture. The father explains why they ought to be rejoicing and the scene finishes without ever telling us what ultimate response the older brother made. I am convinced that our Lord told this story to urge the self-righteous people of His own day to open their hearts and lives to genuine forgiveness of others. He wanted to help them break through the barriers of bitterness and discover the grace of forgiveness. But He left the decision up to them.

In the same manner, when God deals with our lives today, He leaves the final decision to us. If you have become bitter toward someone else and that bitterness has warped your personality and damaged your relationships with others, it is up to you to decide to do something about it. You can overcome the curse of a bitter spirit. But you can only do so when you allow the love of God to fill your heart and soul with an attitude of understanding which leads to reconciliation and restoration.

PART FOUR

OUT OF THE DEPTHS

Out of the depths have I cried unto thee, O Lord. . . . Let Israel hope in the Lord: for with the Lord there is mercy and with him is plenteous redemption.

—PSALM 130:1, 7

13

Up from the Pit

Life is never all joy and no sadness. While it can be a wonderful and exciting journey of faith, life can still have its own measure of troubled times. There are going to be those times when such problems enter our lives for no apparent reason. You may be sailing along smoothly in life with everything apparently in order, and then unexpectedly you are hit with some great difficulty. That is how life is. Such experience is described in the Book of Acts in the story of Paul's voyage to Rome. The Bible says that "when the south wind blew softly" (Acts 27:13) the sailors set sail against Paul's advice and were eventually caught in a terrible storm which led to their shipwreck. Unfortunately, all too often that is how life is.

When such tragedies come into our lives, we are immediately shaken by the seriousness of such events. Perhaps you have been involved in a car accident or come down with an unexpected illness and you have asked yourself, "Why is this happening to me?" Such questions are an honest expression of the concern that we all experience at a time like that. In our way of thinking, we can understand why bad things would happen to bad people. But we cannot understand why bad things sometimes happen to good people.

One of the most amazing stories in all of Scripture is that of Joseph. He was seventeen years old when his brothers turned against him and sold him into slavery. For some time it had been obvious to his brothers that he was his father's favorite. In resentment, they conspired against him to kill him. But his oldest brother intervened and insisted that they spare his life. Instead of killing him, they decided to sell him to a nomadic trading caravan and deceived their father into thinking that he had been killed by a wild animal. In the meantime, the caravan sold Joseph as a slave in Egypt. While in Egypt, the Bible tells us, Joseph became the chief servant in the household of an Egyptian officer by the name of Potiphar. Because of his abiding faith in the power of God, Joseph remained faithful to the Lord. And even as a slave, he determined to be the best that he could possibly be for the glory of God. While working in the house of Potiphar, Joseph was falsely accused of sexual misconduct by Potiphar's wife. As a result he was thrown into the royal prison. There in the prison, Joseph became a model prisoner and was put in charge of the other prisoners. Eventually he was able to interpret the dreams of two fellow prisoners who were servants of Pharaoh. In time one of them remembered him, and he was eventually brought before Pharaoh himself to interpret the ruler's dream. As a result of God's hand upon Joseph, and in recognition of his special abilities, Pharaoh elevated him to the position of prime minister over the entire land of Egypt. The story of Joseph's rise from the pit and prison to become second only to the Pharaoh himself is indeed one of the most incredible stories in all of Scripture.

I have often wondered what thoughts must have gone through Joseph's mind during those difficult days while he was in slavery and in prison. Surely he must have been tempted to question God. Perhaps he felt that God had turned against him or had abandoned him. Surely he was tempted to discard his faith in the Lord and turn to something else. Most of us, had we been in Joseph's place, would have likely become discouraged, despondent, and depressed, to say the least. Some might even have contemplated suicide. But not this young man. He had an abiding confidence in the purposes of God being accomplished in his life. That is not to say that his was an easy life, for surely it was not. There must have been times of desperation and despair but through it all Joseph remained faithful to the God who loved him.

Perhaps you have recently found yourself in some pit of discouragement. You may even be questioning whether or not God is still with you. It could be that you are almost to the point of giving up on life itself. If so, let me encourage you to come to an understanding of your trouble, learn how to get through it, and use it for a stepping stone to a brighter future.

WHO'S TO BLAME?

I'm sure you realize that human beings have a tendency to want to blame someone else for their difficulties. Some blame themselves, others blame God, some blame the Devil, and some blame another individual. And while others may have contributed to our difficulties, ultimately we must face our own problems squarely and properly. The Word of God not only tells us how to handle the problems of life, but it specifically tells us what attitude to take when bad things happen to us.

First, we need to realize that *many of life's problems are not our fault*. While there are certainly times when we are at fault and deserve to be held accountable for our actions, there are times when life's problems are not our fault at all. Sometimes things simply happen that are beyond our control or responsibility. When these things occur, such as a car accident, we tend to blame ourselves. We start thinking of all the things that we could have done differently to avoid the accident, and before we are finished, we have even accused ourselves of getting out of bed and starting off that day in the wrong manner. You cannot go back and undo the problems that have come into your life. You may be able to undo the actions that caused those problems to result. But you cannot undo the fact that they have already occurred. Learning to accept our problems and face them confidently in the power of God is one of the most important steps we could ever take toward spiritual maturity.

You can blame yourself until you are blue in the face, but that will not remove the problems. You can also "if" yourself to death with a series of statements like, "If this had happened," "If I had only done thus and so." When something happens that is beyond your control, don't start blaming yourself. There are usually enough other people who will falsely accuse you and blame you without your starting in on yourself.

I remember hearing the story about a little boy who always had a tendency to blame himself when something went wrong. He was sitting in Sunday school one day when the teacher decided to ask him a very simple question.

"Where is God?" the teacher asked.

The boy replied, "I don't know where He is."

The teacher looked intently at the boy, and said, "Certainly you know where He is! Tell the class where God is."

Suddenly the boy became so frightened that he jumped up out of his chair, ran out of the classroom, down the hall, out the door, and down the street to his house. When he finally got home, he burst through the front door, ran up the stairs into the bedroom, and shut himself in the closet. His mother, hearing all the noise, went up to his bedroom and tried to get him to come out of the closet, but the boy refused to open the door. "What's wrong with you?" she asked.

"Oh, Momma," he replied, "you will never believe what happened down at the church. God is missing, and they think that I did it!"

Can you imagine Joseph blaming himself for everything that had gone wrong in his life? Can you imagine him saying, "If I had only stayed with my dad"? Or perhaps he could have said, "If I had not offended my brothers." It really does not matter what it was that provoked them to react against him as they did. Chances are, they would have done it regardless. They despised him, and they showed their inner attitude by their outward action. Now we must be careful to recognize that God did not cause them to hate their brother. Their hatred was a reflection of their wrong heart attitude. They were responsible for the way they felt toward their brother. But God overruled their anger and in the long run used it to bring about a greater good than any of them could have ever foreseen. That is why Joseph later told his brothers, "Ye thought evil against me; but God meant it unto good" (Genesis 50:20). Joseph realized that their intentions were evil, but he also realized that God had overruled them all.

If you want to overcome the bad things that happen in life, you must stop blaming everything on yourself. It is time to turn your attention heavenward and realize that God is still at work in your life. He can use even the evil intentions of others to accomplish His good purposes in your life.

Another truth we find is that *life's problems are not God's fault either*. Some people are also quick to blame God for their problems. Their attitude is expressed in questions like, "God, why did you take my family away from me?" or, "God, why did you make me lose my job?" The Bible tells us that God is too good to do anything harmful to us and too wise to do anything foolish to us. He loves you more than you love yourself. He only wants the very best for you. In Joseph's case it was not God who was the source of his problems, but his brothers. They were the ones who had done wrong, and he was suffering the consequence of their wrongdoing.

Blaming God is not a new tactic. Adam tried it way back in the Garden of Eden. After Adam and Eve had sinned, they fled into the Garden to hide from God. When God came pursuing them at the end of the day, He asked them why they had eaten of the tree of the knowledge of good and evil. Adam's response was to blame both Eve and God for what had gone wrong. First of all, he said, "The woman whom thou gavest me to be with me, she gave me of the tree, and I did eat" (Genesis 3:12). Adam took no responsibility for what had happened. He blamed Eve for enticing him and then he blamed God for giving Eve to him in the first place. In his attempt to blame everyone else for the problem, he was showing the typical human reaction to dealing with difficulties. We might call it Adam's Law: When things go wrong, blame somebody else.

Even in the area of insurance there are statements that refer to "acts of God." These are generally such things as lightning, fire, floods, and earthquakes. While God may certainly send these things at times, we must also remember that this present sin-cursed world is under the control of Satan. God can overrule him at any time, but that does not mean that every natural disaster is God's fault.

Then, *whatever your problem, God is near*. Five times in the story of Joseph we read the words, "And the Lord was with Joseph." God was with him in the pit, in the prison, and in the palace. The Lord was standing by Joseph despite his outward circumstances. The presence of God in Joseph's life was so evident that when he stood before the Pharaoh of Egypt, the ruler remarked, "Can we find such a one as this is, a man in whom the Spirit of God is?" (Genesis 41:38).

Most of us, when we go through difficulties in life, tend to complain about our problems. This was not the case with Joseph. Regardless of what inner turmoil he may have faced, he never let it show on the surface of his life. It became evident to everyone that he was indeed a man of God. When you are struggling with the problems of life, I wonder if others can see the evidence of God at work in you. If they cannot, then you are so caught up in the struggle that you have shifted your attention from the Savior to the difficulties. You are focused on the problem and not the solution. The Word of God tells us that God is with us at all times. In your darkest night, when it seems that nobody else cares or understands, God is with you to meet your needs.

The promise of Scripture is that God will never leave us or forsake us. Jesus told His disciples, "Lo, I am with you alway, even unto the end of the world" (Matthew 28:20). It does not matter how deep your struggles may be, nor how far away from God you may feel; Christ has promised never to leave you or forsake you. In your darkest hour, even if family and friends may have turned their backs on you, God is still standing by your side. Even if you have to face the indignity of false accusation or unjust suffering, He will never forsake you. Your life is co-eternal with the life of God. Because He lives, you shall live forever also. This truth reminds us that God will right some of the wrongs of life during this lifetime, but He will right them all in the next.

Lastly, remind yourself that *your present problem is not the final outcome.* For thirteen years Joseph remained a victim of circumstances over which he had no control. During that time he was either serving as a household slave or enduring the shame of a filthy dungeon. He was only seventeen years old when his brothers turned against him and threw him in an empty pit and eventually sold him to a slave-trading caravan. At some point in his early twenties he was falsely accused and condemned to prison. During this long and difficult imprisonment, Joseph never gave up on God despite the fact that there was no quick or easy solution to his problem.

During his imprisonment, Joseph certainly could have blamed God for abandoning him. He could have developed an intense hatred toward his brothers, or he could have been overcome with depression, grief, and self-pity. But somehow Joseph understood that it wasn't over for him. Even in slavery he became the best possible slave. In prison, he became the best possible prisoner. He was a model of spiritual vitality and personal integrity. Most of us would have cracked under these circumstances. But Joseph understood that God's purposes were still being accomplished and that the story of his life had not yet come to an end. It is no wonder that when he finally had the opportunity to stand before Pharaoh, the ruler of Egypt was deeply impressed with the qualities of this young man. In him, he recognized the presence of God Himself.

Years later, when Joseph's brothers arrived in Egypt, they could not even recognize him. They had no way of knowing that their brother had risen to the position of prime minister under the Pharaoh. He looked like an Egyptian. Most men, if they had gone through what Joseph had experienced and had risen to the level of power and authority to which he had risen, would have vindictively treated their own brothers with scorn and cruelty. But not Joseph. He broke down and wept before them and hugged and kissed them and forgave them for selling him into slavery. He was able to do this because he realized that through it all God had a greater purpose than they could have ever begun to comprehend.

Joseph understood that God was in control of the final outcome of life. Long before Romans 8:28 was ever written in the Bible, Joseph knew the truth that "all things work together for good to those who love God, to those who are the called according to His purpose!" (NKJV).

You and I will never be able to handle the terrible problems of life that will come our way until we understand as Joseph did that God is fully in control of the circumstances of our life. Life is not an accident. It is not mere chance meandering down the meaningless river of time. Life is a daily adventure with the living God. And if God be for us, who can be against us?

HOW TO GET THROUGH THE BAD TIMES

We cannot always understand the purposes of God from our finite perspective. Even though we may attempt to stretch our minds to comprehend the infinite purposes of God, we will always fall short of understanding what He is really accomplishing in our lives. But there are three things that will help you through the bad times.

1. *Trust God to Do What Is Right.*
When God announced to Abraham that He was about to destroy the city of Sodom, Abraham pleaded with Him to spare the city and said, "Shall not the Judge of all the earth do right?" (Genesis 18:25). In spite of Abraham's pleading, the city was destroyed in an act of divine judgment. When Abraham awoke the next morning and saw the smoke of the destruction in the distance, he understood that God does indeed do what is right, whether we understand it or not.

God is a righteous God. He is the antithesis of sin and evil. While He may permit evil to exist in the world, He is not the author of sin and evil. Everything in His nature hates sin and evil. But God allows us the free choice of determining what we will do with our lives as free moral agents. We are not pre-programmed human robots.

One day God is going to settle the score for time and eternity. I am convinced that Joseph did not worry about his present circumstances because he understood that very clearly. He probably never dreamed that he would rise to the heights to which he did in his lifetime. But somehow he knew that God was still in control, and whether He made it right in this life or in the next, he knew that God would do that which is right.

2. *In Time You Will Understand Why.*
Contemplating the future, Paul said, "For now we see through a glass darkly; but then face to face: now I know in part; but then shall I know even as also I am known" (1 Corinthians 13:12). Time

is a marvelous thing. It enables us to gain a better perspective on the activity of God in our lives. Perhaps you can recall a time in your life when you were going through a great difficulty and questioned whether you would ever make it. But as you look back now, you can see that God was leading you every step of the way. It is important that we recall the struggling process that eventually brought us through to victory, so that we can sensitively share with others who are hurting along life's road. We must learn how to reach out with compassion and understanding to those who are struggling with the Christian walk. God has not called us to condemn them for their failures but to lift them up and help them along their way.

When we are young and immature we think that a problem is not having a date every night of the week or not being able to buy the car that we've had our heart set on for so long. But at that age we don't understand what real problems are about at all. Later in life, we focus on our marriage, our children, our jobs, or our future. It is only as the years of life roll by that we gain a better perspective on what our lives are really all about in the first place. You and I do not have the opportunity to see our individual lives from the standpoint of eternity. Ours is a limited human perspective. But God, who sees all things from the perspective of the eternal, clearly understands the significance of every experience in your life. We serve a righteous God who is also a loving God. He loves us so much that He will not place any load upon us that we cannot bear. A. M. Overton wrote this comforting poem:

> My father's way may twist and turn,
> My heart may throb and ache,
> But in my soul I'm glad I know,
> He maketh no mistake.
>
> My cherished plans may go awry,
> My hopes may fade away.
> But still I'll trust my Lord to lead
> For He doth know the way.
>
> Tho' night be dark and it may seem
> That day will never break;
> I'll pin my faith, my all, in Him,
> He maketh no mistake.

There's so much now I cannot see,
My eyesight's far too dim;
But come what may, I'll simply trust
And leave it all to Him.

For by and by the mist will lift
And plain it all He'll make,
Through all the way, tho' dark to me,
He made not one mistake.

3. Trust Christ to See You Through.

Some of the greatest promises in all of Scripture come from the words of our Lord Jesus Christ Himself. It was He who said, "Come unto me, all ye that labour and are heavy laden, and I will give you rest" (Matthew 11:28). He also said, "I am the good shepherd: the good shepherd giveth his life for the sheep . . . and I give unto them eternal life; and they shall never perish, neither shall any man pluck them out of my hand" (John 10:11, 28). In regard to His ascension and second coming, He said, "I go to prepare a place for you. And if I go and prepare a place for you, I will come again, and receive you unto myself; that where I am, there ye may be also" (John 14:2-3). He also said, "Ye have not chosen me, but I have chosen you, and ordained you, that ye should go and bring forth fruit, and that your fruit should remain; that whatsoever ye shall ask of the Father in my name, he may give it you" (John 15:16). Peter put it like this, "Casting all your care upon him; for he careth for you" (1 Peter 5:7). And the writer of Hebrews declared, "He hath said, I will never leave thee, nor forsake thee" (Hebrews 13:5).

If you belong to Christ, no matter what trials or difficulties you may go through in life, He is there to bring you through it all. You have become a child of God, and God will not forsake His children. You are a joint heir with Jesus Christ, and He will not forsake you. When we struggle with the serious problems of life and question why certain things happen to us, we are only revealing our humanity. But when we learn to trust in God no matter what the circumstances, we reveal the work of God within our hearts. God is at work in your life. He is not limited by external circumstances or human problems and difficulties. Whatever may seem to be going wrong, remember, He is working to set it right. Trust Him and He will not fail you.

14

Maintaining Moral Purity

Joseph trusted God in the depths and was raised to the heights. But some of you may be envying him even in his prison cell. After all, he was there through no fault of his own and could at least take comfort in his integrity. Often we don't have that consolation. We have to acknowledge that our own choices have put us where we are. The believer who has succumbed to sexual immorality, the prodigal son who has wasted his inheritance, the person whose life has been poisoned by bitterness—these often feel that the promises of God no longer apply to them.

But when the psalmist cried to the Lord "out of the depths," he came to realize that "with the Lord there is mercy and with him is plenteous redemption" (Psalm 130:1, 7). In the next few chapters we will be looking at the God who delights to restore and redeem.

America is a nation that is experiencing an explosion of pornography. This explosion is destroying our homes, marriages, communities, and young people. It is flaming the fires of rape, molestation, and sexual abuse. No community, regardless of its size, and no age group, has escaped its destructive effects. We are living with a mentality that is based upon selfish humanistic principles and is expressed in the popular phrase "If it feels good, do it."

A recent government report on pornography pointed out the already evident fact that we are plagued with the greatest moral crisis we as a nation have ever known. The number of teenage pregnancies is at an all-time high, as is the number of abortions. The reason is simple: More people are involved in illicit sexual relationships than ever before. Our television programs promote it, cable television channels offer to pipe it into our homes, movies graphically depict it, and books that describe it fill the shelves in our local bookstores. The tragedy of our time is that we are destroying ourselves. AIDS threatens to cut the world population in half by the middle of the next century. That means that billions could die. If something is not done soon to turn the moral tide in our country, we can only expect to reap the penalty of our gross immorality.

I am approached time and time again by sincere people who genuinely want to avoid moral disaster in their lives. They tell me of the sexual temptations that seem to be always around them. They wonder how they can have strength to resist these daily assaults on their morality. Others, who have already made mistakes, seek God's way of forgiveness and the hope that they might have the strength and understanding never to fall again. They seem to express a desperate fear that they will not be able to withstand the pressures for immorality exerted daily upon them. I understand their concerns. There was a time when ministers devoted most of their attention in these matters to teenagers. Teens are still under tremendous pressure to give in to illicit sexual encounters, and they have plenty of opportunity to do so. But what is different today is that not only teens but people of all ages, even young children and older adults, are falling prey. Only God knows the consequences that are ahead for our society, which seems determined to engage itself in every kind of perverse sexual experimentation that lust can imagine.

Moral purity is one area in which the Scripture is very clear in its statements. The Bible says, "Flee fornication. Every sin that a man doeth is without the body; but he that committeth fornication sinneth against his own body" (1 Corinthians 6:18). You can't say it much more directly than that. In other words, the Bible clearly tells us to avoid any involvement in illicit sex. The word *fornication* is a translation of the Greek word *porneia*, from which we also get the word *pornographic*. It means sexual sins of all kinds. It is not limited to any particular sexual indiscretion, but is a general term covering every type and kind of illicit sexual involvement. The Scripture clearly states that God's boundary for sexual involvement is within the bond of marriage. This gives the greatest possible protection and security to every member of the family. It also elevates sex to its proper place of beauty within marriage as God intended it in the first place.

When the Scripture tells us to flee from sexual sin, I believe it means exactly what it is saying. We are to stay away from any and every potential opportunity to do wrong. For some, that may mean the need to flee from certain friendships and acquaintances. For others, temptation may come through a movie, or a video, or a picture.

Whatever the source of temptation may be, it is essential to stay away from it. A person who is inclined to succumb to sexual temptation is no different from an alcoholic who is tempted to get drunk. If someone is sincerely trying to conquer the problem of drinking, the worst thing that person can do is to go sit in a bar where everyone else is drinking. The same is true of those who are battling with the problem of sexual temptation. It is vital that they stay away from people and places where they know the opportunity for temptation is going to arise. God does not tell us to get as close to temptation as we can without giving in to it. On the contrary, He tells us to stay as far away from it as we can possibly get!

Notice that God demands moral purity. He does not make any exceptions at all. While He is a God of forgiveness, who can forgive even the worst of sins, He nevertheless urges us to maintain moral purity at all costs. One of the reasons is that the consequences of sexual sin can be so devastating. They can destroy an individual, a marriage, a family, or an entire society. God does not make this demand because He is a cruel dictator. Some people think that God is sitting on a throne in Heaven in a white robe and a long beard, trying to decide how to make people miserable. Unfortunately, that is the picture that they have of religion. What they do not understand is that God commands that we abstain from those things which He knows will ultimately harm us. God's rules and standards are truly for our own good. He only wants the very best for our life.

PURITY PROTECTS

When God first gave His commandments to the children of Israel at Mount Sinai, He made several strong statements about sexual purity. These laws were to regulate the marital and social relationships of His people. They were also designed to protect His people from the terrible consequences of sexually transmitted diseases and social uncleanness, which were so prevalent among the pagan peoples of that day. In our own time as well, God is providing protection for His people who are willing to follow His guidelines. Really, it isn't difficult to understand why today, perhaps more than ever before, God wants us morally pure.

The first reason God demands moral purity is to *protect our bodies*. The Scripture tells us that whoever commits sexual sin is sinning against his or her own body. Why does it say this? Because illicit sexual involvements all too often lead to sexually transmitted diseases that destroy the body. The so-called "Playboy Philosophy" never shows the real horrors of venereal diseases. Pornographic magazines promote every kind of sexual involvement without ever warning the reader of the real dangers involved. I have personally seen hospital patients whose minds are gone and whose bodies are oozing with sores because of sexually transmitted diseases. And new strains of such diseases are being discovered constantly for which there are no known cures. Once the disease is contracted, all that follows is pain, suffering, and death. We have AIDS victims all around us in society. It will probably be years before we know the real effects of this terrible disease, which is, according to the Centers for Disease Control, spreading more rapidly than any plague known in human history.

It is in this context that God demands moral purity. He is saying in essence that He wants us to have a healthy, pure body so that we might love and serve Him and enjoy the blessings that He provides for us. Therefore, His command to flee from sexual sins is a warning to protect us from the terrible consequences of such sin. I realize that it is difficult to talk someone out of a desire with an argument. The real tragedy of sexual desires is that they can dominate the mind just as severely as the physical desires of an alcoholic. But there is no temptation that life can throw at us for which God has not made provision for escape.

The Scriptures say:

> I beseech you therefore, brethren, by the mercies of God, that ye present your bodies a living sacrifice, holy, acceptable unto God, which is your reasonable service. (Romans 12:1)

In this text the Apostle Paul is pleading with us to present our bodies as a living sacrifice unto God Himself. The concept conveyed here is that of placing oneself on an altar of sacrifice. The idea is that we must die to self in order to live for God effectively. What Paul is urging us to do is to put to death all of our physical desires and place our body in submission to the will of God. Notice that he makes his appeal on the basis of the "mercies of God." These are the mercies that God displays to us in His grace and in His love. It is His mercy as well as His holiness which demands that we separate ourselves from sinful people and sinful practices. God's appeal to His children is that they maintain a morally pure relationship with others so that they might be better equipped to serve Him.

Moral purity also *protects our minds*. Immorality warps and twists the human mind. People need to realize that the more they indulge in immoral practices, the more they will plunge themselves into situations they never dreamed possible. In the first chapter of Romans, the Apostle Paul describes a process of degradation and immorality. In that description he makes the statement, "God gave them over to a reprobate mind" (Romans 1:28). That process begins with vain imaginations in the heart, leads to lust and uncleanness in the sexual use of the body, and continues until a person is given over to vile affections and finally to a reprobate mind. The Scriptures describe the resulting condition as "being filled with all unrighteousness" (and "fornication," meaning sexual sins, heads the list) (Romans 1:29).

The tragedy with sexual sin is that it not only destroys the body but it also destroys the mind. I recently talked with a university student in his early twenties whose mind was being warped and destroyed by pornography. "Every day, all day long—every minute I'm awake—all I can think of is lust and pornographic acts," he told me. "When I lay my head on the pillow at night, I cannot go to sleep because of my fear of having lustful dreams." As we talked together about his problem, it was evident that it actually possessed his thinking. Whether he was driving the car, sitting in the classroom, or talking to another individual, he found himself constantly filled with terrible thoughts. "I don't know what's happening to me," he would say. "I think I'm losing my mind!"

While there are those who try to say that he was not losing his mind, I believe there was a sense in which he was. His continual indulgence in pornography was turning him into a reprobate mentally. Lust destroys the mind. If you live on the level of lust constantly, your mind will become a reprobate mind. The tragedy is that sexual sins begin in the mind and are then translated into actions. That means that in order to control sexual temptation you must learn how to control your mind.

God also demands moral purity to *protect our affections*. Sexual desire is a part of our physical being. God Himself gave us that desire to love and to be loved. It is not an ugly, vulgar, or dirty thing. It is a beautiful thing that God has placed within us. And the reason that God created this desire is to cause men and women to come together in the beautiful institution of marriage and to know love at its fullest. I am convinced that God wants us to know how to give and receive the gift of love in the highest possible expression. But in order to protect our ability to love, He demands that we abstain from lustful and sinful practices.

One of the great tragedies of the sexual indulgence that is going on today is that people are becoming involved sexually without even becoming involved romantically. There was a time when most people felt love should come first, before any physical expression. Today people have sex with total strangers. They fall into bed with people that they hardly know, let alone love, and end up with an empty, meaningless relationship. When real love comes along, they don't understand it because they have involved themselves with so many other people in unloving relationships. You can never know and appreciate true love until you have loved in a truly holy manner.

The Bible has a great deal to say about "natural affection." This natural desire for physical love is inherent within us all. It involves an attraction to the opposite sex that enables us to develop a permanent relationship and bond in marriage. It is a desire that brings joy and satisfaction when used as God intended. But it is the misuse of that desire by allowing oneself to become involved with a person to whom one is not married that guarantees tragedy.

Perhaps you are already convinced that moral purity is essential for your life. But you are struggling with the fact that sexual temptation is so readily available in our society. People at the office are talking about it, ladies at the beauty shop are talking about it, magazines are promoting it, and the television is beaming it across the nation.

GUIDELINES TO MORAL PURITY

"I want to live right," a young businesswoman once told me, "but how can I when everyone else is doing wrong?"

Unfortunately, she had been listening to the advice of friends and business associates, rather than following the guidelines of the Word of God. The end result was that she had gotten herself into a very complicated illicit relationship, which was slowly destroying her. Let me share with you six guidelines to moral purity that I shared with her.

1. Recognize Your Own Potential for Moral Failure.

Believe it or not, I am convinced that many Christians fall into immorality because they never believed they ever could. The Bible says, "Let him that thinketh he standeth take heed lest he fall"

(1 Corinthians 10:12). Not only does the Scripture warn us of the direct assault of temptation in our lives, but it also reminds us that when we have resisted temptation and think that we are standing firm, we need to be careful that we do not become overconfident. The potential for moral failure is real within each one of us. We still have an active fleshly nature, which, at times, does all it can to resist the work of the Spirit of God within us.

There are those who believe that once a person becomes a Christian he or she will never again succumb to blatant sin. I do not believe that the Bible teaches that, nor have I observed that in the lives of people. Born-again Christians are susceptible to the same temptations as everyone else and have the potential of giving in to sin. On the one hand, the Bible clearly implies that those who have been born again will not live in deliberate sin and rebellion against God consistently in their lives. But that does not mean that the believer cannot fall into acts of sin at specific times. I believe this is a very important concept for us to understand. When we think that we cannot give in to a certain kind of sin, we will not make the proper kind of preparation to defend ourselves against it. If you think you are above the sin of immorality, you are sadly mistaken. Many of the people that I have counseled over the years had the same attitude. They thought that they were the last ones who would ever give in to such a thing, but they allowed themselves to be put into a place of compromise which led to capitulation. Once we realize that the potential to be wrong is very real in our lives, we will be better prepared to deal with temptation when it comes.

It is often the person who thinks, "I would never do anything like that," who ends up involved in some kind of sexual sin. There is just something about the self-righteousness of thinking that you are above that sort of thing that actually weakens you and contributes to doing the very thing that you despise. Don't be so overconfident or self-sufficient that you are not prepared. All of us need to go out of our way to avoid any kind of compromising situations that could lead to sexual temptation. Once you admit that you could be tempted, you are much more likely to prepare yourself to deal with temptation when it comes.

2. Commit Your Life to Clear Moral Standards.

You will never make it through the maze of temptation that is so much a part of our world unless you determine specific moral standards for your life. Know where you stand morally and determine not

Maintaining Moral Purity

to compromise your convictions. I am convinced that we need to know what we are going to do even before temptation comes. And if it does come, then you need to act according to the principles and convictions you have established. I think of the tragic story of David's daughter Tamar, who was raped by her own half-brother, Amnon (2 Samuel 13:1–20). She was tricked into putting herself into a compromising situation with him. And when he attempted to tempt her, instead of fleeing, she foolishly tried to talk him out of it. There is no indication in the text that she screamed for help or tried to run out of the room. Because she did not flee from temptation, she became its victim.

By contrast, I think of Joseph, who, as we have already learned, was sold by his own brothers as a slave. Even though Joseph was a slave of an Egyptian official, he was a young man of godly character. As he rose to authority and influence in the home of Potiphar, his master's wife began to lust for him. In time, she made an all-out attempt to talk him into a sexual encounter, and the Bible says that Joseph fled from her presence (Genesis 39:12). Though he suffered the indignity of her false accusations, he, nevertheless, escaped the worst disaster of illicit sin.

3. Flee Every Temptation of Sin.

The one point that is so clearly made in Scripture is that we are to flee from temptation. Don't remain in a place of vulnerability. Stay away from people and places that you know are going to cause you to fall. In Joseph's case, he was a slave in the house of Potiphar. He was not free to leave. The Bible says that Potiphar's wife appealed to him day after day to become involved with her. Finally she made a desperate attempt to seduce Joseph and grabbed him by his coat. When he fled, he left the coat in her hands and escaped.

Joseph had the right idea. Even if it cost him his position, he knew that in order to maintain his morality he could not continue in the situation. Something had to change! And the change that was brought about by his flight not only saved his morality but eventually won him his place in the kingdom.

There is a story about a man who lived in Texas in the days of the Old West. He would often come into town, hitch his horse in front of the saloon, and go in and get drunk. One night he was converted at a Baptist camp meeting. The next morning the saloonkeeper was walking down the street and noticed the man hitching his horse in front of the Baptist church. He shouted, "Hey, why are you hitching your horse here instead of at the saloon?"

The man looked him in the eye and said, "Well, I was converted at a Baptist camp meeting last night and now I've changed my hitching posts."

This man understood the way to handle temptation. That is to change your hitching posts. Whatever or whoever is tempting you, keep away from them before they destroy you.

If certain television programs lead you to evil thoughts, turn them off. Better yet, never turn them on. If certain magazines have a lustful appeal, throw them in the wastebasket. In some cases, it may even be necessary to resign from your job in order to get away from temptation. If you cannot deal with it where you are presently, you would be better off to remove yourself from that situation than to stay there and allow yourself to be destroyed. If you are a teenager, be careful whom you date. Learn to say no to the kind of guys or girls who have a bad reputation. Don't put yourself in a position of vulnerability and expect God to bail you out.

4. *Practice Self-Control in Your Life.*

Self-control is a quality that is developed to its full by the indwelling Holy Spirit within us. He is the One who enables us to control our natural drives and desires. We need to make a practice of controlling these desires. Just as you have to learn to control your appetite for food, so you have to learn to control your appetite for anything else. Once you lose self-control you are going to lose the battle with temptation. That is why the Bible says, "He that ruleth his spirit [is greater] than he that taketh a city" (Proverbs 16:32). *The Living Bible* puts it this way, "It is better to have self-control than to control an army." If you can learn through the power of the Holy Spirit to control the desires within you, you will be greater than a general of an entire army.

Self-control is not something that we develop easily or automatically. It comes with discipline and determination. It is only in the denying of that which is tempting us to do wrong that we develop the ability to live above temptation. I realize that life is filled with tremendous pressures in this regard. But only as you allow God to control your desires will you ever be able to control them yourself.

5. *Fill Your Life with the Things of God.*

Not only do we need to learn to avoid temptation, but we also need to fill our lives with positive things that can effectively prepare us to live for God. In writing to his spiritual son, Timothy, the Apostle Paul said, "Flee also youthful lusts: but follow righteousness, faith, charity, peace, with them that call on the Lord out of a pure heart (2 Timothy 2:22). Notice that Paul advises Timothy to fill his life with real love, faith, righteousness, and peace in place of youthful or sensual lusts.

It is only as we begin to fill our lives with the positive qualities which can be produced by the Spirit of God within us that we have no need for those things which we once desired. In other words, the Apostle Paul is clearly telling us that we must replace that which we removed. That means that there is a twofold aspect to dealing with the problem of sexual temptation. On the one hand, we must learn to deny its desire, and on the other hand, we must fill our lives with inner qualities that are much greater. Paul's advice even touches the area of our friends and associations. He refers to those who call on the Lord out of a pure heart. I believe if we build our personal friendships with those kinds of people, we will be providing a social ring of spiritual protection around our lives.

Learning to live above the level of temptation involves learning to say no to that which you know will ultimately harm you. Once you have experienced the wonderful blessings of God in your life, you are not as likely to be tempted to go back to what you know can never satisfy you. To put it another way, once you ride in a Rolls Royce you can hardly be satisfied with a skateboard! Don't believe those people who say that they've given up so much to serve Jesus. The truth is, you haven't given up anything that was ever worth having in the first place. And in Him, you have found everything that you could never have known without Him.

6. *Remember, One Day You Will Give an Account to God.*

One of the real truths of Scripture is the fact of a final judgment. The Bible tells us that God will judge us for every action and even every word we have spoken. Nothing will be hidden and everything will be made known by Him. One of the reasons God expects the moral purity of His children is that we will all be judged for our personal conduct. Not only will moral purity protect you physically and mentally and emotionally, but it will also prepare you for Heaven and the life to come. Do not foolishly tell yourself that somehow it will go better for you on the Day of Judgment than it will now. Over the years I have counseled with people who have taken exactly that attitude. They have said that they would be horrified if their family knew what they had done, but they seemed rather lax about having to face the judgment of God. Perhaps we sometimes think that as Christians we will never really be judged by God, but that is not what the Bible teaches. While it is true that the blood of Christ covers our sins and cleanses us from sin, that does not mean that we can merely walk away without having to give account to God for our lives.

I believe that there is a beautiful twofold truth taught in Scripture. First, the Bible clearly tells us that God honors and blesses those who obey His Word. Second, Scripture also teaches that He extends forgiveness and the opportunity for a second chance to those who have failed his standards. In one sense we have all failed and come short of the glory of God because we have all sinned. But on the other hand, there are those who have fallen into deep moral sins. Perhaps you are saying to yourself, "I am one of those people." And you are asking the question, "What can I do now that I have already failed?"

There is no sin which is beyond the grace of God. This truth is not an excuse to enable us to continue sinning. Rather, it is the beautiful expression of the love, grace, and mercy of God toward sinners. David was a child of God who fell into the sin of adultery and confessed that sin openly in Psalm 32 and Psalm 51. In the latter psalm he said, "Wash me, and I shall be whiter than snow." Despite the tragic failure which had occurred in his life, David understood the reality of the power of God's forgiveness. Having confessed his sin, he clung to the promise of God. It was after this experience that God called him a man after His own heart. Why? Because David understood the grace that is available from the heart of God.

Whatever your moral problem may be, there is freedom and forgiveness in Jesus Christ. God is still in the business of forgiving sin and cleansing lives. Stop trying to resolve this problem within yourself by your own human effort alone. Come to God in prayer. Whatever it takes, break away from that sin, acknowledge your need, and receive the gift of cleansing which He so willingly provides. He can put your life back together again.

From our childhood we have all heard the story of "Humpty Dumpty." It goes like this:

> Humpty Dumpty sat on a wall,
>   Humpty Dumpty had a great fall,
> All the king's horses and all the king's men
>   Couldn't put Humpty together again.

Someone may be reading this today who feels somewhat like poor Humpty Dumpty. Perhaps your life has been broken by a sexual sin and you have tried everything you know to put it together again. I'll agree with the rhyme, everything of the world, "all the king's horses and all the king's men," could never put your life together again—but THE KING CAN! No matter what your mistake, you can once again be morally pure. Virtue is something that can be lost, but through Christ, the King of Kings, it is also something that can be regained. Why not let Him help you today?

15

How to Get Out of a Mess

Perhaps you have gotten your life into a mess. Things have gone wrong and couldn't be much worse. Let me remind you that you are not alone. There are millions of people in today's world who feel just like you. One day everything was going fine for them, and then, suddenly, the bottom fell out!

No matter how empty you may feel, God cares about you even in your most desperate hour. Although you are down you don't have to stay down. You can always find a way up through Jesus Christ. The whole message of the Bible is one of hope. It is the story of God's love reaching down to the point of our greatest need. No matter how many times you have blown it or how entangled in mistakes you have become, there is always a way out by following principles of common sense and God's Word.

THE MAN WHO LOST IT ALL

In a previous chapter, we made reference to the story of the Prodigal Son which is found in Luke 15. It is the story of a young man in trouble. He was about as low as anyone could get, and he was about as far away from God as he could go. The Bible tells us that he came from a home of wealth and comfort. But in his youthful rebellion, he insisted that his father give him his inheritance so that he could leave home. His father complied with his request and the young man left and went "into a far country."

Before long he had wasted his fortune on riotous living. He squandered it all on wine and women and ended up destitute. In desperation, he took a job feeding hogs and ended up in a pigpen. For a Jewish boy, that is about as low as you can go! Abandoned by his so-called friends and left to the consequences of his own indulgence, he was indeed in about as big a mess as you could imagine!

There are several lessons about life that we can learn from this story. In many ways, we ourselves have often done what that young man did. We have made selfish choices and then suffered the consequences of our own mistakes.

How did he get himself in so much trouble? Well, notice first that it is evident *he wanted everything his own way*. When he went to his father prematurely demanding his inheritance, he was violating Jewish law and custom. He was treating his father as though he had already died. His request showed the utmost disrespect. It showed the boy loved himself more than he did his own father. In essence, he was saying, "I want it my way."

We live in a very self-centered world. Some have called this the age of narcissism (self-love). Ours is a self-centered and self-indulgent society. That is one of the major reasons why marriages are falling apart. We have lost our concern for and commitment to others. We care only about ourselves.

This age has also been labeled the "me" generation. People want it all and they want it now. "I want to take care of number one," is what many are saying. They are like the little girl in this familiar poem (author unknown):

> I gave a little party this afternoon at three.
>   'Twas very small, three guests in all,
> Just I, myself, and me.
> Myself ate all the candy,
>   While I drank all the tea,
> And I was the one who ate the pie,
>   And passed the cake to me.

If I were to tape-record the average counseling session, it would be filled with these same three words: I, myself, and me. Think of what people say when they are down: *I* got hurt; *I* got a raw deal; everyone is against *me*; nobody understands *me*; nobody cares about *me*.

A self-centered life is a sorry way to live. It tells everyone around you that you really only care about yourself. "What's in it for me?" and "What can I get out of it?" are attitudes that turn others off. If you are really down and discouraged, perhaps it is time to realize that you're not the only person in the world who has troubles. The first step to getting out of your own despair is to recognize that much of it may be of your own making.

The manner in which the story is told makes it clear that the son also *ignored the will of his father.* Dad knew what was best but the young man didn't care. His very request was contrary to Jewish custom. His father undoubtedly tried to explain all of this to him. I can just hear him saying, "Now, Son, you're too young to do this. If you will wait until the rightful age, we can invest this money properly and provide you with a good living. You could have a marvelous future."

But it was all to no avail. "I want it all now!" was the young man's attitude. I can just hear him now. "Dad, you just don't understand. Don't give me all this advice stuff. I don't need it. I know what I'm doing. I wasn't born yesterday. Besides, I'm not like everybody else. I'm different. I won't turn out like others. I can make it on my own."

Sounds familiar, doesn't it? It first sounds familiar because those of us who are parents have heard it from our own kids and second, because we have all said it ourselves at some time. If not to our parents, we have certainly said it to God before. "Lord, I know what I'm doing, so stop convicting me. I can handle it. I'm not like other people," we have rationalized to ourselves and then tried to pass those excuses on to God.

It is a wonder to me that God puts up with us at all. We are the biggest excuse makers that have ever existed. It is only His love and grace that keeps Him from discarding the whole human race. This may come as a shock to you or it may burst your ego, but we are all alike. We are all the same. Once you strip away the veneer of education, prestige, income, and popularity, we are all about the same inside. We have the same kind of selfishness, the same needs, and the same problems.

Scripture describes us like this, "For all have sinned, and come short of the glory of God" (Romans 3:23). Nobody is excepted; we have all sinned. No matter what your social status or your intellectual capacity, you are still a selfish sinner without God and without hope until you come to Christ. You may be an educated sinner or an ignorant sinner. The result is still the same. You may be a wealthy sinner or a poor sinner, but you're still a sinner.

The great tragedy of our sin is the cost involved. The Bible says, "The wages of sin is death" (Romans 6:23). Sin exacts a terrible payment, both now and in eternity. It costs us a clear conscience and leaves us burdened with guilt. It robs us of our joy and peace and leaves us questioning whether life is really worth it.

The young man in our story lost everything because he would not listen to his father. He ignored his advice and rejected his will. As a consequence, he paid with his own human dignity. All the time he was in rebellion, his father only wanted the best for him. In the same way, God never said one thing intended for your harm. He only wants the best for you, but you will never receive it as long as you are wallowing in rebellion and self-pity.

Once you reject your heavenly Father's will, you place yourself under the terrible consequences of your own sin. While God can sovereignly overrule those consequences, there is a sense in which He is limited by your sin. He is limited by His own holy nature as well. For example, if you rob a bank and kill the teller in the process, you may repent and God may forgive you, but you are still going to go to jail. When you rebel against God's direction for your life, you place yourself in complete vulnerability to the consequences of your sin.

Finally, to make things worse, the young man also *wasted his resources*. When he ran out of money, he was totally destitute. Remember, when he first arrived in that far country, he had all the friends money could buy. But when his money ran out, his friends deserted him.

This young man had big plans, but he left God out of his plans. It wasn't long until his dreams faded like a vapor. There are countless businessmen who could testify that they thought they had it all together in life. But something went wrong and they lost it all. There are countless women who could testify to the same thing: "Everything was going so well for me in life. My husband had a good job. My children were healthy. I was happy. Everything seemed perfect, and then the bottom fell out."

The Bible reminds us that life is a vapor. It is here one moment and gone the next. And the things of this life are a vapor as well. They disappear about as easily as they come. One day we have them, and the next day they are gone. The only things that last are those done in God's will.

The Prodigal Son thought his inheritance would last him a lifetime, but it was quickly gone. He was destitute and impoverished. In desperation he took a job feeding swine. The Bible tells us that he was so desperate that he "would . . . have filled his belly with the husks that the swine did eat: and no man gave unto him" (Luke 15:16). What a pathetic picture! Here was a young man who had been raised in the lap of luxury. He had known all the conveniences money could buy. But now he was so destitute that he would have eaten the pig's food, but no one would even give that to him.

Here was this Jewish boy, mired in the slop of the pigpen. All the dignity of his life was gone. No one now could even recognize him to be his former self. All his hopes and dreams were shattered. His life was devastated. Things could not have been worse for him.

"Pastor, you just don't know how low a man can sink," a middle-aged man once said to me. "I'd trade places with the Prodigal Son in a moment," he continued. He went on to tell me a story that made my heart sick. He had fallen to the lowest depths to which a man can fall.

COMING HOME

No matter how great our problems may be, God's grace is always greater. His mercy is deeper, His love is wider, and His forgiveness is stronger than anything we could ever know. The same God who reached out to the Prodigal Son is still reaching out in love to men today.

1. *Come to Yourself.*

In his most desperate hour, the young man found the solution to all of his problems. We have no idea how long he remained in that pigpen, but the Scriptures tells us that he finally "came to himself" (Luke 15:17). A modern paraphrase would be that "he came to his senses." But the truth here is even deeper. He came to see himself for what he really was. He saw the awful consequences of his mistakes, but he also realized afresh that he was a child of his father. He came to a full appreciation of who and what his father was.

In this parable, our Lord said:

> And when he came to himself, he said, How many hired servants of my father's have bread enough and to spare, and I perish with hunger! I will arise and go to my father, and will say unto him, Father, I have sinned against heaven, and before thee, and am no more worthy to be called thy son: make me as one of thy hired servants. And he arose, and came to his father. (Luke 15:17-20)

Perhaps you need to wake up and come to your senses. It is time to come to the end of yourself and turn to your heavenly Father.

You may need to realize that the problems in your life are not all caused by someone else. Many of them may be the consequence of your own wrong decisions.

Some years ago I was greeting people as they left the church, and an elderly lady approached me and said, "Your sermon was excellent. Everything you said reminded me of a friend of mine. She really needed to hear that."

Isn't that just like human nature! We can always see the flaw in someone else more quickly than we can see it in ourselves. Yet, our Lord reminded us to remove the beam from our own eye before attempting to remove a splinter from our brother's eye (see Matthew 7:3).

In Psalm 51, we see a beautiful picture of a broken man who came to the end of himself and turned to God. The psalm was written by David after his sin with Bathsheba. Prior to his confession and repentance, David testifies, he had lost the joy of his salvation (v. 12) and he actually feared being cast off by God (v. 11). He was still God's child, but the guilt of his sin had robbed him of his joy and shaken his security. He even describes his physical and emotional distress.

In his prayer, David calls upon God to purge and wash him, to cleanse his sins and blot out his transgressions, to create in him a clean heart and renew in him a right spirit. It is a prayer of repentance that leads to restoration to service.

Have you ever prayed until you couldn't think of anything else to pray? Have you ever sobbed until you couldn't cry any more tears? When you are at the bottom of the barrel that is how you will feel. Only when we have a "broken spirit" and a "contrite heart" will God hear us, turn us around, and bring us out of the pit of self-affliction. That's the way it was with David; only after this process was completed could he say "then will I teach transgressors thy ways" (v. 13).

David was called "a man after God's own heart" (1 Samuel 13:14), despite his human failures. Why? Because he, like the Prodigal Son, came to the end of himself, came to his senses, and turned to God.

2. Remember Your Father's Resources.

Home never seemed so good to this young man as it did when he was starving in the pigpen. It was then that he remembered his father's great resources. They were such that even the servants had plenty to eat.

Why am I sitting here starving? he thought to himself. *My father's servants are better off than I am.*

With a fresh awareness of his desperation and a new appreciation for his father, he determined to go home and throw himself on his father's mercy. Now, here is the key to his attitude. He did not merely return home making excuses for his failure. He came asking forgiveness for his disobedience. Neither did he return home demanding to be restored to his former position. He came home willing to work as a hired servant.

You see, even in the midst of your most desperate hour and your most despicable rebellion you who know the Father are still children of the King. Do not forget who you are and who your Father is. He is the Lord of Glory, merciful and full of grace. His resources are limitless!

In his letter to the Ephesians, the Apostle Paul captured this concept of our sonship in the Father when he wrote, "that ye may know what is the hope of his calling, and what the riches of the glory of his inheritance in the saints" (1:18). In other words, Paul was praying that our eyes might be opened to see who we are and what we have in Christ. We are not paupers. Our Father is the King of Heaven.

Satan loves nothing more than to smash us underfoot and make us feel less than worthless. He loves to beat us down spiritually with the guilt of our own failures. But we must learn to resist his onslaughts. We are no longer his children; we belong to the King.

3. Decide to Do Something about It.

Finally, the young man arose from his humiliation and decided to return to his father. He said, in essence, "I've come to my senses, I know who I am, I know what my father's provisions are, and I am going home." If you are waiting on a miracle from God, believe me when I tell you it will never come until you get up out of self-pity and are willing to do something about it.

There must come a point of decision in your life where you determine that by faith you are going to get out of your mess. One day Jesus walked by the pool of Bethesda and saw a man who had been lame for thirty-eight years. In mercy, He stopped and had compassion on him. Jesus commanded him to rise, take up his bed, and walk. The man did not lie there debating the whole issue. He just got up as Jesus had commanded, and he was healed.

In Acts 3, we read the story of how Peter and John took mercy on a crippled man who was begging for money. "Silver and gold have I none," Peter replied, "but such as I have give I thee: In the name of Jesus Christ of Nazareth rise up and walk" (v. 6). The Bible goes on to tell us that the beggar leaped up and went running and leaping about the temple. He had been touched by the power of God because he moved when God said to move.

There is a story about an angry fan at a basketball game. His team had been losing all four quarters and he was irate, to say the least. Although he was so far back in the stands that he couldn't see who was on the floor playing, he had been constantly yelling at the top of his lungs at the coach for most of the game, "Come on, coach, if you wanna win, put John in, put John in." On and on he yelled until the coach had finally had enough. Looking up into the stand he shouted back, "John *is* in, you dummy, he's been in all the game!"

Then the fan replied, "Then take John out, take him out, take him out." What was he saying? He was saying, "Come on, coach, when we're losing, do something, just do something."

If you want to get out of the mess you are in, then do something. Get up and start moving toward God. Don't wait for something to happen. Move out by faith now and *do something!*

4. Receive What Your Father Has to Offer.

The Prodigal returned home, willing to receive whatever his father would give him. As he journeyed home, the Scriptures tell us, his father saw him a "long way off" (Luke 15:20, NIV). No doubt he had been searching for his son on the horizon day after day, hoping he would return. Then on the certain day, as he strained his eyes to see, he could hardly believe it. It was his son, returning home. The Bible tells us that the father ran to meet the boy and, rejoicing to see him, embraced his son and kissed his neck. Then he ordered his servants to place a ring on his finger, a coat on his back, and shoes on his feet. "Kill the fatted calf," he commanded and prepared a banquet feast to welcome him home.

Though the lad had offered to become one of his father's servants, he was restored to the full status of sonship. Though he offered to work for hire, he was made an heir. Why? Because the father loved him. He was forgiven, his confidence was restored, he was reminded of who he was, and he was given a brand-new beginning.

In the game of baseball there is a term for the player who has the talent but hasn't gotten a hit in some time. We call that player "overdue." Some of you are "overdue" with God. He's been waiting for you to return to Him. He wants to pick you up, to love you, to restore you, and to get you out of your mess. He wants to give you what is rightfully yours. But you must do your part:

- Come to yourself.
- Remember God's bountiful resources.
- Arise and come to the Father.
- Receive the blessings He has to offer.

16

What to Do When You Feel Like Quitting

I had no sooner settled in behind my desk one Monday morning, planning to get my day started, when my secretary's voice came through the intercom. "Tom and Janet are here, and they are really upset."

"Send them in right away," I answered.

Tom burst through the door in a bolt of anger and frustration, with Janet following behind.

"I've had it with him," she announced abruptly as she sat down. "He's impossible to live with anymore."

"Well, I'm the one who has had it," Tom replied angrily. "I just don't want this marriage. I've tried and I'm tired of trying."

"Can we talk about it, without exploding?" I asked.

"I'll talk about it," Tom said, "but I still want out."

As we talked together about their problems, it became obvious that they were both burning out on life. Their routines of living had become dull and meaningless. The pressures of their work and of their poorly managed finances had them both on edge, and they were taking it out on each other. The kids were getting older and making greater demands on their time, and that wasn't helping the situation either.

"Have you ever heard of electrical overload?" I asked them after a while. Before they could answer, I went on to explain that is what happens when we plug too many appliances into the same electrical outlet. The circuit overloads and usually throws the breaker or blows a fuse.

"That's what you both are doing," I told them bluntly. "You are so overloaded with responsibility and pressure that your emotional circuits are overloaded and you're trying to call time-out on life."

Unfortunately, situations like this happen frequently. Many

couples appear highly successful but are under so much stress that they are about to explode. Husband and wife lash out at each other in frustration, and their marriage starts to fall apart—even though in many cases their problems are not being caused by their marriage. Rather, the marriage has become the battleground where they take their frustrations out on each other. But stress overload is not unique to married couples.

THE BURNOUT SYNDROME

Burnout is a serious problem throughout our fast-paced, high-stress society. It affects everyone. It seems every time I turn around I'm reading another book or article on burnout. Businessmen and women are burning out on their jobs. Housewives are burning out on the home. Single parents are put under an almost unbearable load. Numbers of teenagers are leaving home, trying to walk away from it all, trying to escape, only to find it much worse on the streets.

Often we see Christians who aren't doing much better than the rest of the world on this account. We who ought to know how to find inner peace and strength often fall victim to the same pressures as everyone else. Jesus said, "Peace I leave with you, my peace I give unto you. . . . Let not your heart be troubled, neither let it be afraid" (John 14:27).

Christ Himself promised to give us peace in the midst of life's pressures. But in giving this promise, He never said there would be *no* pressures at all. Rather, He promised to give us enduring strength during our times of stress and pressure.

The mature knowledge of this is the key to overcoming burnout. When you feel like quitting, you are focusing on your problems, not God's solutions. When stress has you rattled, your attention is not on God. As believers, we are supposed to be different from the world. We are supposed to know how to live under pressure. People should be able to watch our lives and ask themselves, "How do they remain so cool and calm in these situations?" Their curiosity ought to be attracted to the reality of God's peace in our innermost being.

The real issue comes down to one of pressures or priorities. Your life is going to be dominated by one of these two factors. Every morning when you wake up and start your day, you will be dominated by pressures or priorities. Throughout each day you will be controlled by one or the other.

When we let our lives become driven by pressure, every decision we make reflects that constant badgering within us. And though you may outwardly begin to taste success, the end result will be a bitterness within because your soul will begin to dry up. Driven people never take time to spiritually refresh themselves. They keep moving hurriedly from one project to another, driven by the desire for conquest and success. When they finally arrive at their goals, they are usually burned out and washed up on life. The wreckage lies all along their pathway to success: a frustrated outlook, neglected loved ones, and a loss of everything that is real in life.

On the other hand, when we properly define our priorities (those factors we consider to come foremost in our personal well-being) and make our decisions accordingly, we can better keep our living in balance. When we put God first in our lives, we are beginning with a spiritual priority which says that those things which help us grow in our daily walk with God are most important. These cannot be neglected on the excuse that we are too busy.

When our priorities include such matters as family togetherness, physical and emotional health, and a positive quality of life, we will learn to say no to those things which would rob us of the vitality of life. But when our priorities are wrong, we will readily sacrifice all of these for that which has little lasting importance. We only live to satisfy those unrelenting pressures that can never be satisfied anyway.

ENDURING THE PRESSURES

A revealing scripture found in Hebrews 11:24–27 tells us how we may endure the pressures of life. It tells us of Moses, who chose the right priorities for his life. Despite having been raised by the daughter of the Egyptian Pharaoh, Moses refused his royal heritage, "choosing rather to suffer affliction with the people of God." The author of Hebrews then tells us that Moses denied the treasures of Egypt and forsook its material wealth and prosperity for the will of God.

From the Old Testament we know that he was condemned by Pharaoh and fled into the wilderness for forty years. Later, he returned to lead the children of Israel out of bondage into freedom. Along the way, he had many problems and struggles. Pharaoh's army pursued them and they were trapped at the edge of the Red Sea.

Moses prayed and God miraculously delivered them by parting the water. Then in the wilderness of Sinai they ran out of food and faced starvation. Again, God miraculously supplied their need by sending the manna. Every step of the way, although the people complained, Moses remained fixed on God. He never turned back, despite all the obstacles.

What was Moses' secret? Hebrews 11:27 tells us, "For he endured, as seeing him who is invisible." He endured all the pressures of life by faith in God. He went on with such confidence in God's promises that it was as though he could actually see Him. His faith enabled him to visualize God at work in his life. If we are going to endure the pressures of life, we must do the same.

1. Identity: *Know Who You Are.*

In spite of being raised in Pharaoh's home, Moses knew he was an Israelite. He understood that he had been born into a Hebrew family and that his real mother hid him in a basket during a time of persecution. In desperation she placed the basket in the Nile River and let it go. Eventually, Pharaoh's daughter found the baby in the basket. She assumed he was a gift from the gods, since the Egyptians believed the Nile was a god and the source of all life. She accepted the baby as a gift of divine providence, and Moses was raised in Pharaoh's court as a member of the royal family. As such, he enjoyed all the privileges of wealth and royalty. He may well have been in line to inherit the throne of Egypt itself.

But one day Moses came to the realization of who he really was. He came to a point of spiritual self-identity. He realized that he was an Israelite and a child of God. He could not deny his identity with his own people, so he turned his back on Egypt. He refused to be called the son of Pharaoh's daughter because he wanted to be who he really was.

Today, many people seem to want to be someone they're not. "If I could only be like him," they will often say to me, wishing they were better looking, happier, or wealthier. This is a problem that affects teenagers and adults alike. They think that if they could be somebody else they would be happy. But they are wrong. You can only be truly happy when you accept yourself for who and what you are in Christ. He alone can transform you into the best person you could ever become by His grace.

A television commercial soliciting recruits for the United States Army says, "Be all that you can be." I want to tell you that you can be all you ought to be and need to be through Jesus Christ. You don't need to be anything other than what He has planned for you to be to His glory.

Some of us get down on ourselves to the point that we become so depressed that we are useless. We don't believe we are worth anything, so we act accordingly. I remember my high-school chemistry teacher telling me that the chemical elements of my body were only worth about ninety-five cents. That was always pretty discouraging to me until I heard a scientist say that each pound of the human body has within it enough atoms to produce 11.4 million kilowatt-hours of electricity. Now, according to the Georgia Power Company, that much energy would cost about $798,000. Think about it: I weigh 170 pounds. That means I'm worth about $135,660,000! It all depends on how you look at it.

In fact, you are worth more than money can buy. The worth of your soul is so great that God's own Son took your sins upon Himself and died in your place on the cross. God cared enough about you that He gave His own Son to die for you. Your worth is not determined by your material prosperity, the house you live in, or the car you drive. Your real worth has been determined by Almighty God, who gave all that He had that you might become His child.

2. Relationship: Learn Whose You Are.

The world can be classified into two groups of people: the saved and the lost. Men classify each other by race, nationality, locality, or socioeconomic status. We tend to view people as black or white, red or yellow, rich or poor, white-collar or blue-collar. But God sees only two classes of people in the eyes of eternity: those who know Him and those who do not.

The Scripture teaches that there are only two ways into eternity. One is broad and leads to destruction. The other is narrow and leads to eternal life. The Bible also declares that there are two foundations to life: one of solid rock and one of shifting sand. The sand represents the unstable ideologies and philosophies of the world, while the solid rock represents Jesus Christ. Unfortunately, many people have built their lives on materialism and the pursuit of self-gratification, only to find it all blown away like the sand when they come to life's end.

The laws of God are specific and relentless. They always work one way or the other. The law of gravity teaches us why things are held to this earth. Gravity keeps us all from hurtling into outer space. But gravity will also cause you to fall down to the ground if you jump off a tall building. Its force can be positive or destructive, depending upon our choices. Similarly, the law of aerodynamics teaches us how things fly; but when violated, it also tells us why things crash. The laws of physics tell us how things are made, but they can also be used to blow things apart.

Jesus said, "I am the way, the truth, and the life: no man cometh unto the Father, but by me" (John 14:6). That may seem narrow to some, but it is the law of God. If you are going to overcome discouragement, you must know to whom you belong. Moses knew that he belonged with the children of God and acted accordingly. We must do the same. Stop putting yourself down and start acting like a child of the King!

3. *Purpose: Understand Whom You Are Trying to Please.*

Moses had his hands full once he got the children of Israel across the Red Sea. They complained about everything. They didn't like the food, they ran out of water, they questioned Moses' leadership, and some of them even rebelled. The pressures upon him must have been incredible. But Moses was only interested in pleasing God. Otherwise, he would have cracked under the load.

Can you imagine people coming to Moses with their requests? I can just imagine that it may have begun with the "Let's Not Leave Egypt" committee. Perhaps they thought he had taken things a bit too far and wondered how they would all survive out there in the wilderness. Perhaps next it was the "Red Sea Crossing" committee. I can just hear them trying to talk him out of using his rod and into trying something more conventional. Next might have come the "Wilderness-Wandering Planning Committee." They decided it might be a good idea to stay in the wilderness permanently and build a settlement. Perhaps they envisioned something like "Six Flags Over Sinai."

We do know from Scripture that Moses faced tremendous resistance from the people at every turn. They always seemed to be complaining about something. But Moses never gave in to their complaints. He was not a perfect man, but he was a man determined to please God. Moses had his weaknesses, too. He needed Aaron and Hur to hold up his arms, and he appointed seventy elders to help him judge the people's requests. And on one occasion, he became angry and smote the rock with his staff, although God had commanded him merely to speak to it. But over all, Moses was a great leader because he kept his focus on God.

You and I can never please everyone. When we try, we only exhaust ourselves in the process. Some people are just impossible to please no matter how hard you try. Someone told me once of a woman who had a grouchy husband who was hard to please. But she loved him dearly and was determined to please him. She got up early one morning, fixed herself up, and asked him what he wanted for breakfast.

"I'll fix whatever you want," she announced.

"All right," he responded, "I'll take freshly brewed coffee, freshly squeezed orange juice, toast, bacon and two eggs—one fried and one scrambled."

Desiring to please him, she set about the task of preparing breakfast. She brewed the coffee, squeezed the orange juice, and fried the bacon. Then she cracked one egg and scrambled it and cracked the other egg and fried it. When everything was ready, she called him to breakfast. He walked in, sat down, and looked at the two eggs. A big frown came over his face. He looked up at her and snarled, "Just as I thought. You fried the wrong egg!"

As incredible as it may seem, that is about how ridiculous some people are. No matter what you do for them, you can't please them. So, you are better off not trying to please them. I had to learn early in my ministry to quit trying to please everybody. People would come to me saying, "Now don't offend this person because he is related to that person." The requests were endless. Finally, I had to realize there was only one person I needed to please and that was God. Once I got that settled in my mind, a spirit of peace settled over me.

Often the stress and pressure of life comes from trying to please others. It may be your boss, your husband, your wife, your kids, or your family. But whoever they are, you will never be able to completely satisfy their needs. Only God can do that, and He doesn't want you wearing yourself out trying to do His job. He alone can meet their needs. All you have to do is concentrate on pleasing Him.

The Bible promises, "When a man's ways please the Lord, he maketh even his enemies to be at peace with him" (Proverbs 16:7). When you and I concentrate on pleasing God, He takes care of satisfying everyone else. You don't have to please everyone. Chances are that you can't anyhow. Simply trust God with your pressures and determine to please Him with your life.

4. Direction: Know Where You Are Going.

Most people think the Israelites stayed in the wilderness for forty years because they were lost. Not so! The Scripture tells us that they knew where they were going. Their destiny was the land of Canaan, known to them as the "Promised Land" because of God's covenant with their forefathers. They remained in the wilderness for forty years because of rebellion against God's direction in their lives.

But despite all their problems, Moses never lost sight of their ultimate goal. He knew that their final destiny was worth the wait and that it was well worth the struggle. He kept his eyes focused on the eternal reward of God. You and I must do the same. Whenever it appears outwardly that all has failed, that the journey is too difficult, or that the road is too rough, remember where you're going. Pressures seem to ease greatly when our purpose lies clearly before us and we know where we are headed.

My father had a little poem (author unknown) that he would often say to his children in our times of self-pity and discouragement. I've remembered it through the years—especially when I felt like giving up or thought the winds of good fortune were blowing in everyone else's direction but mine. It goes like this:

> One ship sailed east
>   Another sailed west,
> Impelled by the self-same blow.
> For it's not the gale
>   But the set of the sail,
> That determines where they go!

God will not give up on you as long as you don't give up on yourself. Set your sail and keep on. There will always be rivers to cross and mountains to climb. But God is with you every step of the way. When you falter or stumble, He will hold you up. He will give you direction. He will see you through.

When the great conqueror Napoleon and his armies crossed the Alps, his troops came into battle with the enemy. Napoleon's troops found themselves trapped in a valley, and many began to die in battle.

The great leader's heart went out to his men, so he turned to his bugler boy and said, "Son, sound the retreat." The boy did nothing. Again Napoleon said, "Son, blow the retreat or our men will die."

Then the bugler looked at his great general and said, "I'm sorry, sir, but I have forgotten the sound of retreat." Napoleon snapped back, "Then blow whatever you know how to blow!"

The boy placed the bugle to his lips and blew—charge, charge, charge! The troops of Napoleon thought, "Help is coming," and they fought with all their might. The enemy thought, "We must flee because reinforcements must be on their way." Thus the battle was won and eventually the war, because one little bugler boy had forgotten the sound of retreat.

Quitting is not an option for the Christian. We have been set free from our old life and we must press on to our new destination. Like the children of Israel, we can't go back to Egypt; it isn't wise to stay in the wilderness; so we must press on to the Promised Land. Like the bugler boy, we must forget the sound of retreat. No matter how long or difficult the journey, it's never right to quit. Keep your focus on the goal and keep pressing on, for victory is straight ahead.

PART FIVE

ON TO VICTORY

One man of you shall chase a thousand: for the LORD your God, he it is that fighteth for you, as he hath promised you.

—JOSHUA 23:10

PART FIVE

ON TO
VICTORY

17

Claim Your Mountain

Travel back in time with me to the days of Joshua and the children of Israel. Moses had died and Joshua had taken over as the leader of the people of Israel as they prepared to enter their Promised Land.

Forty years earlier Moses had sent twelve men to spy out the land of Canaan. Among these were Joshua and Caleb. While the others brought back a negative report, only Joshua and Caleb had the faith to believe that God could help them take the land. They all had agreed that it was a wonderful place that "flowed with milk and honey." But the others were fearful of the awesome power of the Canaanites and urged the children of Israel to turn back. It was this incident which caused them to waste nearly forty years wandering in the wilderness. Now, Joshua is preparing a new generation of Israelites to enter the land.

The initial conquest was overwhelmingly successful as Joshua and his armies put the Canaanites to flight. As they marched across the land in a triumphal victory, Caleb came to Joshua to remind him of a promise that Moses had made to him some forty-five years earlier. We find his request recorded in Joshua 14:7-12.

> Forty years old was I when Moses the servant of the Lord sent me from Kadesh-barnea to espy out the land; and I brought him word again as it was in mine heart. Nevertheless my brethren that went up with me made the heart of the people melt: but I wholly followed the Lord my God. And Moses sware on that day, saying, Surely the land whereon thy feet have trodden shall be thine inheritance, and thy children's for ever, because thou hast wholly followed the Lord my God. And now, behold, the Lord hath kept me alive, as he said, these forty and five years, even since the Lord spake this word unto Moses, while the children of Israel wandered in the wilderness: and now, lo, I am this day fourscore and five years old. As yet I am as strong this day

as I was in the day that Moses sent me: as my strength was then, even so is my strength now, for war, both to go out, and to come in. Now therefore give me this mountain, whereof the Lord spake in that day; for thou heardest in that day how the Anakims were there, and that the cities were great and fenced: if so be the Lord will be with me, then I shall be able to drive them out, as the Lord said.

Caleb was now standing in the Promised Land. How his heart must have pounded within him as he was reminded of Moses' promise to give him the mountain city of Hebron, a stronghold of giants known as the Anakim. Caleb requested that Joshua allow him the opportunity to take the city in the will of God. He wanted to possess that which was rightfully his. But there were incredible obstacles to overcome. The place Caleb chose was probably the most difficult place in all of Israel to conquer. It was a high mountain fortress city, south of Jerusalem, which later would become the chief city of the tribe of Judah.

Not only did Caleb have his possession in mind, but he had a plan in mind as well. It is never enough simply to want something, you must know how you can get it. You have to go after it with determination to pay whatever sacrifice is necessary to accomplish the deed, and you have to be willing to understand how you are going to bring it about.

You may have a particular goal in mind that you wish to achieve in life, but there may be obstacles standing between you and that goal. It may be the goal of a higher education, or starting your own business, or owning a new home, or some other personal goal. Whatever the objective is, there is a right way and a wrong way to go about it. God has laid out a plan in His Word to help us clearly understand how to possess our possessions.

From Caleb's example, I want to suggest a simple plan to help you claim the promises of God in your life. There are many wonderful things which God has stated belong to His children, but many people never possess them because they do not understand how to go about acquiring them from God. Caleb gives us the key to understanding that process.

1. He Identified What He Wanted.

Caleb knew exactly what he wanted. He did not come to Joshua and say that he would like to have something nice if it could be worked out. He knew exactly what he was after. He wanted a particular mountain, and he was willing to do whatever was necessary to possess that mountain.

A lot of people talk about conquering mountains in their lives, but notice that Caleb was interested in conquering a certain mountain of his own choice. He was not even satisfied with conquering the territory in general; he wanted to possess that mountain in particular. I am convinced that this is imperative for the believer today as well. We need to understand exactly what it is we are asking from God. The Bible clearly identifies specific spiritual blessings which are available by faith to the children of God if we will only claim them. Our need is to be informed as to what is available to us, so that we can make the commitment to do what is necessary to claim that blessing in our lives.

Suppose a millionaire came to your house tomorrow morning, carrying in his hand a beautiful catalog of the most wonderful things that you could possibly imagine. And suppose that he handed you the catalog and said to you, "I like you so much that I am going to present you with this catalog of riches. I want you to study this catalog for a whole week, and next Monday I'll come back to your house and give you everything that you have selected to meet your needs." What do you think you would do? I know what most people would do. They would search that catalog from one end to the other to discover what things they needed the most. I also think that I know what you would not do with the catalog. You would not likely throw it on the coffee table and leave it to gather dust for the week. But that is exactly what we do with the catalog of blessings that God has made available to us in His Word. Here in the Scriptures are the proclamations of great divine promises of God, which are made available to all who will claim them. Most of us are too lazy even to make the effort to find out what is available to us.

I am convinced that we need to identify specifically the things that we want from God. We need to know what God has made available to us and what it is that we can claim from Him by faith. I think of the blind man who was sitting on the roadside near Jericho as Jesus passed by him. The Bible says that he cried out, "Jesus, thou Son of David, have mercy on me" (Mark 10:47). The Bible tells us that Jesus stopped and called for the blind man to come to Him. He stood up and cast off his outer garment and walked toward Jesus. The Lord looked at him and asked, "What wilt thou that I should do unto thee?" (Mark 10:51). Obviously our Lord knew that the man was blind, both by his appearance and his actions. He must have known that he wanted to be healed of his blindness, yet our Lord asked him what it was that he wanted.

Jesus was asking the blind man, whose name was Bartimaeus, to identify his request specifically. When the blind man responded, "Lord, that I might receive my sight," he was specifically targeting his request.

Obviously God knows what our needs are before we ask Him. But there is nothing more important than being willing to ask specifically. Too many people pray in vague generalities rather than in specific requests. If you have a need, clearly identify your need when you express it to God in prayer.

2. He Claimed What He Was Promised.

Even though he had to wait forty-five years for the fulfillment of the promise that Moses had made to him, Caleb never lost sight of that promise. He had apparently seen Hebron on his first visit to the land of Canaan. This rocky mountain fortress had so captured his mind and attention that he never forgot it. I can imagine that it was in his dreams night after night. Every day as the people of Israel trudged through the sands of the Sinai Desert, his heart beat with anticipation for the day that place would be his. In his mind, he never forgot the promise that Moses had made to him. Despite all the obstacles (and there were many), he never let go of the dream. There was the mixed report by the spies, with the ten bringing a negative report against him and Joshua. There was the disappointment of turning back at Kadesh-barnea and the subsequent forty years in the wilderness. There was the incredible difficulty of the initial conquest of the land of Canaan. Finally, there were the Anakim who currently held the mountain fortress. We do not know much about these people, but we do know that they were extremely large in size and that some of them later merged with the Philistines, probably including Goliath. These were enormous people whose height reached anywhere from seven to nine feet. Of all the places that Caleb could have chosen, this had to be the most difficult. Yet, his faith never wavered because he believed the promise of God.

The key to Caleb's success was not merely in his own determination, but in his firm conviction that God was the source of the promise. He knew that the promise would be fulfilled because he knew who had made it. A promise is only as good as the word of the one who makes it. Therefore, if God has made a promise to you and me, we have every reason to believe that it will be fulfilled.

Claim Your Mountain

There are certain people that I am convinced will always keep their promises, while there are others that I am convinced will rarely do so. If the latter group were to promise me little, I would never really expect to see it. But if others I know made me a promise, I would have complete confidence that it would come to pass. Why is that? Because I have confidence in the character of those who are making the promise. That is why we can have such confidence in the promises of God. There is not one promise in the Word of God that He has ever failed to keep. Our Lord Jesus had such confidence in the promises of God in Scripture that He said not one of them would ever be broken. It is for that reason that we can trust God in the most ultimate concerns of our lives to fulfill His promises to us. Even though forty-five years had elapsed, Caleb was still convinced that the promise of God was as good as it ever had been. With that confidence he stepped forward to make his request known to all.

3. He Never Stopped Believing.

Three times in the fourteenth chapter of Joshua we read that Caleb "wholly followed the Lord." This gives us a key insight to his character. He was a deeply committed individual. During the forty years of the wilderness wandering he had watched the entire adult generation die off with the exception of Joshua and himself. Yet, he never lost confidence in the promise that had been made to him. He refused to give up on God.

I can imagine Caleb trudging across the sands of the desert for forty years with a smile on his face, a gleam in his eyes, and this promise in his heart. People were dropping dead daily, and yet he was marching on with hope for the future. I can imagine some of them thinking that he was getting too old to conquer anything. Others may have told him that after all these years the promise wasn't any longer in effect. Someone else may have suggested that he shouldn't take the promise so literally in the first place. Perhaps it was merely symbolic of God's general concerns for the people of Israel. But Caleb never saw it that way. He always viewed the promise as a literal promise from God which he could expect to be literally fulfilled in his own lifetime. He never stopped believing.

Too many people have a half-hearted faith that never activates the promises of God. They question the reality of what God has promised and then toss up a prayer with little or no expectation of any kind at all. There is a principle in Scripture that says, "According to your faith be it unto you" (Matthew 9:29). There is a definite sense in which God responds to our faith. The more we are willing to believe Him, the more He is willing to move on our behalf. The Scripture expresses this in the statement, "But without faith it is impossible to please him" (Hebrews 11:6). This has always been the attitude of great men and women of faith who were willing to believe God for the impossible simply because He said that it was so.

Throughout Caleb's life, he never lost sight of the reality of the promise of God. The most wonderful epitaph that could ever be recorded of any individual was summed up in the simple statement, "He wholly followed the Lord." That meant that regardless of the discouraging words of others, the many reasons that seemed to say he would never succeed, he maintained his faith that God would do as He said He would do. When everything and everyone else would have given up, he kept on believing by faith. But that is what believing in God is all about, isn't it? Having faith in that which cannot now be seen, which cannot now be touched, but can only be felt by belief in one's heart. There are many things that by human standards we cannot prove; the proof lies only within our hearts as we believe. That is what Tennyson had in mind when he wrote the opening lines of *In Memoriam:*

> Strong Son of God, immortal Love
> Whom we, that have not seen thy face,
> By faith, and faith alone, embrace,
> Believing where we cannot prove.

4. He Made Known His Plea.

There was nothing vague about Caleb's request. The words "give me this mountain" made it totally clear to all Israel that he was claiming a specific possession as a result of his belief in a specific promise. Caleb identified his request to Joshua and the people of Israel and ultimately to God Himself. I am convinced that we cannot expect God to meet our needs unless we are willing to make them clearly known. This is not because God does not know what our needs are; rather, it's because Scripture clearly teaches the principle of activating our faith in response to His promises by making specific requests. The Bible says, "Call unto me, and I will answer thee, and shew thee great and mighty things, which thou knowest not" (Jeremiah 33:3). Notice that God asks us to call upon Him in order to activate His power in our lives. The New Testament expresses the same concept when it says, "Ye have not, because ye ask not" (James 4:2). Our Lord Jesus said the same thing when He promised, "Ask, and ye shall receive, that your joy may be full" (John 16:24).

You might reason within yourself, "God knows what I need, so why should I have to ask Him for it?" Now it is true that He does know what you need and in some cases He even meets our needs in His grace when we fail to ask Him. But in most cases, God responds to our specific requests. Whatever we are willing to believe Him for in our lives is what He does on our behalf. God does this in order to increase our faith and confidence in Him. If He were to answer our prayers before we ever prayed them, we would never bother to pray them at all. Therefore, we would take His blessings for granted and never realize that they were coming in answer to our prayers. This would discourage spiritual communication with God, rather than encourage it. In reality, our spoken words are an outward manifestation of the attitude of our hearts. By specifically formulating our request in prayer, we are demonstrating the sincerity of our own hearts toward God.

5. He Relied Upon God's Presence.

Caleb's confidence in God was an expression of true and sincere faith. He was not even presumptuous enough to assume that God was automatically on his side. He said, "If so be the LORD will be with me" (Joshua 14:12). He fully understood that God had to be with him in order to drive out the enemy and possess the mountain. It is also clear that Caleb was not depending upon his own ability as a warrior to win this victory. While he was willing to make whatever effort was necessary in order to be successful, he clearly recognized that God was the source of his strength and his success. It is a marvelous thing when we come to the place of spiritual maturity that we realize that God is the One who is in control. Caleb was expressing the same kind of confidence in God that the Apostle Paul had when he said, "I can do all things through Christ which strengtheneth me" (Philippians 4:13). These are not mere human boastings in one's own abilities, but rather, they are expressions of faith and confidence in the power and promises of God.

The truth of Scripture is very clear. Without God you can never win, but with God you can never lose. If God is on our side, then the victory is already assured. We must go out and win it, but we do so with the confidence that it will be won.

6. He Took His Possessions.
Caleb had been given this place by promise. It was his inheritance to claim. But he still had to take hold of his possession personally. There is a vast difference between an inheritance and a possession. An inheritance is something someone promises to give to us. They may even be legally bound to that promise, but to make it a possession you personally have to take it for yourself.

Suppose that I had left you a million dollars in an inheritance. I signed all the legal papers to make it guaranteed to you. Then I deposited the money in a bank where it would be held until you claimed it. That would be an inheritance. It has been provided for you and the price has already been paid. It is merely waiting for you to claim it. But it would only become your possession when you went to the bank, withdrew the money, and used it for yourself.

Caleb was convinced that Mount Hebron was his inheritance, and now he was willing to go and take possession of it for himself. He engaged the giants of the Anakim in battle and defeated them and took the city for his own. From that day even until now, Hebron is known as *the place of great determination*.

Our Lord died on the cross that He might give us a spiritual inheritance. The Bible tells us that He has provided all that we need for this life and the next. He has "blessed us with all spiritual blessings in heavenly places" (Ephesians 1:3). God has made every provision for our every need. Jesus bought and paid for our spiritual inheritance with His death on the cross. The problem with many of us is that we simply have not gone out and claimed the promises and possessed our inheritance. I am convinced that at times we actually insult God by refusing to claim what is rightfully ours. We act as though we are too timid to even ask Him for that which He has already promised to do for us. By contrast, the Bible tells us that we may "come boldly unto the throne of grace, that we may obtain mercy, and find grace to help in time of need" (Hebrews 4:16).

Several years ago I read the true story of an incident in the life of the great French conqueror Napoleon. It made such an impression upon me that I have never forgotten it. Napoleon and his soldiers overcame an island in the Mediterranean Sea with great casualties. They had fought for many days to take the island and finally succeeded. After it had been captured at the cost of many lives, Napoleon and his generals gathered for a celebration. As they were seated around a great table talking about the victory that they had won, they heard an interruption as a young officer approached the guards.

"Let me see Napoleon," he insisted. But the guards would not let him through. Finally Napoleon himself told the guards to allow the young man to enter the tent and he would speak with him personally. The young officer walked into the tent and stood looking down the table toward Napoleon, waiting for the emperor to speak. Napoleon looked and said, "What do you want?"

The young man looked Napoleon in the eyes and said, "Give me this island."

The generals began to laugh. They could not believe that he was asking Napoleon for the island that they had all fought so hard to win. They thought to themselves, *Who does he think he is?* Anyone with the audacity to make such a request of Napoleon was certainly putting his own life in jeopardy.

But history records that Napoleon turned to one of his aides and asked for pen and paper. He wrote out a deed to the island, signed it, and gave it to the young man. He put it under his arm and walked out, leaving the generals stunned and amazed.

"How could you do it?" one of them asked Napoleon. "What made him worthy to receive this great island?"

"I gave him this island," Napoleon replied, "because he honored me by the magnitude of his request."

We too need to honor God by the magnitude of our requests. He does not expect us to live a life of defeat which is far below the standard He has set for us. Neither does He expect us to be satisfied with asking for the mere crumbs of this life. I am convinced that God has made great provisions for us and He expects us to make great requests and experience great joy when He answers our prayers. Through faith, you too can claim your mountain!

> And this is the confidence that we have in him, that, if we ask anything according to his will, he heareth us: And if we know that he hear us, whatsoever we ask, we know that we have the petitions that we desired of him. (1 John 5:14-15)

18

Finding Perfect Peace

The world knows little about genuine peace and contentment. Its values are usually based upon social success and material prosperity. The deep, settled peace of mind and soul often eludes the average American. Most of us are disturbed by the plunge of the stock market or the instability of world affairs. Our own president has said, "We live on the verge of Armageddon." Last year alone, according to the U.S. Department of Vital Statistics, 31,482 Americans decided they had had enough and took their own lives.

Yet, our Lord Jesus promised us a peace that surpasses human comprehension. He said, "Peace I leave with you, my peace I give unto you: not as the world giveth, give I unto you. Let not your heart be troubled, neither let it be afraid" (John 14:27). He has promised us peace of heart and mind. This is a peace that is rooted deep within the soul of those who know Him as their Lord and Master.

I would like to share with you some principles for peace that I have found helpful in my own life. I am convinced that you too can know this deep and abiding peace that comes from God. It is the automatic result of His Spirit living within you.

1. *Come to Terms with Your Past.*
Many people are haunted by something in their past that prevents them from having peace in the present. Some will say, "Just forget it and go on." But it's not that easy. Most of us get bogged down by guilt and can't seem to shake it. When we try to suppress our feelings we only rob ourselves of true joy and peace. The stress of guilt robs us of peace and leaves us with the heartache of unconfessed sin.

Until you come to terms with sin in your life, you will never conquer it. By this I mean that you must admit (confess) your sin and turn away from it (repent). Only then can you really forget it because it is under the blood of Christ.

Remember, David tried to hide his sin and it didn't work. He had committed the multiple sin of adultery and murder. He had taken Bathsheba and then had her husband Uriah killed. In his mind he rationalized that he had made a mistake, but he would simply marry Bathsheba and go on with his life. However, the Scripture reveals that he was grieved in his heart because guilt was tearing at his soul.

The Living Bible describes his plight like this:

> There was a time when I wouldn't admit what a sinner I was. But my dishonesty made me miserable and filled my days with frustration. All day and all night your hand was heavy on me. My strength evaporated like water on a sunny day until I finally admitted all my sins to you and stopped trying to hide them. I said to myself, "I will confess them to the Lord." And you forgave me! All my guilt is gone. (Psalm 32:3-5)

What a marvelous statement this is of the power of forgiveness and the peace that it brings. The key to finding inner peace is to confess your sins and lay them at the foot of the Cross. Trying to forget them will not remove them from your memory. Only God can erase them from your heart and set you free.

Perhaps you have made a serious mistake recently. Perhaps it was an error in judgment or a character weakness that has flawed your life. You have tried to forget it, but its memory still haunts your soul. It may be a particular day you would like to forget. Perhaps it was a night of sin that you wish had never occurred.

"I'll just put it behind me," you have tried to tell yourself. But somehow it won't go away. Let me remind you again that you can't rid yourself of guilt alone. You must turn it over to God by confession and submission to Him. Only then will you find true and lasting peace. He offers you more than temporary relief. He offers you everlasting forgiveness and peace.

Forgiveness comes in two stages. They are distinct, but inseparable, acts. First, *we must seek forgiveness from God*, and second, *we must forgive ourselves*.

Dr. Charles Allen tells an amusing story he read in a newspaper in Wichita, Kansas. It was about a man who tried to forgive himself for a speeding ticket. A terrible snowstorm hit the city on the day he was scheduled to go to court. When he arrived, the court was closed because of the inclement weather. He waited for the judge and the accusing officer, but they never showed up. So the man finally penned a letter to the judge and left it on the door. It went like this:

> I was scheduled to be in court on February 23 at 12:15 P.M. It was concerning a traffic ticket. Well, when I arrived, I was surprised to find I was the only one there. No one called to tell me the court would be closed, so I decided I would go ahead with the hearing as scheduled, which meant that I would have to be the officer in charge, the accused, and the judge.
>
> Now, as officer in charge, I had given the accused a ticket for going 45 in a 35 MPH zone. But I had to admit I was only estimating his speed. As the accused, I admitted I was going more than the speed limit of 35, but just a few miles per hour faster. As the judge, I was angered that this accusing officer would only estimate the speed, so being the understanding man that I am, I decided to throw the case out of court. But I better not let it happen again.*

Although I'm sure this judge didn't forgive the offense so easily, at least it is evident that the man had forgiven himself. But our eternal God, the judge of all humankind, is willing and wanting to forgive us if we ask Him. And once forgiveness is sought with repentance, then and only then can we honestly, fully, and finally come to terms with our past.

Remember, when God forgives, He forgets. Someone told of a man who came to God trying to bring up a sin that had long been repented of. He said, "God, I want to talk to you about this particular sin." To which God replied, "What sin?" God had forgotten. You don't need to be hindered by your past. You don't have a sinful past. It has all been washed away by the blood of Jesus Christ.

2. Accept God's Value System.

We hear a lot today about prosperity. Most Americans live for the almighty dollar. Ours is a society that is intoxicated with material prosperity.

If I could only get that mink coat or diamond bracelet, many women think, *then I'd be happy.*

If I could just afford a new Mercedes or a Jaguar, the men think, *then I'd really be somebody.*

---

*Charles L. Allen, *Victory in the Valleys of Life* (Old Tappan, NJ: Fleming H. Revell Co., 1984).

Many of our families are pushing themselves to work more and more in order to get ahead financially. But in their pursuit of prosperity, they often drive themselves to personal and emotional collapse. In other words, the means (overwork) destroys the goal (financial success).

Not only are we consumed with consuming, but some have even tried to get God to help them in this obsession. Prosperity theology has become very popular today. Some people call it "name it and claim it." Others call it "blab it and grab it." Either way, the concept says that God has promised to bless us if we trust Him by faith. Based upon this, they distort the idea of God's blessings to mean that if you take God at His Word, you can get all you want from Him by holding Him ransom to His own promises. It is really a theology of greed that is built upon the faulty premise that we deserve material blessings from God.

God's value system is quite different from that of the world. His view of prosperity is essentially spiritual, not material. His view is expressed in 1 Timothy 6:6, "But godliness with contentment is great gain." God's view of prosperity ("great gain") is based upon two spiritual qualities: (1) godliness and (2) contentment. Godliness is the quality of spiritual piety that enables us to be like God in the character of our lives. Contentment is the quality of satisfaction and sufficiency. In this context it is derived from God Himself. Thus, the truly successful person is the one who has found contentment in a godly life. Being able to put your head on a pillow at night and know that your soul is clean is the real key to peace with God and yourself.

Godliness is not something we can attain or produce by ourselves. It is that God-like quality which results from a heart that is clean before God. It comes as a result of confession and repentance. Contentment is the inner, abiding peace of God regardless of outward circumstances.

The Apostle Paul understood this kind of inner peace. Despite being beaten, imprisoned, rejected, shipwrecked and even left for dead, he knew the true source of peace. He said, "I have learned, in whatsoever state I am, therewith to be content" (Philippians 4:11). It was in this context of talking about his sufferings and difficulties that Paul wrote: "I can do all things through Christ which strengtheneth me" (Philippians 4:13).

If you want to talk about true prosperity, this is it! True prosperity is the peace and contentment God gives to us in the face of adversity. Knowing that your sins are forgiven and that you can have inner peace and strength for today is the greatest success anyone could ever know. This peace is greater than wealth or riches. It is the most valuable quality we could ever possess.

On Monday, October 19, 1987, (a day that has been labeled "Black Monday") the stock market took a terrible plunge and nearly collapsed. It was the worst day for many investors in recent history. The results were catastrophic. People took their own lives in violent acts of suicide. One man walked into his stockbroker's agency and shot and killed his broker. Then he turned the gun on himself and killed himself. Why? All because of money. That poor, confused man thought that money was the key to prosperity. And in that tragic moment he lost what life is really all about.

Money and material possessions can never buy you peace of mind. That kind of peace only comes from God working in your soul. Only when He is in control of your life will you experience the great prosperity of godliness and contentment.

3. *Concentrate on the Present.*

You cannot go back and relive the past. It is over and gone. Nor can you live tomorrow until it comes. Too many people are so caught between the failures of yesterday and the fears of tomorrow that they cannot really enjoy today. But today is your only guarantee. Learn to live it to the fulfillment of God's will. The psalmist said, "This is the day which the Lord hath made; we will rejoice and be glad in it" (Psalm 118:24). He was talking about learning to find our joy in the blessings of today.

Our Lord said, "Don't be anxious about tomorrow. God will take care of your tomorrow too. Live one day at a time" (Matthew 6:34, TLB). When we become overwhelmed by the pressures of life, we get bogged down by the failures of the past or worried about the fears of the future. Either way, we lose the joy of today.

Worry has been defined as "building bridges over rivers you will never cross." True peace comes when we stop worrying and start trusting God to meet our needs. The country singer was right when she sang, "One day at a time, sweet Jesus, that's all I'm asking from you. Lord, help me today, show me the way, one day at a time."[*]

---

[*] "One Day at a Time," written by Marijohn Wilkin and Kris Kristofferson. Copyright © 1973, 1975 by BUCKHORN MUSIC PUBLISHERS, INC. (BMI) International Copyright Secured. All Rights Reserved. Used by permission.

4. Discover Life's Purpose.
God has saved you for a purpose. Find out what it is and give yourself wholly to it. Life is not a meaningless journey. It is an opportunity to discover God's will and purpose for your life. People often feel that their life is a merry-go-round that keeps going in circles but never goes anywhere. They get up in the morning, go to work, come home, eat dinner, watch television, and go to bed—only to get up the next day and do it all over again.

While that may be a necessary part of a daily routine, it is not the ultimate purpose of your existence. God created you as a unique individual to fulfill a specific purpose in life. When He redeemed you by faith in Christ, He established a purpose for you that no one else can ever fulfill.

The Bible is filled with examples of people who discovered God's purpose for their lives. Abraham was a nomadic herdsman who became the father of the Hebrew nation. Joseph was a slave in Egypt who became the grand vizier, second only to Pharaoh. Gideon was a cowardly thresher of wheat who became a mighty warrior that delivered Israel. Ruth was a Moabitess whose devotion to her mother-in-law resulted in her becoming an ancestor of the Messiah. Esther was a Jewish orphan who became queen of Persia and saved the Jews in that empire from destruction. Mary was a young virgin in Nazareth of Galilee who gave birth to God's Son. Peter was a simple fisherman who caught a vision of what God wanted to do with his life and became one of the apostles. Paul was a legalistic Pharisee who discovered Christ on the road to Damascus and became the greatest missionary evangelist of all time.

Each of these individuals discovered God's divine purpose for his or her life. Each learned that God is no respecter of persons. He will use all those who willingly surrender their lives to Him. The same is true for you and me. There was a time when I simply and routinely went about my daily duties. I was faithful, but my life had no zeal or zest. I had no ultimate purpose to what I was doing. I wasn't even very excited about life. But one day God clearly revealed His cause and purpose for my life.

When I learned why I was here, I began to get excited about life. I made His cause my cause, and I made His purpose my purpose. I learned that God had a specific plan for my life. I began to realize that I was called of God to serve Him and that no one else could fulfill that service like I could. Once you come to grips with that truth, you will never be the same again—never! Helen Steiner Rice said it like this:

> Life without purpose
> is barren indeed—
> There can't be a harvest
> unless you plant seed,
> There can't be attainment
> unless there's a goal,
> And man's but a robot
> unless there's a soul . . .
> If we send no ships out,
> no ships will come in,
> And unless there's a contest,
> nobody can win . . .
> For games can't be won
> unless they are played,
> And prayers can't be answered
> unless they are prayed . . .
> So whatever is wrong
> with your life today,
> You'll find a solution
> if you kneel down and pray
> Not just for pleasure,
> enjoyment and health,
> Not just for honors
> and prestige and wealth . . .
> But pray for a purpose
> to make life worth living,
> And pray for the joy
> of unselfish giving,
> For great is your gladness
> and rich your reward
> When you make your life's purpose
> the choice of the Lord.*

5. Depend upon God's Promises.

The Bible is filled with the promises of God. We need to claim each one by faith and activate its truth in our lives. Some folks like to say, "If God said it, I believe it, and that settles it!" The fact

---

* From *Gifts from the Heart* by Helen Steiner Rice (p. 51). Copyright © 1981. Published by Fleming H. Revell Company. Used by permission of the Helen Steiner Rice Foundation.

of the matter is, if God said it, that settles it, whether we believe it or not.

Someone will question, "How can I be sure God really said this?" or, "How can I be sure this is what it means?" I realize we must interpret each promise in its proper context. But I also believe that we need to take those promises which apply to us and activate them by faith.

In Hebrews 4:3, we read an amazing truth. It says there that God's works were "finished from the foundation of the world." In other words, God had already provided the answer to your every need before the world was ever formed. With His divine foreknowledge He looked down the corridor of time to come, saw your coming problem and provided just exactly what you would need. Just think of it, since the beginning of the world, God has had in His storehouse of blessings the perfect provision for your problem.

"But you don't know how big my problem is," you may object. Perhaps I don't fully understand. But God does and He is greater than all your problems combined. Your problem is that you have your attention focused on your problems instead of having it focused on God. Once you comprehend the greatness and magnitude of God, you will see how tiny that problem really is.

We live on a planet that is part of a solar system that is part of a galaxy called the Milky Way. Scientists tell us that if we could travel at the speed of light (186,281 miles per second), it would take over one hundred thousand years to travel from one end of the Milky Way to the other! And those same scientists tell us that there are millions of galaxies, like the Milky Way, in our universe. It is almost beyond what the human mind can comprehend.

But as big as our universe is, it is not as big as God. He is the One who spoke it all into existence. He is the One whose majesty and greatness go beyond the stars. And, yet, He is the One who knows your name, who numbers the hairs of your head, and who loves you and cares about your problems.

Do you really think you have a problem that He cannot handle? When all the personal, emotional, financial, and spiritual problems of life come upon you, remember that He who lives within you is greater than all of them.

How can we find peace in a troubled world? We can find it in a personal relationship with the God who made this world. Even when the world threatens to blow itself apart, we can rest assured that God is in control. That means He is in control of the details of your life as well. You need not spend fruitless hours worrying about life. You have the gift of eternal life within your soul. Your life is co-eternal with the life of God. You shall live forever in His care and keeping.

Pause for a moment of reflection. Think on the majesty and magnitude of God. Focus on the promises He has given you in His Word. Turn your attention to fulfilling His purpose for your life. Live in the confidence that He is in control. Now you can relax, for there is nothing to worry about. God cares and He keeps His promises to help.

~§ 19 §~

Causing Heaven to Hear

Prayer is one of the great privileges of the Christian life. It is an opportunity for us to communicate with God Himself. It includes expressions of praise and petition, thanksgiving and request. Prayer is the verbal expression of our innermost being.

Despite the blessing that prayer brings into our lives, there are times when it seems that Heaven does not hear us no matter how long or sincerely we pray. The psalmist expressed this concern when he wrote, "Do not keep silent, O God! Do not hold to Your peace, And do not be still O God!" (Psalm 83:1, NKJV). Have you ever felt like that? Have you ever come to a place in your life when it seemed as though Heaven had shut its doors against you? It doesn't happen often, but there are times in the life of a believer when it seems as though God is suddenly very far away. No matter how much you cry to God or how much you pray, you can't seem to break through to Heaven. If that has been your experience, consider with me several reasons why God does not answer our prayers. Let's discover why and what we can do about it.

1. *Heaven Doesn't Hear Us When We Fail to Pray.*

"That is obvious!" a man once said to me. "How can people expect God to hear them if they do not pray?"

That is exactly my point! There are many people who never verbally express prayer to God and then cannot figure out why God never answers their prayers. It is as though they merely expect God to intervene on their behalf without their ever calling upon Him. I have actually heard some people say, "God knows everything and He knows my needs, so He will take care of them whether I ask Him to or not." I have also heard other people say, "I will just imagine in my mind what my needs and requests are, and God will understand and He will answer me." Now I realize that every prayer does not have to be verbally expressed with our lips. Certainly we can pray in our heart or mind. But I believe that all too often people use these kinds of statements as excuses for not taking the time to discipline themselves to actually spend time alone with God. If you are expecting God to answer that kind of prayer, I think you are in for a big disappointment.

Prayer is not something that comes easily. It takes discipline, diligence, and commitment. Jesus' own disciples said, "Lord, teach us to pray" (Luke 11:1). Why would they make such a request? Isn't prayer something that is obvious to everyone? Certainly no one prayed more than the people of Jesus' own day. But most of their prayers were nothing more than vain repetitions. The disciples realized that people were saying words without touching the power of Heaven. Therefore, they wanted to know how to communicate with God. It is evident by their request and our Lord's response that true prayer takes effort and discipline on our part.

The Apostle James made a marvelous and profound statement about prayer when he wrote, "Ye have not, because ye ask not" (James 4:2). Our Lord Jesus made a similar statement when He said, "Hitherto have ye asked nothing in my name: ask, and ye shall receive, that your joy may be full" (John 16:24). Our Lord's messages to His disciples are filled with admonitions to ask in prayer. He said:

> Ask, and it shall be given you; seek, and ye shall find; knock, and it shall be opened unto you: for every one that asketh receiveth; and he that seeketh findeth; and to him that knocketh it shall be opened. (Matthew 7:7-8)

Another time He said, "And all things, whatsoever ye shall ask in prayer, believing, ye shall receive" (Matthew 21:22). On yet another occasion, He said,

> And whatsoever ye shall ask in my name, that will I do, that the Father may be glorified in the Son. If ye shall ask any thing in my name, I will do it. (John 14:13-14)

Prayer is not designed to become a selfish process by which we simply demand things from God. Nor is it the kind of process by which we simply state our needs by faith and demand that God fulfill them. However, it is more than clear that prayer involves asking God for specific things. Those things may be material or immaterial, but they are, nevertheless, specific things for which we are making our requests. If you are going to expect God to give you something, you must ask Him for it.

I have a son who is now away at college. We have always had a wonderful relationship. He knows that when he has a need he can usually come to me, ask for help, and get it. But if he were to encounter a serious need while away at school and never share that need with me, it would be impossible for me to help. If he has the need and I have the resources to meet the need, then the most natural thing in the world is for him to tell me what the need is.

I remember hearing the great preacher Vance Havner speak on the subject of prayer. During his message he told the story of a factory that had this sign hung over the machines: When the Threads Get Tangled, Call for the Foreman. One day, sure enough, the threads got tangled on one of the machines. The operator thought she would take care of the problem herself and began to try to untangle them. Just then the foreman came by and asked why she hadn't called him to help. "Can't you read the sign?" he asked. "Oh yes," she replied, "but I'm doing my best to take care of it myself." Looking at the mess she had made, he retorted, "Doing the best you can always means calling for the foreman."

Of course, I realize that God is sovereign and that He is omniscient. He knows our need before we express it to Him. But He still delights to hear us express it. Unfortunately, some people are so lazy spiritually that they will not even take the time to articulate their requests before the Lord. I am convinced that Heaven is closed to those who refuse to pray.

2. God Doesn't Hear Us When We Ignore His Will.

We cannot expect to flagrantly disobey the commands of God and ignore His will for our lives and still expect Him to answer our prayers. The Bible says:

> And this is the confidence that we have in him, that, if we ask any thing according to his will, he heareth us: And if we know that he hear us, whatsoever we ask, we know that we have the petitions that we desired of him. (1 John 5:14-15)

This passage makes it clear that answered prayer is dependent upon our obedience to the will of God for our lives. It expresses both a positive and negative truth. On the one hand, if we ask anything according to His will, He will grant it to us. On the other hand, however, if we ask for anything out of His will, He will not respond.

"But I really want to do the will of God," a young man said to me once. "I just don't know what it is."

"How often do you read your Bible?" I asked him.

"Well, I bring it with me every Sunday," he responded.

"But do you read it for yourself during the week?" I asked.

"No, not really," he replied.

"If you really want to know the will of God, then you must read it!" I insisted.

I went on to explain to the young man that the Bible itself is divided into two testaments. A testament is a statement of a will or covenant. In a sense, it is the last will and testament of God to humanity. If someone had written a will and died and you thought there was any possibility that you might receive something in that will, I am sure that you would make certain that you read it or had someone read it to you. The same is true of the Word of God. If we really want to know the will of God, then we must be willing to read the Word of God. This is the book that tells us God's will for our lives. Every word—every verse, every chapter—is an expression of God's will for your life. The tragedy is that many Christians are content to carry this wonderful document with them to church on Sunday and then place it on a shelf for the rest of the week and never take it down again until the following Sunday.

Most of the problems we confront in life are dealt with in the Word of God. The Bible is God's manual for effective living on this planet. If you really want to experience God's very best for your life, you need to fill your mind and soul with the truths of His Word.

Jesus said, "If ye abide in me, and my words abide in you, ye shall ask what ye will, and it shall be done unto you" (John 15:7). He made this promise about as clear and straightforward as anything could ever be. He knew that if His Word was abiding in you, you would be asking according to the Father's will, instead of against His will. Therefore, He could have the confidence to know that your prayers would be answered because they were being asked in accordance with the Father's will. But again, the opposite is also true; if we ask anything contrary to the will of God, He is not going to hear us.

3. *God Doesn't Hear Us When We Pray Selfishly.*

Unfortunately, there are times when we pray out of nothing more than our selfish desires. We have decided that there is something that we just must have, and we are convinced that God will agree. However, if the thing for which we are making our request is not really best for us, God will deny it for our own good. The Epistle of James puts it like this, "Ye ask, and receive not, because ye ask amiss, that ye may consume it upon your lusts" (James 4:3). The point of this verse is very clear. You are not going to receive an answer from God in order to fulfill your own selfish desires. Many times we pray for things that we think we need and God knows that they are not for our best, so He denies the request. I can remember as a teenager praying for a car before I even had a driver's license. There was no way God was going to answer that prayer. God is not going to give us answers to prayer just to fulfill our foolish desires.

The word *amiss* is a translation of the Greek word *kakōs*, which is used by James as an adverb, meaning "evil" or "foolish." I have observed Christians who have asked God for some of the most foolish things imaginable. It was evident that they were not part of God's will and when He did not answer, they became all upset and mad at God! I know people who have stopped attending church, and stopped tithing, and stopped witnessing to others, simply because they are angry at God. Let me remind you that God is not impressed by our little spiritual tantrums.

When I was a boy there was another boy in our neighborhood who was one of those kids who are able to manipulate their parents with tantrums. He could get just about anything he wanted in life by pitching a fit. He would throw himself on the ground and pound on it, screaming and hollering and gasping for breath. His mother would rush out and say, "Oh, _____, please don't do that. You can have whatever you want." Afterwards the boy would brush himself off, and his poor mother would give in to his demands.

One day my friend's mother had to be gone for the day, so she left him at our house. I will never forget it. My mother was in the kitchen washing dishes when this kid came in and punched her in the back. He made a demand, and Mother said, "No." Suddenly he threw himself to the floor and started kicking and screaming and holding his breath. My mother turned around, wiped her hands off, folded her arms, and started laughing as loudly as she could. The boy was stunned. He did not seem to know what to do. My mother told him to get up and get out of her way before she took a paddle to him. She wasn't one bit impressed with his little tantrum.

God is not impressed with our little tantrums either. We can kick and scream and squawk all we want to, but if God has decided not to give us our request because it was based upon selfish desires, our fit will not impress Him one bit. In fact, such an attitude closes Heaven to our prayers.

4. God Doesn't Hear Us When We Harbor Bitterness Toward Others.

In our Lord's teaching on prayer (Matthew 5:21-24), He made it clear that there is a direct connection between forgiveness and answered prayer. He made it clear to His disciples that even bringing their gifts to the altar was inadequate if they were holding bitterness in their hearts toward others. In fact, He told them to go and "be reconciled to thy brother" before attempting to offer their gifts. On another occasion, Jesus told His disciples that they would not be forgiven themselves until they were willing to forgive the trespasses that others had committed against them (Matthew 18:35).

In 1 Peter 3:7, Scripture tells husbands to dwell with their wives according to knowledge, honor, and grace, "that your prayers be not hindered." God takes it seriously how we treat our family because the family is His creation. I am convinced that He takes very seriously how we treat one another within the family. That is especially true of the relationship between husbands and wives. We cannot expect God to answer our prayers when things are not right at home.

Bitterness is a very terrible thing. I have discussed it in depth in another chapter. It is like a cancer of the soul. It not only poisons a person's attitude toward others, but it spreads like a plague and poisons the attitude of others as well. Once bitterness becomes lodged in your heart, it will destroy all other relationships in your life. The Bible warns us against a "root of bitterness" springing up in our lives (Hebrews 12:15). Bitterness is the most dangerous of all attitudes to healthy Christian living. It eats away the vitality of your spiritual life and leaves you cold and empty. It is the opposite of forgiveness, which is God's powerful principle for resolving the hurt and pain of human relationships. When we truly learn to forgive one another, we are putting the grace of God into operation in our lives.

The second part of the verse in Hebrews 12:15 reminds us that bitterness defiles our lives. The word *defile* (Greek, *miaiño*) means to "stain" as with a dye. The term can be properly translated "pollute" or "contaminate." The concept communicated in this passage is that when we allow bitterness to remain in our lives it contaminates our relationship to others. It not only pollutes our own soul, but the lives of all who come in contact with us. If you really want to get your prayers answered, confess your bitterness, seek forgiveness, and make reconciliation with those who have wronged you.

5. God Doesn't Hear Us When We Refuse Wise Counsel.

In the Book of Zechariah we read that the prophet preached to the people who were hearing with their ears, but not responding with their hearts. He preached; they listened; but nobody responded to the message. For that reason, "I would not hear, saith the Lord of hosts" (Zechariah 7:13). Because they would not heed God's counsel through His prophet, He refused to listen to their cries.

Scripture has much to say about wise counsel. The Book of Proverbs is filled with statements urging us to heed the advice of spiritual leaders. When we reject the advice of godly men and women, we are placing ourselves in a very precarious position. It is unfortunate when someone insists that he or she is right and everyone else is wrong. But that is rarely the case. The Bible warns:

> Then shall they call upon me, but I will not answer; they shall seek me early, but they shall not find me: for that they hated knowledge, and did not choose the fear of the Lord: they would none of my counsel: they despised all my reproof. (Proverbs 1:28-30)

We cannot go against the Word of God or the advice of godly people and expect God to answer our prayers. Such stubbornness will certainly close the door of Heaven to our requests.

6. God Doesn't Hear Us When We Regard Iniquity in Our Hearts.

The psalmist said, "If I regard iniquity in my heart, the Lord will not hear me" (Psalm 66:18). To regard something means to cherish it in one's inmost being. Unfortunately, we are often beset with habitual sins which we refuse to surrender to the will of God. It is those besetting sins which defeat us and often keep us from getting our prayers answered.

For many, these sins are little things, and for others, they are very serious things. Whichever the case may be, such sin prohibits us from having real power with God. He refuses to hear because He is a holy God. He cannot tolerate sin because it is against His nature to do so. Therefore, God will not answer our prayers when we deliberately cling to sinful habits in our lives.

There is a story told about the king of England years ago who was visiting in a small town in the southern part of his kingdom. While he was there, he broke a heel on one of his boots. Wanting to get it fixed as quickly as possible, he took it to the local cobbler shop to have it repaired. As he walked through the door, he noticed the walls were dirty, the floors were unswept, and everything was in disarray. Suddenly, the cobbler came out from behind the counter and was stunned to see the king. He fell down before him and said, "Oh, King, if I had know you were coming I would have cleaned my house." The king looked down at the cobbler and said, "Sir, clean your house, for tomorrow I will return."

The cobbler worked feverishly all night long to clean the walls, mop the floors, and dust everything in sight. When the king returned the next day, he noticed that the shop was spotlessly clean. Everything was appropriately put in its proper place. Therefore, the king said to his servant, "Bring me the banner." So the servant brought in the banner, and the king placed it across the counter where everyone could see it. It contained four simple words: "Approved by the King." From then on, the cobbler never lacked for business. Everyone in town came to see the place that was "Approved by the King."

If you lack power with God in prayer, perhaps you would do well to examine your heart. Is it clean before God? Are sins confessed up to date? Are all things in their proper order? When your life is clean before Him, you will find yourself "Approved by the King." When you pray, all of Heaven will stand at attention. You will be received through the blood of Jesus Christ and be granted the privilege of coming boldly before the throne of grace (see Hebrews 4:16). It is there that we may find "grace to help in time of need."

These are the many reasons that God does not hear us when we pray. But the ultimate desire of God's heart is to hear us and to grant our request. He is a loving Father who delights to meet the needs of His children. You do not have to exhaust yourself in order to get His attention. It is not the saying of certain words in a certain order that brings response, but it is the heart that is pure before Him. I don't know who wrote the following words, but they express perfectly what I'm trying to say:

> It's not the Length of your Prayers—how long they may be
> It's not the Number of your Prayers—how many there are
> It's not the Words of your Prayers—how pleasant to hear
> It's not the Eloquence of your Prayers—how many they please

It's not the Height of your Prayers—how high they sound
It's not the Breadth of your Prayers—how far reaching they may be
But it's the Power of your Prayers from the heart right with God!

The clean pure heart has power with God! His prayers literally shake Heaven into action. Augustine said, "When a man's life is like lightning, his prayers are like thunder." It is such a praying out of the sincere depths of the righteous heart, that God will not reject. In fact, He delights in answering to show forth His power.

I am especially fond of a verse found in 2 Chronicles 16:9. Read it and let it speak to your heart.

For the eyes of the Lord run to and fro throughout the whole earth, to shew himself strong in the behalf of them whose heart is perfect toward him . . .

Just think of it—God is looking for someone to bless. Why not give Him an opportunity? If your heart is pure, He is seeking you. Why not start praying right now!

God Can Use You, Too

Recently, I had one of those terrible days. Everything seemed to go wrong. It reminded me of the infamous Murphy's Law: "Whatever can go wrong, will go wrong." All that day I felt that people were ignoring me. I even received a fund-raising letter from a television evangelist with my name misspelled. I was so discouraged and frustrated by late afternoon that I developed a splitting headache. Finally, I decided to leave the office and stop at a nearby drugstore for some aspirin.

As I entered the door, a little boy skidded past me, being chased by his mother. As he slid into the counter, she caught him by the arm, yanked him up, and dragged him over to where I was standing. Grabbing his cheeks, she pointed his face toward me and said, "Billy, if I've told you once, I've told you a thousand times, don't run in front of nobody again!"

Suddenly it occurred to me that she had called me a "nobody." That was about all I needed to let the bottom fall out of my day. The woman tried desperately to get the boy to apologize to me, but he wouldn't do it. I really felt low. Even this child wouldn't treat me decently. I thought, "Maybe it is true. Maybe my life doesn't count at all."

Have you ever felt like that? That the world could just as easily go on without you? Have you wondered if you were really loved or needed by anyone at all? Perhaps you have told yourself that you are not much good to anyone. Maybe you don't have the talent, ability, or personality that others have. Perhaps you think that nobody really cares about you.

When we get to feeling like this, we are filled with self-pity. We let our minds dwell on all the negative factors of life and overlook all the good things of life. Self-pity is ultimately an expression of self-centeredness. It is actually our way of admitting how selfish we really are inside. Self-pity is the protest of self against the goodness of God.

It is the refusal to be content with God's provision in your life. It is a selfishness that demands the right to have more, be more, and do more. In time, it is an attitude that leads to rebellion, despair, and depression.

But it is right here in the midst of our self-pity and self-condemnation that God enters into our lives. It is here that He belongs for He is the One who made us and who understands us. If anyone has the right to speak to the issue of our self-worth, most certainly it is God. He knows us for what we really are and yet He loves us more than we could ever love ourselves.

If you are discouraged and wondering if God could ever use you, consider these thoughts in 1 Corinthians 1:25-31. Perhaps you have failed in your walk with God, and you want to give up and run away from it all. Maybe things have not gone well at home or on the job, and it has made you feel like throwing in the towel. Well, hang in there, because it is evident in these verses that God can still use you.

The Apostle Paul wrote this letter to the church at Corinth, which he helped establish on one of his missionary journeys. He knew the Corinthian believers well. They were a cross section of every element of society in that seaport city. Some were of noble birth and some were wealthy merchants, but most of them were ordinary common people who came from the lowest levels of society. Some were even slaves.

As he wrote this letter, Paul reminded the believers at Corinth that what often appears to be foolish to men is really the wisdom of God. To the world it seemed foolish that God let His Son die on the cross, but in His death He conquered sin and death for all men. He turned apparent defeat into glorious victory. Then the apostle reminded them of what God had done for them personally:

> Because the foolishness of God is wiser than men; and the weakness of God is stronger than men. For ye see your calling, brethren, how that not many wise men after the flesh, not many mighty, not many noble, are called: But God hath chosen the foolish things of the world to confound the wise; and God hath chosen the weak things of the world to confound the things which are mighty; And base things of the world, and things which are despised, hath God chosen, yea, and things which are not, to bring to nought things that are: That no flesh should glory in his presence. But of him are ye in Christ Jesus, who of God is made unto us wisdom, and righteousness, and sanctification, and redemption: That, according as it is written, He that glorieth, let him glory in the Lord. (1 Corinthians 1:25-31)

Do you find yourself in this text? Are you among the foolish, the weak, the base, or the despised ones? If so, I have good news for you. God can use you to His glory. He is not seeking just the intellectual, the personable, the aristocrat, or the successful. He is seeking the weak that He might reveal His power. He is seeking the lowly that He might lift them up. He is seeking the rejected that He might accept them. In reality He is seeking all of us, no matter what our situation, that He might save us and use us for His glory. Let's take a closer look at those God is willing to use.

1. The Foolish: No Dignity.

The word *foolish* comes from the Greek word *mōros*, from which we also get the English word *moron*. It means those who are stupid, silly, and unpredictable. They are the opposite of the wise (sophos), thus they are the unsophisticated ones. The apostle reminded the Corinthians that most of them were considered foolish by the world because of their faith in Christ. The phrase *"ye see your calling"* means "you see in what manner you are called" to salvation. The idea communicated in this text is that God chooses the foolish things of the world in order to confound—that is, put to shame—the wise. *"After the flesh"* is a Greek idiom that simply means "in your humanity." In other words, Paul is saying that in our humanity (in ourselves) we are nothing, but in Christ we are everything.

Whenever I think of God using the unpredictable, I think of the baseball-player-turned-evangelist named Billy Sunday. He was one of the most powerful preachers of all time. Over one hundred million people heard him preach in the early twentieth century and over one million of them came to faith in Christ.

Billy Sunday was also one of the most unpredictable preachers who ever lived. He threw chairs around on the platform and simulated a boxing match with the Devil. It is said that while he was preaching at an evangelistic crusade on a hot summer day the people began to fall asleep. To get their attention, he hurled a chair through a stained-glass window. As it crashed and glass spattered everywhere, it sent a message that no one was to sleep while he preached!

On another occasion Sunday gave an invitation for people to come forward to publicly announce their faith in Christ. During the invitation, an old man with a long pointed beard came forward and stood at the edge of the platform. Sunday noticed the beard and couldn't keep

God Can Use You, Too

his eyes off it. Finally, he walked over to the edge of the platform, reached down, grabbed the man's beard, gave it a couple of tugs, and yelled, "Honk, honk!"

Billy Sunday was certainly unpredictable. Some might even have called him foolish, but God used him mightily. He was one of those trophies of God's grace who brought variety and spice to Christianity in an era when it was needed most to overcome the image that Christians were dull and old-fashioned.

2. The Weak: No Strength.

The word translated "weak" *(asthenēs)* comes from the Greek word for physical weakness. It means "feeble" or "without strength." In our text it refers to those who have little power or physical strength on their side. They are the opposite of the powerful *(dunatos)* or strong and dignified ones. The idea conveyed here is that God delights in using the physically weak and seemingly powerless that His power might be displayed in their lives.

Let me illustrate with a story. A true story of my very own uncle, my mother's brother, George Hitt. Until his death in 1958, George was a silhouette artist of world renown. He would use a special black paper and through the process of his own imagination create a beautiful scene that he wished to bring forth. With no preliminary drawings, just envisioning the finished product in his mind, he would use surgical scissors to cut the silhouette with all its intricacy out of the black paper. The results were amazing. Pictures that almost came to life would seemingly come out of the page.

It might be a silhouette of a dancer gracefully moving across the stage, a deer standing in a flowery meadow, or even the portrait of some famous individual. In fact, it was his skill in portraits that caused President Franklin D. Roosevelt to invite George to the White House to do silhouette profiles of the entire Roosevelt family. His cuttings hang in the White House today.

During his lifetime, George was proclaimed by many to be the greatest silhouette artist in the world. *Guidepost* magazine ran stories on his accomplishments and Robert Ripley made him a topic of *Ripley's Believe It Or Not.*

But what was so special about George was not just that he was a great artist, nor that he had received great acclaim, but the fact that since he was a seven-year-old boy he had been severely crippled by rheumatoid arthritis. His head, arms, legs, and feet were held rigid in the vise-like grip of this incurable disease. Confined to his bed or his wheelchair, he could not feed or dress himself. The only movement he had in his body was the slight use of his left arm and thumb. Yet with the special surgical scissors placed tightly between his thumb and index finger, he reproduced scenes and characters in silhouette with unbelievable precision and reality.

In George, God had chosen the weak, the handicapped, to confound the wise. His favorite saying, often quoted by those who interviewed him, tells it all, "Don't worry about what you think you can't do but with all your heart and soul do those things that God wants to do through you."

3. The Base: No Position.

The base ones (*agenēs*) are those of low birth; hence they are of no reputation. They are the unimportant people who are the opposite of the noble ones (*eugenēs*), who are of high birth. These are the common people. They have no special pedigree. They are not part of the "jet set" or the "country club" crowd. They are the people Will Rogers, the famous American humorist, was talking about when he said, "God must have loved ordinary people, because He made so many of them."

Jesus Himself had a great ministry to the common people of His day. He preached to fishermen, farmers, and laborers. The Bible says, "the common people heard him gladly" (Mark 12:37). God has never made the lack of wealth or position an obstacle to the gospel. His love is available to all persons regardless of their social standing.

One of the greatest examples in Scripture of God's using an ordinary person is Gideon. God called him to lead the nation of Israel during the time of the judges when the Israelites were severely oppressed by their enemies. Gideon was so fearful of the Midianites and Amalekites that he was actually trying to thresh grain in a winepress to hide it from the enemy when God called him. The Lord called this fearful coward a "mighty man of valour" and urged him to rally an army against their enemies.

Shocked by this request, Gideon responded, "Oh my Lord, wherewith shall I save Israel? Behold, my family is poor in Manasseh, and I am the least in my father's house" (Judges 6:15). In other words, he was saying, "I am just ordinary; how can God use me?" But that is exactly what God wanted to do. He wanted to use an ordinary person to accomplish an extraordinary feat so that everyone would realize that God had done it.

God Can Use You, Too

Gideon's exploits are known to every child in Sunday school today. With a force of only three hundred men, he virtually frightened away the entire invading horde of Midianites and Amalekites in his sneak attack during the night by waving torches and blowing trumpets. In panic, the frightened invaders fled before him.

Don't ever tell yourself that you are too ordinary for God to use. While there are times that God raises up people with unusual testimonies and startling life stories, He much more often uses just ordinary people who are willing to be used by Him. No matter how common your life may seem to you, touched by the grace of God it is a life that can bring glory to Him.

4. *The Despised: No Hope.*

The despised are the ones who are of no account. They are viewed by others with contempt either because of some wrong they have done or because they have accomplished little of any real value in life. This is the most difficult group of all for us to imagine God using. We can perhaps understand His willingness to use the foolish, the weak, the lowly, the ordinary, but those who are despised and rejected are beyond our human comprehension.

When God converts the alcoholic, the drug addict, the prostitute, or the gambler, He often makes them into special trophies of His grace. Mel Trotter was just such a man. He seemed to be a hopeless alcoholic who spent every dime he had on liquor. On many occasions his wife and children had to go without the ordinary necessities of life. In time, his infant daughter grew sick and died from neglect. Mel's family was so poor that they couldn't even afford a proper burial. A local church heard of their plight and collected enough money to buy the child's burial clothes and to provide for the funeral.

The night before the burial, Mel Trotter stayed at the funeral home until everyone had left. Then thirsting for a drink of alcohol, he went to the casket and removed the shoes from the little feet of his baby daughter. Clutching them to his chest, he sped away into the night to sell the shoes to get the money for a shot of whiskey.

If there was ever a man who was despised for his selfish deeds it was Mel Trotter. Yet, years later Mel came to know Christ and his life was transformed. He became one of the great preachers of the twentieth century. Thousands of alcoholics were converted under his ministry.

I have known people who refused to come to Christ because they thought they were too bad to be converted. But that is simply not true. The Scriptures assure us that "where sin abounded, grace did much more abound" (Romans 5:20). As a young man, John Bunyan's life was so vile and profane that his vulgar language once brought a rebuke from a passing prostitute. But after he gave his life to Christ, he became a preacher of God's grace, and from the Bedford jail, while being persecuted for his faith, he authored the spiritual classic *Pilgrim's Progress*.

Understand, God never gives up on anyone. Often I have seen those whom society has avoided and whose families have rejected them come to faith in Christ. Although others thought they would never amount to anything, out of their despair they found God and their lives were transformed.

5. *Those Who Are Not: No Significance.*

Finally, Paul points to the most insignificant group of all—the nobodies. He calls them "those who are not," meaning those who have no meaningful or significant existence. This was a contemptible expression to the Greeks, to whom existence was everything. The apostle uses it in our text to denote those people who are less than ordinary; they are nothing! They are the people who really don't count for anything in this world. They are the ones nobody cares about at all.

It is interesting to me that the apostle added this last group because that is where I used to see myself. I really believed that I was just a nobody. I was always the silent, bashful type. Even in school, I seldom spoke in class unless I was called upon to answer a question. As a result, no one ever paid any attention to me.

I can still remember an elementary teacher who skipped my name every morning when she read the roll. Every day it frustrated me, but I was so bashful I never said anything. This went on all year until I finally got up enough courage to go and tell her what had been happening. She apologized and said, "Son, I'm sure sorry that I've skipped over you." Then she added, "Now what was your name again?" I had been in her class all year, and she still didn't know my name!

The wonderful thing about God is that He knows all about us, and we can be sure that He knows our name. God always called people by name in Scripture. He never once said, "Hey, you." We are all important to Him.

Dr. Bailey Smith, former president of the Southern Baptist

Convention, tells about a friend of his who lost his thirty-four-year-old wife in death. After the funeral the man and his little daughter returned home. The little girl became frightened by the empty house without her mother. At bedtime she said, "Daddy, I'm scared. Can I sleep with you tonight?" Her father assured her that she could and put her to bed. After he got ready himself, he turned out the light and slipped into bed. Suddenly, he felt her little hand touch his face.

"Honey, is anything wrong?" he asked.

"No," she replied, "I just wanted to see if your face was turned toward me."

No matter how lonely or insignificant you may feel, I want to assure you that God's face is turned toward you. All may seem dark right now, but through the darkness He is looking toward you. He loves you and is willing to use you. Reach out to Him and you will find He is reaching out to you.

GOD CAN USE YOU

David had always been slow in school. His grades were below average and even then he struggled to do as well as he did. When he was about seven he gave his heart to Christ in our Sunday school. Years later, as a teenager, he was somewhat of a social outcast and often kept to himself. Eventually an evangelist conducted a crusade for teens in our area, and David decided to attend. He quickly became caught up in all the excitement of the meetings. He especially seemed to enjoy seeing other teenagers come to faith in Christ.

On the second night of the crusade, the evangelist urged the teenagers to invite their friends to the meetings. Bewildered, David came to me and asked whom he could invite, since he had no close friends.

"I don't really know anyone," he responded.

"Then it really shouldn't matter whom you ask," I replied.

"All right," he said, "I'll ask the first person I see tomorrow at school."

We both agreed that was a good idea, and after we prayed together, David hurried home. The next night during the service I looked for David but couldn't find him. I was afraid he had been rejected and hadn't come. But during the invitation at the end of the service, I looked up and here came David down the aisle with the captain of the football team.

"He's the first one I saw!" he whispered to me excitedly.

Before the evening was over the football player had given his life to Christ. The other kids were shocked that David had even invited him to the meeting.

"Can you believe it?" one of the teenagers asked me.

Yes, I can, I thought. *That's exactly what the Bible teaches. God uses the weak and lowly to serve Him.*

God delights in using our lives to glorify Him. He is willing to use anyone who will submit to His Lordship. No one is beyond the touch of His grace. God can make you into what you could never be apart from Him. He can take the lowest of people and elevate them to the highest places of leadership.

But God can also take some people of high stature and use them as well. While there may not be many who are the wise, mighty, or noble, certainly there are some. For a long time I could not imagine why God seemed to use so few of these people. Then I realized that it isn't that He won't use them, but that they often will not allow God to use them.

Notice the phrase, *"after the flesh"* in our text. It literally means "in the flesh," or "in one's humanity." It implies that these people are wise, mighty, or noble in their humanity. From a human standpoint, they don't need God and often live drawing attention to themselves. While God is willing to transform them by His grace, He rarely is given the opportunity to use the elite of this world to serve Him. Instead, God allows His grace to be magnified in the poor, lowly, and weak who often have nothing in themselves of which to glory.

Whatever your position in life may be, God can use you, too. Don't ever think that you are not good enough. God doesn't want your "good enoughs." He just wants you, as you are. He will take you with all your frailties, with all your mistakes and limitations, and mold your life and make it into something beyond your wildest dreams.

Often God chooses the lowly people who walk the lonely paths of life to become His servants. We are the pilgrims on the road less traveled. But even on the most lonely road God is there. I like the way Robert Frost put it:

> I shall be telling this with a sigh,
>   Somewhere ages and ages hence;
> Two roads diverged in a yellow wood,
>   And I—
> I took the one less traveled by,
>   And that has made all the difference.*

Now that's what we all want our living to do, isn't it? To make a difference. That the world, our friends, our family—that something will be different, better, because we live. That we are significant. That we count in life for something. And that is exactly what God has promised us: That regardless of what difficulties life has seemingly dealt us, it is really true—God can use us too!

What hope we have in his unfailing promise.

---

* From "The Road Not Taken" by Robert Frost in *Complete Poems of Robert Frost*. Copyright 1930, 1947, 1949 by Henry Holt & Co., Inc. Copyright 1936, 1942 by Robert Frost. Used by permission of the publishers.

Living in Awe!

Copyright © 2012 by Shelli Prindle

Living in Awe!
by Shelli Prindle

Printed in the United States of America

ISBN 9781622301737

All rights reserved solely by the author. The author guarantees all contents are original and do not infringe upon the legal rights of any other person or work. No part of this book may be reproduced in any form without the permission of the author. The views expressed in this book are not necessarily those of the publisher.

Unless otherwise indicated, Bible quotations are taken from the New American Standard Bible, Copyright © 1960, 1962, 1963, 1968, 1971, 1972, 1973, 1975, 1977, 1995 by The Lockman Foundation. Used by permission.

Verses marked KJV are taken from the King James Version of the Bible.

Scripture quotations marked ESV are taken from The Holy Bible, English Standard Version®. Copyright © 2001 by Crossway Bibles, a publishing ministry of Good News Publishers. Used by permission.

Scripture quotations marked NIV are taken from the Holy Bible, New International Version®, NIV®. Copyright © 1973, 1978, 1984 by Biblica, Inc.™ Used by permission of Zondervan. All rights reserved worldwide. www.zondervan.com

Scripture quotations marked NKJV are taken from the New King James Version. Copyright © 1982 by Thomas Nelson, Inc. Used by permission. All rights reserved."

www.xulonpress.com

write down your thoughts
set personal goals
record list of things to do.

*To my nephews, Noah and Jake,
who mean the world to me – and even
more to Jesus; as you continue to grow,
may you truly live in awe of our God!*

Acknowledgements

God is so good to give us brothers and sisters in Christ with which to serve. We work together using our various gifts and strengths for the sake of God's kingdom. I want to thank a few people specifically for helping make this book a reality:

My husband, Jeff, has supported me throughout the years with prayer and provision. He faithfully loves the Lord and me, and I thank him for helping to make this ministry possible.

Karen Fulton has been there since the founding and incorporation of Hope & Passion Ministries. Her dedication to God and His plan is demonstrated beautifully in her behind-the-scenes work in many, many endeavors of Hope & Passion. Her godly friendship and partnership in this labor of love for Jesus is invaluable.

Bria Craycraft has applied her talent tirelessly and meticulously to the manuscript for this book and to many technical aspects of this ministry. Her application of Colossians 3:23 to every task is admirable, and her uplifting friendship is a true blessing in my life.

My parents, Richard & Kay Termin, provided for me a godly home environment and have always supported me in my work for Jesus.

My pastor, Bob Daniels, and the people of Norwin Alliance Church provide a wonderful opportunity for me to grow in Jesus and share the hope of His eternal Word.

Most of all, I thank my Jesus for redeeming me and giving me hope beyond measure. Your love for us sinners is something we cannot quite grasp, and so we delight to bring joy to You by

Living in Awe!

sincerely walking with You and glorifying You in the "everyday stuff" of life. I cannot wait for you to come back, Jesus!

Introduction

~~

David declares in Psalm 33:8, "Let all the earth fear the LORD; Let all the inhabitants of the world stand in **awe** of Him."

The posture of every human heart should be one of awe, a life-altering amazement at the God of the universe. When we are immersed in awareness of His power and truth, we are able to live as He intended – confident that His glory will be the end result of our lives and the ultimate outcome of everything. (I Corinthians 15:28)

Instead, we too often live in a posture of "Aw!" We are consumed by our own selfish desires and a small view of God. We wrongly think that God exists to fit into our plan, when all the while he stands ready to give us true satisfaction by sweeping us into His grand plan for the cosmos. By the grace of Jesus, let us turn our self-centered viewpoints into a truly biblical worldview. We shall be caught up in His greatness and realize that peace comes when our hearts are fixed on who He is, for He is great and above all else!

"By the word of the LORD the heavens were made, And by the breath of His mouth all their host. He gathers the waters of the sea together as a heap; He lays up the deeps in storehouses. Let all the earth fear the LORD; Let all the inhabitants of the world stand in awe of Him. For He spoke, and it was done; he commanded, and it stood fast. The LORD nullifies the counsel of the nations; He frustrates the plans of the peoples. The counsel of the LORD stands forever, The plans of His heart from generation to generation." – Psalm 33:6-11

It is my sincere prayer that these devotions help you to "Live in Awe" of our God.

Living in Awe!

Riding the Updraft

> But those who hope in the Lord will renew their strength.
> They will soar on wings like eagles, they will run and not grow weary,
> they will walk and not be faint.
>
> Isaiah 40:31 (NIV)

As I stepped out of my car and onto my driveway, I looked up into the clear, blue sky and spotted a beautiful, large bird of prey. This hawk was sailing in the expanse above, in that familiar circular motion. Without flapping its large wings at all, the bird floated in a large circle a few times. Soon, the hawk gracefully made its way to yet another area of spherical pattern; it did so seamlessly. One second the creature sailed in one circle, and the next second it veered slightly to begin rotating around the next pattern. At no point in the transfer did the bird ever beat its wings. Amazingly, I watched as the creature continued in this endeavor for more than five minutes, riding from one circle to another, until the bird was on the other side of the sky and nearly out of sight. Not once did it flap its wings!

"How graceful," I thought. As a bird lover, I recognized what was happening. The hawk was engaged in thermal soaring. This flight technique depends on thermal updrafts, which are defined well by Perrins and Elphick (2003), "As the ground warms up in the morning sun, more energy is absorbed by some features than others. This causes the air locally to heat up, forming an invisible, rising bubble. As it rises, more air is sucked in and heats up, and it too rises" (p. 18). The bird I observed that day was literally soaring from updraft to updraft. The hawk migrated by gliding from warm air bubble to warm air bubble – and nearly effortlessly. I cannot even estimate the area it covered without ever flapping its large wings.

Living in Awe!

This hawk is a bird of prey, as is the eagle. These birds of prey – with long, broad wings – are often known for thermal soaring, an efficient way to travel. As I watched that winged creature in the sky at my home, God struck my heart with thoughts of security. He reminded me of Isaiah 40:31 (NIV), "But those who hope in the LORD will renew their strength. They will soar on wings like eagles, they will run and not grow weary, they will walk and not be faint." Why did God mention the eagle here? Perhaps because God means for us to realize we need not frantically flap our own wings as smaller birds do!

The thermal updraft on which we are to securely glide is the warm strength of the Holy Spirit. His power and love are what fills our hearts and provides our way to ride from experience to experience in this life. We need not rapidly or desperately beat our wings to make things happen; our Lord carries us by His own presence. The Holy Spirit is the third Person of the Trinity, fully God. He remains with us here on this earth to guide, comfort, and provide. No matter what "circle" we transition to, it is the Holy Spirit who carries us. Our responsibility is to stay close to Him, listening to Him as He shows us where to glide next. We can take time to hear Him and fellowship with Him, because our energy is not wasted in frenzied movement. We are still, and we know that He is God (Psalm 46:10). We spread our wings and ride on God's strength, and we wait for the day the sphere to which we transfer will be on the updraft to our heavenly home. He will take us there, too.

Does God See My Couch?

> You know when I sit and when I rise . . .
>
> Psalm 139:2 (NIV)

Our sitting and rising are often indicative of a change in circumstance and mindset. When we shift our location or position, it is usually with intention. Therefore, these events mark pivotal moments.

My rising from bed in the morning is a key moment. My attitude at that point often sets the tone for the start of my day. Many factors play into the feeling at my daybreak rising: How well did I sleep? What were my thoughts as I drifted off to rest the evening before? How well does my body feel? What events await me? What appointments will I face today? What human interactions await me today? How much work lies ahead?

Similarly, our sitting down in a particular spot marks important thoughts. Many factors play into our feelings as we sit down in our office chair: Why I am employed here? What is the real purpose of my life? Who will affirm my value today? Who will try my patience? Will my paycheck cover my financial needs? How late do I have to work? Am I smart enough to complete this project? Why don't more people like me? Will I have a job next month? Or, perhaps you are sitting down on the couch in your family room. It is your time to relax . . . or not to relax. Flowing through your mind as you sit in the comfort of your own home may be considerations such as: Why will my mind not stop racing? Will I be lonely again this evening? Why did I make bad decisions today? Why is my house not as nice as someone else's home? What do I need to get done this week? What should I do with the next hour? Why do I feel so overwhelmed at the end of each day?

Living in Awe!

No matter where or when we sit – or where or when we rise – one fact remains . . . the Lord knows all about it. He is not a God removed from His creation. He is ever-present and all-knowing. David confidently proclaimed of the Lord in Psalm 139:2 (NIV), "You know when I sit and when I rise…" What comfort! I face no change in circumstances and no shift in thought alone. My God is with me, taking it all into His consideration. No other person on the face of the earth may understand my heart as I bend my knees to gently sit or plant my feet on the floor to firmly rise, but God – who is both on the face of the earth and above the earth – apprehends my every idea.

God sees every positional transition of my body and every mental activity of my mind. He knows. He knows. He knows. Moreover – to meet every circumstance we face – are the endless thoughts of God toward us. Not only does He see, our Lord is thinking. He is sending His own heart straight to us. The God who is sovereign over the entire universe is thinking innumerable things about you! David said in Psalm 139:17-18 (NIV), "How precious to me are your thoughts, O God! How vast is the sum of them! Were I to count them, they would outnumber the grains of sand."

I recently learned that Lady Gaga has more than twenty million people following her on Twitter. This essentially means that at least eighteen million humans are thinking of her. That astounding fact is nothing compared to God's thoughts aimed at you! His precious ideas for your life cannot even be counted! To meet every question of your heart is a thought of God. To surpass every movement and occurrence of your life is an answer of God. You need not be famous or talented or rich to have the only One who really counts thinking of you always.

Are you sitting and about to rise? Are you standing and about to sit? God knows. Whatever it is you will ponder or have to face in your change of position, God has a thought of His own to meet it and conquer it. He knows when you sit and when you rise, and His thoughts toward you are innumerable! Rise and sit . . . fully assured.

Soul War

> Dear friends, I urge you, as aliens and strangers in the world, to
> abstain from sinful desires, which war against your soul.
> I Peter 2:11 (NIV)

The soul is the essence of who we are. When our body finally succumbs to death, the soul shall not be dissolved. It will rise to God or fall to misery, either way awaiting its reunion with our body. Jesus Christ boldly proclaims, "An hour is coming when all who are in the tombs will hear his voice and come out, those who have done good to the resurrection of life, and those who have done evil to the resurrection of judgment" (John 5:28-29, ESV). Out of the grave will ascend our bodies to be reunited with our souls which preceded them, for even our flesh will experience the unimaginable joy of Heaven or endure the inconceivable misery of Hell.

Though our physical body may await God's final pronouncement, our soul is our core, which not for one moment shall be disengaged. Incredibly essential is the care we take of the soul. Though mysteriously invisible, its present status is ever obvious by our demeanor, words, and deeds. One cannot hide his soul's fundamental bent, for it drives all else. When God breathed into humans the breath of life (Genesis 1:7), He emphatically differentiated us from the animals and made us to walk in solid relationship with Him as we engage the universe He gave to us. Our soul is non-negotiable; it is pinnacle in its importance to our Creator, for by it we walk with God Almighty . . . or we turn and rebel against Him. By it also, we shall give an account of ourselves one day to God (Hebrews 9:27).

The world system presses against the soul. As the current cosmos stands generally in sinful rebellion against the Maker of the soul, we witness a bold disregard for the core of who we are. Tempted to distraction of every sort, the "breath of life" delivered to us straight from God is not only ignored, but viciously attacked. True Christians are not at rest in this world, as we wait the time of Jesus' Second Coming to turn the universe right again. While we anticipate that Day, God tells us unequivocally, "I urge you, as aliens and strangers in the world, to abstain from sinful desires, which war against your soul" (I Peter 2:11, NIV, emphasis mine).

Note those four, unsettling words, "war against your soul." War. The word conjures up a serious picture in our minds. We ponder the gravity of engaged weaponry, hand-to-hand combat, wounded soldiers, the sobering sound of artillery, leveled communities, grieving families, and death. War. The reality of its effects in the physical realm forces a serious approach to its outcome in the spiritual realm.

Sinful desires wage war against our soul. Seemingly mundane places are actually areas of intense battle. My soul is unseen, and a subtle but brutal conflict goes on in that invisible realm. God makes clear that the sinful desires of my flesh initiate a war zone for the heart of me. Imagine, the comfort of our living room is truly a battleground when our flesh is tempted to watch things our eyes should never see. A simple desk adorned with note pads and pencils becomes a place of onslaught, as our godless passions entice our soul to yield to wasted hours browsing needless sites – when all the while we should be seeking God. A school hallway on a Tuesday afternoon is a place of intense battle, as students' fleshly desires pull them to yield to wickedness of all sorts. With cell phone to ear or hand, we may be engaged in conflict as the craving to slander or joke coarsely rages.

Our soul is at war. God tells us we must abstain – say "no" – to sinful longings. An unseen battle for life or death is taking place constantly. The man or woman of God must obey the Lord's commmand to be aware of the onslaught and fight for the life of our soul. Envision the gory mess of war when our base passions arise to choke the soul. So often Christians quote the well-known verse, Ephesians 6:12 (NIV), "For our struggle is not against flesh and blood, but against the rulers, against the authorities, against the powers of this dark world and against the spiritual forces of evil in the heavenly realms." Do we truly comprehend how real this invisible battle is?

Your soul is at stake, and so is mine. Given by God and indestructible, the soul either relates to God by the redemption that comes through Jesus Christ, or the soul stands opposed to God. Following the death of our bodies, our souls will at some appointed time be reunited with our flesh to either be condemned, or to gloriously engage in eternal relationship with God in the universe He remakes. Fight for the welfare of your soul. On ordinary days, take note of the war, and give it everything you have. Did not Jesus say, "What good will it be for a man if he gains the whole world, yet forfeits his soul? Or what can a man give in exchange for his soul?" (Matthew 16:26, NIV)

The Verse AFTER the Favorite Verse

> For those God foreknew he also predestined to be conformed to the likeness of his Son, that he might be the firstborn among many brothers.
> Romans 8:29 (NIV)

As if Bible verses had sensitivity, I feel badly for Romans 8:29. It must be one of the most underrated Scriptures in the Bible. I am sure other verses are quoted just as infrequently, but Romans 8:29 happens to follow one of the most often recited verses. And so, for the next sentence to be commonly overlooked is both odd and unfortunate. Perhaps the less popular nature of Romans 8:29, in comparison to the preceding verse, speaks to our human tendency to cling to what seems to make us feel good, rather than to what is true but difficult for a season. All Scripture should be read and taught in context, and this is also true of Romans 8:28.

Hear the resounding words of God spoken by Paul, "And we know that in all things God works for the good of those who love him, who have been called according to his purpose" (Romans 8:28, NIV). This truth is real comfort to us, as it ought to be. Omnipotent God is able to force each circumstance of a Christian's life to conform to an unbelievable standard: our good. With God, nothing is wasted or given over to evil in the Christian's life. Though the stream of circumstantial working may flow here and there – around mountains and in unexpected ways – each twist and turn takes the path that empties all the waters of life into the ocean of good. When God speaks of our good here in Romans 8:28, the Greek root means "useful, pleasant, excellent, upright, and joyful." Everything I face will work towards a pleasant and excellent outcome. The question is, just exactly what is that outcome?

Living in Awe!

Enter the much overlooked Romans 8:29. Here, we find the answer to what genuinely brings joy. We discover precisely the target for which God aims when He carefully instructs each event to do its work for our good. What is the bull's-eye on which God sets His sights? There is no doubt; the target is my conformity to the likeness of Jesus. Listen to the Word of God: "For those God foreknew he also predestined to be conformed to the likeness of his Son, that he might be the firstborn among many brothers" (Romans 8:29, NIV).

If I go through the Christian life quoting Romans 8:28, but wrongly believe that "my good" can be defined any way I choose; I will be gravely disappointed. But, if I apprehend God's right goal in this miraculous working together of all conditions of my life, I will be both free and satisfied. God's good for my life is not so small as my wealth, prestige, and health. God's good is my likeness to Jesus! This makes logical sense, for Jesus is the sinless Son of God. It is sin which delivers pain, heartache, disappointment, and death. We long for Heaven because sin cannot abide there – only our God and His glory. We long for that sinless residence, knowing its eternal status is joy and excellence! (Recall this is the essence of the Greek root for "good" in Romans 8:28.) Similarly, we ought to aspire to be like Jesus! It is God's "good goal" for us. As more and more of His people conform to the image of Jesus, we will sense what is truly upright and pleasant while we await our conclusive good – Heaven.

When the situations of your Christian life do not seem to fulfill wrong assumptions about Romans 8:28, quote boldly the next verse. Know that God allows pain, discomfort, and factors we cannot understand – all in the process of making us more like Jesus. God's bull's-eye is so much greater than temporal comfort. God's target is the glory of Jesus in my life.

Living in Awe!

Deep Waters of the Heart

O Lord, how many are Your works! In wisdom You have made them all; The earth is full of Your possessions. There is the sea, great and broad, in which are swarms without number, Animals both small and great. There the ships move along, And Leviathan, which You have formed to sport in it. They all wait for You to give them their food in due season. You give to them, they gather it up; You open Your hand, they are satisfied with good. You hide Your face, they are dismayed; You take away their spirit, they expire And return to their dust.

Psalm 104: 24-29

O Lord, You have searched me and known me. You know when I sit down and when I rise up; You understand my thought from afar. You scrutinize my path and my lying down, And are intimately acquainted with all my ways. Even before there is a word on my tongue, behold, O Lord, You know it all.

Psalm 139:1-4

The National Atmospheric and Oceanic Administration reports that 95% of the seas remain unexplored and unseen by human eyes. Yet, Psalm 104:24-29 tells us that our God is currently sustaining every creature of the ocean. Psalm 139:1-4 also proclaims that God has searched each one of us and knows us intimately. What does this mean for our own lives? I pray this poem helps us realize:

>Deep and murky waters
>Yet largely unexplored
>Holding strange and diverse creatures
>Skimming ocean floors.
>
>No human eye has glimpsed
>All your spaces, oh, so broad;
>Your expanse while truly finite
>Is largely left untrod.
>The seas contain such creatures

Living in Awe!

As small as plankton all adrift,
As large as whales whose tails
Above the waves do lift.

Ocean, you are vast
Containing mystery profound,
An environment so odd to us
Who traverse mainly solid ground.

Yet God is ever-watchful
Down in the depths obscure;
He feeds each curious creature
That swims below, beyond the shore.

Though humans stand mainly unaware
Of sundry species in the seas,
God sustains through each second
Every single one of these.

Numbered and known by their Creator
All swimming creatures are fed
By He who told the very oceans
How far their boundaries could spread.

As life above the sea goes on
And we grasp so little of what's below,
So life outside our heart goes on
And our depths we do not show.

How glorious a thought, then,
That God, who feeds the creatures of the deep,
Searches out this heart of mine
Though the crags inside be steep.

Even I do not understand
The depths of my own heart;
But God is down where I cannot see

Living in Awe!

Sustaining every part.

Sea creatures thrive far down below
Without human intervention;
My soul goes on despite confusion
For my life is God's intention.

Swim on, beautiful creature
In the deep waters of the sea;
For God sees every move you make
And sustains you constantly.

Live on, beautiful child of God
Though you do not understand;
For God sees every part of you
And still holds tightly to your hand.

What If Every End Were a Beginning?

In the way of righteousness is life, And in its pathway there is no death.
Proverbs 12:28

What if we could find a way to ensure that every ending is really a beginning? What if we could promise that the phrase, "Something wonderful is right around the corner" is more than just a platitude? After all, is not one of the great dilemmas of humanity the "race against the clock"? Do we not dread the end of what is good even while we enjoy it?

Consider a mind-blowing statement from God: "In the way of righteousness is life, And in its pathway there is no death" (Proverbs 12:28). Right goes on forever; it simply cannot be stopped. When I follow the way of right, I will suffer no final blow of death. My peace cannot die if it is right – based squarely on Jesus' victory; my dreams cannot die if they are right – pleasing to the God who designed me; my hope cannot die if it is right – planted on God's strength, not mine; and my joy cannot die if it is right – based on my God unseen, not on fleeting circumstances. Astoundingly, not even my physical body will ever be overcome by death in any final sense if this body is walking the path of righteousness. My God promises death will be swallowed up in victory, and my body will go on in glory to experiences untold.

Even now, in the minute details of life, right goes on unstopped. Righteousness is the original plan of God; and though a fierce war rages against it, right has unmitigated victory. Our responsibility is to ensure we are walking rightly, holding God's standard as our only benchmark – not the ideas of men.

Though a long-term plan be cut short, do not dismay if you are in the way of righteousness. For right is the continuum of God's

Living in Awe!

plan – the thread stringing this moment of apparent disappointment to the revelation of the good about to burst on the scene. Though it feels your spiritual investment has produced no valuable returns, hang on. If not the passing of years, then Heaven itself will reveal the solidity of the investment. Nothing done on the path of righteousness shall ever be lost.

The power of this promise is stated beautifully in Isaiah 9:7, "There will be no end to the increase of His government or of peace; on the throne of David and over his kingdom, To establish it and to uphold it with justice and righteousness from then on and forevermore." When Jesus finally steps to the throne and God rules this universe unhindered by the devil He will have destroyed, His peace and government will increase eternally. Things will finally be as they ought to have been all along. With Satan and sin conquered, the peace will multiply boundlessly. Our enjoyment of God, His new creation, and His righteous rule will go on forever and ever. We shall love and explore always, with no hindrance of wrong.

My appeal to every reader is that you run into the arms of Him who shed His blood to make you new and right (I John 1:9 and I Corinthians 5:17). Put off no longer the endless promise of a right life, brought to us by the God-Man, Jesus Christ. Live for what never ends.

God of the Lilies

And why are you worried about clothing? Observe how the lilies of the field grow; they do not toil nor do they spin, yet I say to you that not even Solomon in all his glory clothed himself like one of these.
Matthew 6:28-29

As a person fascinated by nature, I love that the Father tells us to "lift up [our] eyes on high and see who has created these stars" (Isaiah 40:26); and the Son tells us, "Observe how the lilies of the field grow" (Matthew 6:28). Clearly, our Creator uses His creation to teach us things about Himself. Romans 1:20 assures us that God is intimating His eternality and divinity through the created order. In other words, the astounding and detailed workings of this world on both a microscopic and telescopic level point to a being who is both infinitely greater than me, ontologically speaking, and whose length of existence I cannot fathom.

Yet, let us go back to the lilies. Jesus spoke to His followers and said, "And why are you worried about clothing? Observe how the lilies of the field grow; they do not toil nor do they spin, yet I say to you that not even Solomon in all his glory clothed himself like one of these" (Matthew 6:28-29). Jesus asks us to observe a component of nature – flowers – in order to understand a deeper truth. Jesus will employ the gladiolus or the iris to shake our world on a spiritual level, so that we come to grips with reality as it truly is – defined by the God of Genesis.

Christ directs us to a specific part of creation in order to affect us in the soul. While Psalm 19:1-4 assures us that the glory of creation speaks to all humans at some level about God's qualities, Psalm 19:7-9 declares that it is the direct Word of God that can restore a soul and give a heart reason to rejoice. Only a radical fear of the Lord is pure, lasts forever, and can make a man or woman fit for everlasting existence. So we ought to heed Jesus' admonition to observe the lily and digest the eternal truth of His verbal instruction.

Jesus tells us that the flower does not toil or spin in order to be made so beautiful. The flower simply exists as God called it to exist. Plants do not have a spirit inside with which to rebel against their Maker, and so they simply do as He directs. In being what God called them to be, the flowers find themselves clothed spectacularly. Who of us has not marveled at the living color, majesty, and intricacy of a wild flower? Jesus reminds us that no human – not even the wildly rich and powerful King Solomon – could ever adorn himself or herself in such a genuine and fitting way. We could attempt to use every monetary and material resource available – wasting time and energy – and still we could not look as splendid as a simple flower clothed by its Creator.

In fact, Jesus goes on to tell us that it is the Gentiles (pagans) who eagerly seek clothing and food (Matthew 6:32). The root word for the pagan search implies "to crave, demand, or clamor for." In other words, the godless go about loudly, continuously, and vehemently seeking to fulfill material needs. However, they seem never to actually be fulfilled. It reminds me of Philippians 3:19, where the enemies of Jesus are described as having their god be their stomach. No sooner is their desire satisfied, than they are empty again and need more.

Are we this way? Do we spend much time and effort trying to "look good"? Do we use too much of our resources trying to accumulate the "right" clothes or the "right" look? How much of our being is absorbed in outward appearances? How much of our thoughts? How much of our disappointment stems from this kind of preoccupation?

Jesus contrasts the clamoring of the Gentiles to the trust of God's children. Christ says, "Your heavenly Father knows that you need all these things" (Matthew 6:32). Our Father is heavenly;

He stands above and beyond this universe and can make things happen for us on an entirely different level! If we honestly "seek first His kingdom and His righteousness, all these things will be added to [us]" (Matthew 6:33).

The key is that my heart's desire for God's kingdom must be at the forefront, and then the supply of the needs of life will automatically follow. Clothing, food, and external appearances are secondary to what is eternal and right – the kingdom of God. He actually reigns supreme! His kingdom has no end! If I make His rule my aim, I have no justified anxieties. If I make His will my goal, I have purpose to live that is grounded in reality and eternality.

All human toiling and wealth cannot do for a person what God can do. He clothes the grass of the field in beauty 24/7. He can provide not only for the physical needs of His own people, but He can supernaturally grant an inner beauty that shines forth on the darkest of days. Money can buy designer clothes and manicures, but only God can restore a soul and fill it with the hope of His kingdom. Where His righteousness prevails, all things necessary to live are granted as a by-product. Do you need a beautiful smile today? Seek His kingdom.

Get a Taste of This Kingdom!

> And he went throughout all Galilee, teaching in their synagogues
> and proclaiming the gospel of the kingdom and healing
> every disease and every affliction among the people.
> Matthew 4:23 (ESV)

Weariness. Struggle. Disappointment. Separation. Helplessness. Grief. Illness. Battle. Pain. Regret. Fear. Disillusionment. Sorrow. These are just a few of the words to describe parts of our experience in the kingdom of this world. By "this world," I mean the aggregate of all things earthly – the entire system of this currently broken cosmos. Temporarily, Satan is permitted to exert influence and humans are free to rebel against God. Hence, the Psalmist notes, "The kings of the earth set themselves, and the rulers take counsel together, against the LORD and against his Anointed" (Psalm 2:2, ESV). The apostle Paul also reminds us of the devil who is "the prince of the power of the air, the spirit that is now at work in the sons of disobedience" (Ephesians 2:2, ESV). The force of evil rebellion is wielded, and God's creation suffers.

Enter Jesus Christ. Diving wholeheartedly into the mess, Jesus began to tread the dirt of this earth two millennia ago. At the inauguration of His ministry, he walked to Capernaum by the Sea of Galilee and began preaching some of the sweetest words I have ever heard, "Repent, for the kingdom of heaven is at hand" (Matthew 4:17, ESV). The kingdom of heaven is at hand! Praise God! We can now begin to sense the infiltration of a kingdom ruled by what is right; the invasion of all we have longed for has begun!

Just in case we are questioning what the rule of God's righteousness is honestly like, Jesus works His way through all of Galilee "teaching in their synagogues and proclaiming the gospel of the kingdom and healing every disease and every affliction among the people" (Matthew 4:23, ESV). Did you catch the wonderment of His action? Jesus healed every disease and affliction that broken humans could present to Him. He single-handedly demonstrated the heart of God . . . to cure what ails and destroys us. This heart of God prevails with the kingdom of heaven, so let us go back to Jesus' prescription for the ushering in of that glorious kingdom.

Jesus exhorted, "Repent, for the kingdom of heaven is at hand." The prerequisite for my part in this kingdom is repentance. I must rightfully acknowledge my guilt in the hellish schemes of a sinful heart. I must confess that I am a sinner, and that I desire to be forgiven of my sins. The gist of repentance bids me go further – to agree to turn away from sin and toward God by the power Jesus grants to me. A repentant heart says, "I run to God and away from sin; and I desire to never look back, even though I know the cost will be great."

You will notice that after calling people to repentance in anticipation of God's kingdom, Jesus approaches individuals and asks them to follow Him (Matthew 4:18-22) – not just in a walk by the lake, but in a walk of self-denial and God-exaltation. He asks Peter and Andrew to come with Him, and both men left their fishing nets and embarked on a relationship with Jesus Christ. They deemed Him worth the adventure and all that would be asked of them.

After the call to repentance and the invitation to follow in the everyday walk of life, Jesus begins to display the heart of the heavenly kingdom with His miracles. How overjoyed the disciples must have been to begin realizing the momentous nature of that which they had become a part. God wants things right! He wants our hearts right, our words right, our actions right, our relationships right, our bodies right, and our universe right! Jesus began in that small province in the Middle East to shine forth hints of what the kingdom of heaven is, and what indescribable joy we shall

Living in Awe!

experience when – finally – "the kingdom of the world [becomes] the kingdom of our Lord and of his Christ" (Revelation 11:15, ESV).

Friends, as surely as the words of John 3:16 are true, the words of Revelation 11:15 are true. One day this world's dark kingdom will be replaced with the kingdom of our Lord. Then we will witness in full what Galileans witnessed in part in the days of Jesus' earthly ministry. We will see with our own eyes afflictions disappear, weariness turn to strength, love prevail without challenge, grief be obliterated, fear become trust, sorrow vanish, regret run away, the earth be restored to perfection . . . and Jesus take charge forever.

Get a taste of this kingdom now, and join me one day when we feast together with our Savior!

Devilish Pondering

> Peter took Him aside and began to rebuke Him, saying, "God forbid it, Lord! This shall never happen to You." But He turned and said to Peter, "Get behind Me, Satan! You are a stumbling block to Me; for you are not setting your mind on God's interests, but man's."
>
> Matthew 16:22-23

Our human interests tend to be very short-sighted and dangerously shallow. Were we to get our own way, apart from the grace of God, we would surely be doomed. In fact, turning to selfish, finite goals puts us in the same mindset category as that of Satan. Remember Peter? He was one of the disciples of Jesus, but after hearing the proclamation of the Lord's impending suffering and crucifixion, he said to Christ, "God forbid it, Lord!" (Matthew 16:22).

What if Peter got his wish? What if God did forbid the horrific betrayal, arrest, crucifixion, and resurrection of His Son? I would be damned. I would die in my sin. And so would you. If Peter's desire had been granted, we would be utterly hopeless. All of humanity would be lost.

No wonder it is that Jesus rebuked Peter sharply by saying, "Get behind me, Satan!" (Matthew 16:23). Peter's selfish, comfort-loving mindset placed him momentarily in the category of devilish pondering. Peter's hope to avoid the temporary pain would result in eternal loss. I have to ask myself, "How often have I chosen the path of least resistance to the detriment of eternal accomplishments?" When we want what we want instead of what God knows is best, could we possibly be stepping into satanic territory? Imagine – Peter was bold enough to tell Jesus that God's plan was wrong. How insolent have I ever been in my emotional reactions to God-ordained difficulty?

Jesus went on to say to Peter, "You are a stumbling block to Me; for you are not setting your mind on God's interests, but man's" (Matthew 16:23). Directly related to a satanic mindset is concentrating on human interest rather than on God's interest. Jesus is implying that a great battle is taking place in the minds of believers. Even those who closely follow Jesus must check carefully their focus. Do we have in mind the eternal and costly plan of God or the temporal and indulgent plan of humans?

If God had done things the way Peter that day thought they ought to be done, Peter's life would have possibly been less heartbreaking and confusing for a short period of time. Jesus certainly would have avoided more spiritual, emotional, and physical pain than ever could be imagined. However, Satan would have gained the victory! In the long run, all would be lost for creation.

Peter's devilish pondering did not last forever. Jesus' rebuke settled into Peter's heart somewhere. Peter came to realize his selfish, shortsighted reaction. He wrote beautifully in his first epistle (chapter one, verse three) of the living hope we have only because of the resurrection of Jesus from the dead. Looking back, Peter recognized the everlasting value of God's paradoxical plan.

Soon after the pointed interaction of Peter and Jesus, our Lord reminded all His followers of the cost of discipleship. In the context of rebuking the horror of a self-centered, satanically motivated mindset, Jesus proclaims the need for every follower to take up their own cross for God's kingdom. Have I taken up my cross? When God calls me to sacrifice time, money, emotion, status, relationship – or anything else – for His sake, do I? Even though it is temporarily painful, do I put God's will first? If not what is being lost?

Our everyday decisions are critical and fall into one of two categories: God's eternal focus or devilish pondering.

Living in Awe!

Outside the Box

I pray that you . . . may have power . . . to grasp how
wide and long and high and deep is the love of Christ.
Ephesians 3:17-18 (NIV)

He measured the city with the rod and found it to be . . . as wide and
high as it is long . . .I did not see a temple in the city, because the
Lord God Almighty and the Lamb are its temple.
Revelation 21:16,22 (NIV)

A simple square
Of length and width,
So distinct, and very clear.

If it is raised
And given height,
A cube it now becomes.

In three dimensions,
Volume calculated
By length times width times height.

I can determine
The amount of space
My cube occupies.

Multiply, I will
The length by width by height.

My basic math procedures
Will not suffice, however,
To measure the amount of love
My God has for me.
Little cubes

Living in Awe!

In the three space dimensions I know
Have capacity determined
By how long and wide and high.

But the love of God,
In dimensions unknown,
Has magnitude unbelievable!

Paul prayed
That we would have the power to grasp
How long and wide and high and deep
Is the love of Christ.

Four dimensions to the expanse of God's love!
Exceeding all I know in this world alone,
Defying my calculations,
His love goes a dimension deeper.

Oh, Lord,
We need your love
To be as long as our lives endure,
As wide as our unfaithfulness,
As high as Heaven can take us,
And as deep as human misery goes.

Oh, Lord,
Your love's volume
Covers all I know,
And all I don't know.

We read of your love's dimensions
In the vision you gave to John.

He saw the New Jerusalem
Come down from Heaven,
Measuring as long as it is wide as it is high -
A perfect cube.
And then He saw,

Living in Awe!

In that glorious city
Of length and width and height,
No temple did abide.

For the fourth dimension -
The depth of that city -
Is the Lord God Almighty and the Lamb.

Beyond all comprehension,
Deeper than any physical glory could ever be,
Stands the love of God in Jesus,
The Lamb slain for you and me.

So when tempted to think
All is lost -
That we could have possibly exhausted
The length and width and height of
The love we grasp,

Remember the added dimension -
The depth -
The unfathomable depth -
That passes our understanding -
The depth of the love of Christ.

How long, how wide, how high
And – gloriously -
How deep
Is the love that makes me think
"Outside the box."

God of the Means and the Extremes

Do you not know? Have you not heard? The Everlasting God,
the LORD, the Creator of the ends of the earth
Does not become weary or tired. His understanding is inscrutable.

Isaiah 40:28

Did you realize that the God who created the earth also created the ends of the earth? Isaiah 40:28 says, "Do you not know? Have you not heard? The Everlasting God, the LORD, the Creator of the ends of the earth Does not become weary or tired. His understanding is inscrutable."

If you are just an "average" person in "average" circumstances of life, God's presence and sovereignty at and over the extremes may not matter much to you. But if, like me, you find yourself at least at times needing God in the extreme and difficult places, His identification as the "Creator of the ends of the earth" bears comforting significance.

God understands the extremes of existence. He is not shocked by problems and sins of all depth and descriptions. No remote or hopeless case exists as far as God is concerned. He fashioned with His own hands not only the earth, but the ends of the earth. The Hebrew root for "ends" means extremity or end. It comes from another word which includes the notion of the border, the outskirts, or the margin. Do you ever feel you are on the margin of the page, instead of inside the story? No fears! God is present even there, for no location exists – physically or emotionally – where the Creator is not the moment-by-moment Sustainer. He is there at the margin.

When I think of the Ark of the Covenant*, that powerful image of the work of Jesus Christ to blot out the power of sin in our lives, I have to think of our God of the extremes. The same Hebrew word used in the aforementioned Isaiah phrase is the term used in Exodus 25:18 "You shall make two cherubim of gold, make them of hammered work at the two ends of the mercy seat." God intended the image of these magnificent, angelic creatures to loom over the mercy seat from the very edges. God does not tell us the reason, but I wonder if He is beautifully picturing for our simple minds the fact of His merciful covering from one end or extreme of existence to the other. There is no place His mercy cannot go, and even the angels are privy to this compassion and long to see all God does for pitiful humans.

Psalm 139:7-8 affirms that God is with us at the highest height (Heaven) and the lowest depth (Sheol or the nether world). Surely, these positions are the extremes. As if to solidify the miracle of His inexhaustible, merciful presence, the Psalmist adds in verse nine, "If I dwell in the remotest part of the sea, even there Your hand will lead me." I have never plunged the depths of the sea, but I know it can be very dark, cold, and strange in that world, with odd creatures all about. Have you ever been in a dark and cold place, spiritually and emotionally speaking? God is not only in average situations with average people (if any truly exist!); He is in the depths.

Mathematically speaking, a mean is an average. When I take a list of numbers, add them together, and divide by the total number of numbers, I derive an average (or a mean). So, for example, the average of 0, 5, 10, 50, and 10,000 is 2,013. This seems strange, because 2,013 does not reflect well the extreme numbers of zero and ten thousand. Averages – or means – are funny things. Often, in mathematics, they give us little information. Therefore, statisticians prefer more complicated calculations such as variances and standard deviations. The point, however, is simple; average is sometimes an elusive concept and does not always represent the extremes. Do not think it strange if you do not feel average; rather thank the God of the extremes! He is with you at "0" and at "10,000"!

God accounted for the extremities in His plan for the world. I Peter 1:20 (NIV) says of Jesus, "He was chosen before the creation of the world, but was revealed in these last times for your sake." Jesus agreed to come to this world and die for our sins before He ever laid the foundation of this universe (see also Revelation 13:8). The Creator of the ends of the earth knew He was coming because He "so loved the world" (John 3:16, NIV). Our God saw all the world's best and worst. He looked down through the annals of time and recognized all the extremes of sin and difficulty, and He still came! Why? Peter boldly declares, "for your sake."

All of us who have feared that the extremities of our life are too "out of bounds" for God's help need to pray today and call on the Creator of the ends of the earth.

* For more understanding of the Ark of the Covenant, please visit: www.hopeandpassion.org/?p=759/

Close to His Heart

> He tends his flock like a shepherd: He gathers the lambs in his arms and carries them close to his heart; he gently leads those that have young.
> Isaiah 40:11 (NIV)

Have you realized that your God is not a God of religion, but of relationship? He knows you not only need to comprehend His truth, but you desire also to feel His heart. Though at times we may not sense His presence, God is holding us through all seasons. Often – if we are honestly focused on Him – God will bless us with an acute recognition of His nearness and care.

The prophet Isaiah proclaimed this simple truth in Isaiah 40:11 (NIV): "[God] gathers the lambs in his arms and carries them close to his heart." Take a moment to process the thought that God "carries you close to His heart." The God who placed our solar system in the Milky Way Galaxy and upholds the universe by His Word is the One who by His own arms presses us in until we rest in the safety of His embrace. We are close enough to hear His heartbeat, and a deeply-rooted calm washes over us.

We must cease striving for the sake of effort and allow God to gather us in His arms. The Lord who carries us close to His heart is not a God who is pleased with obligatory, religious exertion. He wants us to love Him because He loves us. He wants us to listen to His heart and be consoled by Him in a world of distress.

Weakened, disillusioned, and injured lambs need to be lifted up to the heart of the Shepherd. Peace will come when we little lambs gaze into the eyes of our God and adore Him for who He truly is. His arms are strong enough to hold the weightiest of burdened souls. His arms are nimble enough to snatch from harm those of us in the most precarious of situations. His arms are long enough to reach the most wayward among us.

The goal of his outstretched arms in every case is an intimate relationship. He loves us. He wants us to know Him. Let Him lift you close, and then listen for His heartbeat.

Leaving Space

> When you reap the harvest of your land, you shall not reap your field right up to its edge, neither shall you gather the gleanings after your harvest. And you shall not strip your vineyard bare, neither shall you gather the fallen grapes of your vineyard. You shall leave them for the poor and for the sojourner: I am the LORD your God.
> Leviticus 19:9-10 (ESV)

Leave a margin. Do not hold on with a tight fist to every last bit of resource. Strive to give room for the needs of others. Do not depend on every last minute of time or ounce of strength just to make it through the day. God would have us live in such a way that others can glean from the surplus of our lives.

Even in the Old Testament book of Leviticus, we see clearly the heart of God. The biblical principle behind this command given to an agricultural people 3,500 years ago is timeless. The Lord made clear that when His people harvested their own crops, they were to leave the edges or the corners for the poor and the sojourners. In other words, His people should insure that a margin of their intake was available to those who needed food due to poverty or lack of residency. One implication is clear: the Israelite family should be able to live on the main portion of the harvest, without having to cling to the edges of it.

Similarly, our God's desire is that we thrive beneath our means if possible – on less than we have financially, physically, emotionally, and in regards to time. When we are able to function on just a portion of the harvest, we are joyfully able to contribute to the well-being of others. In all societies, poor people and sojourners will exist; God wants His people to be part of the provision for them. In the same way, people deficient in hope and those wandering in emotional deserts exist with us always.

God's will is that His people are living in such a way so that we can give to them.

The question becomes, "Have I stripped my vineyard bare?" Is there currently no room in my life to give to the spiritual, emotional, or physical needs of others? Have I given in to the cultural lie that grabbing everything I possibly can for myself is a critical element in the pursuit of "happiness"? Perhaps we do not need to be involved in every activity or have all the latest gadgets. Perhaps we should leave grapes in our vineyard for others. Do I have strength to concentrate and hear the hurts of others? Do I have the emotional resources to stretch beyond my own needs? Do I have money with which to bless someone for whom a blessing will demonstrate the love of Christ?

Crystal clear is the reason behind God's directive of margin: "I am the LORD your God." Let us make absolutely sure we understand this precept – God is the only reason I have anything. Providing a portion of my crop for others reminds me that whatever I possess comes from God through grace. The book of Exodus precedes Leviticus, and God proclaimed in Exodus 6:8 (ESV), "I will bring you into the land that I swore to give to Abraham, to Isaac, and to Jacob. I will give it to you for a possession. I am the LORD." Here we realize that our possessions are really God's possessions, granted to us by an all-powerful God of grace. When I share of my joy, my physical presence, my wisdom, or my money, I am only sharing what ultimately belongs to God. He kindly allows us to manage these belongings for the glory of His name and the growth of His kingdom. When I have "room to give," God is exalted and I am blessed because I am following His design for life.

Inherent, also, in God's directive for margin is the recognition – even under the Old Testament law – that people will be needy in a world currently operating in anticipation of God's future redemption of all things. This cosmos simply is not right. At times, we will harvest a crop, and at times we will need someone's crop shared with us. Our loving God understands this, and He is not ashamed

Living in Awe!

to require His people to be givers; for that is what He is! God is the greatest Giver! When we are called to create a buffer of resources, time, and energy for others; we ought to recall the sacrifice of God. Owing to no one – and answering to not a soul – God gave His own Son for our redemption and future inheritance of all the unimaginable wonder of Heaven.

Wonderfully, we recall that Ruth, the great-grandmother of King David and ancestor of Jesus Christ, was a woman who benefitted from the margin of a good man named Boaz (Ruth 2:2-3). Imagine, Ruth is in the lineage of Jesus, and she found provision because of the righteous perimeters of another person.

God asks us to leave space so that we may help others. Since both the core and the margin of all we have come from Him, freely giving the edges makes sense.

The Answer to Self-Esteem Issues

He who began a good work in you will perfect it until the day of Christ Jesus.
Philippians 1:6

True confidence for living comes only from God, the One who invests Himself in us. Self-esteem is not necessary when a person comes to understand who he is in Christ; for that individual will know Jesus-esteem! She will realize that God, who fashioned the universe, has now taken her up as an enterprise!

Philippians 1:6b states clearly, "He who began a good work in you will perfect it until the day of Christ Jesus." The Greek root behind "work" in this verse implies "business, employment, that with which anyone is occupied, enterprise; an accomplishment of hand, art, industry, or mind." Wow! Imagine that a single human being on this celestial orb can be an enterprise of God! You can be an accomplishment of the very mind and hand of the Almighty!

Not only can we be a work of God; we are a "good" work of God. "Good" in this context means "useful, pleasant, excellent, distinguished, or honorable." When a man comes to Jesus for salvation, his life becomes a good life, in the sense that his life is now honorable and excellent. His life now serves the purpose of bringing God's ways to the forefront. Our life now brings with it wherever we go the sweet fragrance of grace and the excellence of truth. A woman finds reason to live in the fact that she is useful to her Creator and to every part of the world to which He has commissioned her to take His glory and righteousness.

Amazingly, this good work of God in us will be completed – despite all the troubles of the world and the inconsistencies of humanity. Philippians 1:6 declares that "[God] will perfect it until the day of Christ Jesus." The concept of "perfect" implies "bringing to fulfillment or completion." It is the same root behind Hebrews 12:2, which promises that Jesus is both the Author and the Finisher of our faith. What He starts, He will surely complete. Many a project of man has been left in the dust – to disintegrate and be forgotten. Not so the project of God!

In fact, contrast happily the work of God to the work of the devil. No matter how diligently, methodically, and diabolically Satan labors to bring about his destructive desires; we know that his work comes to an end. I John 3:8 is a verse of huge and comforting proportions: "The Son of God appeared for this purpose, to destroy the works of the devil." The business of Satan is the promotion of sin and its ultimate outcome – death. Well, his enterprise is crushed by Jesus!

When John here tells us that Satan's work is destroyed by Jesus, the Greek root means, "loosen, undo, dissolve." Whatever the devil assumes he has accomplished, God absolutely undoes it. The Creator of all reality can dissolve whatever Satan has tried to assemble. A pivotal example is Jesus' prophetic claim when He spoke of His body as a temple in John 2:19, "Destroy this temple, and in three days I will raise it up." In other words, it is as if God said, "Go ahead, devil, and do your work. It will be undone. I will dissolve your effort and raise mine up forever."

Thank you, God, that the good work you do in your people will be brought to completion; it will not fail. Conversely, whatever the enemy tries to do will be undone. What an awesome God! And – to think – He works in you and me.

Living in Awe!

Why Doesn't God Do Something?

> The LORD looks from heaven; He sees all the sons of men;
> From His dwelling place He looks out on all the inhabitants of the earth,
> He who fashions the hearts of them all, He who understands all their works.
> Psalm 33:13-15

I had the recent privilege of sitting with a young lady after I had preached the Word of God at a women's event. The woman was crying, and she told me she was angry. After having endured the drug overdose death of a friend and having witnessed the neglect and disability of children, she wanted to know, "Why doesn't God do something?" She added, "Why does God not hear the cries of people?"

We sat for some time as I listened and shared. Our productive time ended in sincere prayer and led me to think through more thoroughly the Bible's clues to what God is doing; because, my friends, He is doing something, and He will do something. Our human inability to see and understand it all does not negate the reality of a supernatural God's working.

First, God sees what happens. "The LORD looks from heaven; He sees all the sons of men; From His dwelling place He looks out on all the inhabitants of the earth, He who fashions the hearts of them all, He who understand all their works, " declares Psalm 33:13-15. God is fully aware of the good and bad deeds of all people. He is cognizant of every pain suffered, every injustice endured, every sin committed, every oversight, every evil scheme, and every disappointment. He takes it all into account. In fact, I was recently encouraged while reviewing Bible passages I have memorized. I came to Ephesians 3:17 and was reminded it is God's desire that "Christ may dwell in your hearts through faith." Christ dwells in my heart! He is right there in the mix with all the emotions I experience! Of course He knows exactly how I feel. Of course He is paying special attention to all the feelings of His people! He understands the works of all people, and He dwells particularly in the midst of His children's hearts.

Second, God is waiting to bring final judgment. Although it does not appear that God is correcting wrongs and answering desperate pleas, He will act one day with finality and accuracy. For now, He is waiting because "[He] is patient toward you, not wishing for any to perish but for all to come to repentance" (II Peter 3:9). God's judgment of the horror of sin and its effects is so terrible, so final, and so unimaginable that He wants to ensure all have had a chance to repent and turn to Him. Please do not be disturbed by the unimaginable nature of His judgment, for you know the indescribable horror resulting from sin throughout the centuries. The judgment is commensurate with the gravity of sin. Somehow, God's waiting provides a way for all to have opportunity to repent before facing God's wrath.

Third, the judgment lies on the other side. The essence of Biblical Christianity is faith. Hebrews 11:6 proclaims, "And without faith it is impossible to please Him, for he who comes to God must believe that He exists and that He is a rewarder of those who seek Him." Faith declares that God's people will be rewarded – on the other side of death. Likewise, Revelation 20:13-14 states, "Death and Hades gave up the dead which were in them; and they were judged, every one according to their deeds. Then death and Hades were thrown into the lake of fire. This is the second death, the lake of fire." Faith also declares that God's enemies will be punished on the other side of death. While we reap natural consequences in part in this present world, precise and comprehensive judgment and reward takes place at another time.

Do you believe this? Can you affirm what Paul said in I Corinthians 13:12, "For now we see in a mirror dimly, but then face to face"? Do you believe that the next world is the right world? (II Peter 3:11-13, Revelation 21:1-5) Do you believe that the God who made everything out of nothing actually has a New Heaven and a New Earth to follow an accurate and final judgment? Do you believe that the omniscient God of the universe can sort out the rights and wrongs of every human heart? Do you believe that He will serve justice because He is – by His very nature – just?

If you believe these things, then you will be most miserable unless you also believe that Jesus Christ stands waiting to absorb your guilt! As I counseled that sobbing young lady, allow me to tell you that you also can "throw your sin on Jesus, because He can handle it; you cannot!" II Corinthians 5:21 says, "[God] made [Jesus] who knew no sin to be sin on our behalf, so that we might become the righteousness of God in Him." Only an infinitely powerful and completely holy God can handle our sin. We cannot pay for it. We cannot hold it inside. If we do not take it to God now, then He will judge us later. Sin demands payment. An infinite, holy God can absorb that sin in one, finite moment of time (just as He did on the Cross). On the other hand, a finite, sinful human being could never pay for his or her own sin. A person would have to go on forever, in complete separation from God without ever finding rest or resolution for the sin problem. Hell is as logical as Heaven, and both lie on the other side.

God has done something, He is doing something, and He will do something. Trust the work of Jesus on the Cross two thousand years ago as payment for your sin, assist God in the mission to see others repent while we await the final judgment, and – finally – hope in the realities of the other side!

Which Fire?

> Just as the weeds are gathered and burned with fire, so will it be at the end of the age. The Son of Man will send His angels, and they will gather out of His kingdom all causes of sin and all law-breakers, and throw them into the fiery furnace. In that place there will be weeping and gnashing of teeth.
> Matthew 13:40-42 (ESV)

> When you walk through the fire, you will not be burned; the flames will not set you ablaze. For I am the LORD, your God, the Holy One of Israel, your Savior.
> Isaiah 43:2-3 (NIV)

Let's focus on two instances in the Bible where God speaks to us about a "fiery furnace." Though both situations are ominous, they are infinitely different. One leads to a closer relationship with Jesus, and one leads to eternal damnation. A night and day difference is clear. The question is: of which fire will you be a part?

At one point in his book, Erasing Hell, Francis Chan contemplates the day-to-day implications of the reality of Hell. After discussing the conflict he undergoes while considering the destinies of passers-by, Mr. Chan explains about Hell,

> This is not just about doctrine; it's about destinies. And if you're reading this book and wrestling with what the Bible says about hell, you cannot let this be a mere academic exercise. You must let Jesus' very real teaching on hell sober you up. You must let Jesus' words reconfigure the way you live, the way you talk, and the way you see the world and the people around you. (p. 72)

Obviously, Francis Chan believes (as I do) that our Bible teaches a non-negotiable reality of a just God – Hell. Jesus once told the "Parable of the Weeds" to crowds of listeners. Later, the Lord took his disciples aside and explained the parable. Jesus

Living in Awe!

made clear that the sower of the good seed is the Son of Man, the field is the world, and the good seed represents true Christians. The weeds, however, are the sons of the devil. When the close of this world occurs, angels will gather in the "harvest." Jesus soberly proclaimed in Matthew 13:40-42 (ESV), "Just as the weeds are gathered and burned with fire, so will it be at the end of the age. The Son of Man will send His angels, and they will gather out of His kingdom all causes of sin and all law-breakers, and throw them into the fiery furnace. In that place there will be weeping and gnashing of teeth."

Certainly, God is communicating through His Word a truth many would rather ignore. Nonetheless, it is apparent throughout Scripture that evildoers (without the redemption that comes through Jesus Christ) will be going to a place of misery. In the New Testament, we find Hell described as a place of fire, darkness, weeping, and unimaginable regret. In Matthew 25:41 (ESV), Jesus describes hell as a place of "eternal fire prepared for the devil and his angels." In this context, Jesus explains that unrighteous people will go to this place of punishment; though it was originally designed as the final abode of the most wicked one.

Okay, so very sadly we discover that there is a fiery furnace to be endured by those who reject God's salvation through Jesus and continue on in their sinfulness. This fiery furnace is one where pain is felt to a degree currently unknown to us. Crystal clear is the fact that this fire is one of which we do not want to be a part. We are given no hope in Scripture of assistance or comfort there.

Travel back to the Old Testament book of Daniel. Three young men – Shadrach, Meshach, and Abednego – refuse to give in to the wicked decree of King Nebuchadnezzar, demanding that all people bow down to a golden idol he had built. These men decided to remain faithful to the one, true God. Knowing the punishment for disobedience was to be thrown into a fiery furnace; Shadrach, Meshach, and Abednego obeyed God still. Furious at their refusal to do his bidding, Nebuchadnezzar had the furnace overheated so that the flame of the fire killed even the men who took Shadrach, Meshach, and Abednego to the furnace! Even so, the righteous young men were bound and thrown in.

Contrast what happens next to the description of Hell we have discussed already. In astonishment, King Nebuchadnezzar quickly rose and observed what was happening in the fire. In Daniel 3:24-25 (ESV) we read, "[King Nebuchadnezzar] declared to his counselors, 'Did we not cast three men bound into the fire?' They answered and said to the king, 'True, O king.' He answered and said, 'But I see four men unbound, walking in the midst of the fire, and they are not hurt; and the appearance of the fourth is like a son of the gods.'" Later, in verse 27 we discover, "The fire had not had any power over the bodies of those men. The hair of their heads was not singed, their cloaks were not harmed, and no smell of fire had come upon them."

Unbelievable! THIS fire did no harm to the lovers of the true God. In fact, Jesus Himself appeared in the fire with them! This was a furnace of testing – meant to refine and draw men closer to God – not to destroy them. We note particularly that the fire had no effect on their physical bodies, so that not a hair was singed, nor did even a faint smell of smoke arise. In this furnace, God is with us. This fire is not OUR end or THE end; it is part of the process of learning to trust Him. We come out of this one unharmed . . . and more confident in our God!

Of which fire do you want to be a part? The one of punishment and separation from God? Or the one of testing and drawing nearer to God? One continues on in hopelessness and suffering untold. The other is one in which Jesus walks with us and protects us. We come out to a glorious end! I think this fire is the one of which the prophet Isaiah spoke in 43:2-3 (NIV), "When you walk through the fire, you will not be burned; the flames will not set you ablaze. For I am the LORD, your God, the Holy One of Israel, your Savior."

Living in Awe!

If you choose the fire of testing and drawing nearer to God, you must choose Jesus. He is the only one who can cover your sin, because He took the payment for your wickedness at Calvary. Call on Him, and He will surely deliver you from Hell, and walk with you through the temporary, testing fires of this life.

Living in Awe!

Sinking and Swimming

> "Come," he said. Then Peter got down out of the boat, walked on the water and came toward Jesus. But when he saw the wind, he was afraid and, beginning to sink, cried out, "Lord, save me!"
> Matthew 14:29-30 (NIV)

> Then the disciple whom Jesus loved said to Peter, "It is the Lord!"
> As soon as Simon Peter heard him say,
> "It is the Lord," he wrapped his outer garment around him
> (for he had taken it off) and jumped into the water.
> John 21:7 (NIV)

This poem is based on Matthew 14:22-33 and John 21:1-19.

Peter, how did it feel to watch Jesus on that sea?
Walking on water as if it were earth?
Demonstrating so clearly who gave the oceans their birth?

Peter, how did it feel to know He was the Master?
Taking charge of creation as He saw fit?
Showing by Whose hand all substance was knit?

Peter, how excited were you to step towards Him that night?
Though battered by wind and tossed by wave?
Heading toward Jesus who can make weary men brave?

Peter, how glorious did it feel to walk those few steps on water?
Looking at your Savior with a steady gaze?
Allowing His loving strength your heart to amaze?

Peter, did you catch a glimpse of His creative power
in those moments?

Living in Awe!

Your feet defying gravity and scientific law?
Your heart awash with worship and newly-found awe?

Peter, what made you look away from Him and rather
toward the storm?
Though He was right in front of you, I think I understand.
For often I am distracted though my Master is at hand.

Peter, what was it like when He stretched forth
His hand as you cried?
Without allowing you to drown, though lack of faith
was your own fault?
Without forsaking you because He knew the ultimate,
victorious result?

Peter, did you cry with joy as He lifted you back into the boat?
Getting in Himself, without abandoning you?
Taming wind and wave so that both sky and water stood
clear and blue?

Peter, were you amazed at Jesus' faithfulness though
you had denied Him thrice?
Running to the tomb to find only His wrappings of linen?
Marveling that your Lord could possibly have risen?

Peter, what was it like to see Him on the shore
after His resurrection?
When He stood on the beach and instructed
where the net should be cast?
When He prepared a fire and fish and bread now that His time of
suffering was past?

Peter, why did you – and you alone – jump into the sea
when you saw Him on the beach?
Not waiting with the others to sail to Him by boat?
Rather, throwing yourself into the waters and swimming
stroke by stroke?

Living in Awe!

Peter, when you dove in, were you thinking of that
former day upon the sea?
When you looked to Jesus and walked on water,
but then quickly slipped away?
Were you wanting to demonstrate your undying love
on this new day?

Peter, how did it feel to abandon yourself to the water
for your Lord?
Not fearing the sea because Jesus mastered it on
your behalf before?
Not delaying your progress toward your Savior anymore?

Peter, how did it feel after breakfast on that beach?
When Jesus asked you if you loved Him three times in a row?
When He explained that one day someone would lead you where
you did not want to go?

Peter, I know from history that you did love Him.
You died for Jesus' sake after preaching all your days.
I have to think of you and the sea when by the faithfulness of
Christ I am amazed.

What Is the Good Life?

> There are many who say, "Who will show us some good?
> Lift up the light of your face upon us, O Lord!"
> You have put more joy in my heart than they have when
> their grain and wine abound.
>
> Psalm 4:6-7 (ESV)

Living in the presence of God. Enjoying His eternal favor because of Jesus Christ. Knowing that the Almighty is moving in all the details of my life. This is the good life – the truly good life.

The Psalmist tells us in 4:6 (ESV), that many are asking, "Who will show us some good?" These people have not even an idea of whom it is to which they should be looking. The aimless crowds are desperate to find anyone who can lead them to a measure of satisfaction – some genuine hope – in this confusing life. As verse seven testifies, the questioning people mistakenly believe the satisfaction must certainly derive from material things: in this case, a bounty of grain and wine.

How desperate the seekers will remain who search for good in the accumulation, use, or enjoyment of things without the presence of God Himself! It is a constant, vibrant, all-pervasive relationship with our Creator that brings a joy – a good – that is beyond description and brings the only genuine comfort in which a soul can rest.

The good life. I spent a large part of an afternoon playing "Nerf guns" with my nephews, Noah and Jake. This game is physical, as I needed to run around my parents' home either chasing or being chased. Jake often partnered with me, as we found unique places to hide together until Noah came at us, fully armed and ready for battle! As Jake and I crawled behind tables, crouched beside appliances, and stood for what seemed to be hours in the laundry room awaiting the attacks; we giggled together. When Noah would find us, a barrage of Nerf darts flew through the air as we all laughed and enjoyed the simplicity of time together doing what the boys really love. That is the good life.

God created us to love Him and enjoy the creation He has graciously provided according to His plan and in His presence. And so, Jesus has willingly entered our world in order that we might actually have God with us for all the stuff of life; just as I entered the world of my nephews so that they could have me with them for the stuff of their lives. The Nerf game is not a complicated one; rather, its beauty was the simplicity of love and presence. I love my nephews enough to be with them, even at the cost of my time and my being. The good life is not complicated; rather, its beauty is the simplicity of basking always in the presence of God's Spirit. His very real presence in the details of our lives came at the immeasurable cost of Jesus' life.

The Psalmist answers the aimless crowds by asserting in 4:6-7 (ESV), "Lift up the light of your face upon us, O LORD! You have put more joy in my heart than they have when their grain and wine abound." The answer to the question of what is good and what will satisfy is simply this: we need God's presence. We need Him to be pleased with us because we depend on Jesus for our redemption and every breath we take. We need to seek the favor of God Himself. When He is right with us – invited to be at every turn – our joy will be much more than the fleeting happiness of aimless questioners.

Chokehold or Mercy?

I forgave you all that debt because you pleaded with me. And should not you have had mercy on your fellow servant, as I had mercy on you?
Matthew 18:32-33 (ESV)

Who has wronged you? What is owed to you? How badly have you been mistreated? These are questions on which we can focus. However, the outcome of human bitterness is never beneficial. In fact, the results of refusing to forgive are absolutely damning when viewed in the light of divine perspective. As we ponder the teaching of Jesus Christ in Matthew 18:23-31, the choice is, "Chokehold or mercy?"

In the Parable of the Unforgiving Servant, Jesus likens the kingdom of heaven to a king who wished to settle accounts with his servants. This seems reasonable to us, as the human heart cries out for justice. The king confronted a servant who owed him $6 billion in today's terms (obviously, a debt beyond imagination in New Testament times). Since the servant could not rightfully pay his debt, the king ordered him and his family to be sold as payment for what was owed. Surely feeling devastated by the impending slavery, the servant humbly fell to his knees and begged the king to have patience with him so he could feebly work on paying the debt, thereby insuring freedom for his family in the interim. There could be no rational way for this servant to pay his debt by laboring even his entire lifetime. Knowing both the hopeless nature of the servant's proposed plan and the servant's humble request, the king graciously forgave the debt – no strings attached. Jesus tells us the king did so out of compassion.

We gloriously observe the analogy so far. We are the servant faced with the miserable reality of incalculable debt to our King! We have sinned against Him continually in thought, word, and deed. Our hearts are bent against Him from the start. We owe holy God everything, for we have wronged our Creator in every way. Though we were made to magnify Him, we have instead stolen from God by detracting from His glory. He calls for payment from us, but when He sees us fall to our knees and ask for His mercy, everlasting compassion flows from His heart. Aware it is impossible for us to pay this divine debt, He handles the matter Himself . . . and sets us free! (Know that He handled the matter by sending His own, holy Son to die on the cross for our sin so that justice is satisfied.)

So far, the parable is wonderfully assuring. As we continue, a terrible reality comes to the forefront. The very servant who was forgiven by the gracious king is presented with a debt owed to him – a meager $12,000 (compared to the $6 billion he had owed). When the forgiven servant was confronted with the fellow owing him, the forgiven servant grabbed hold of his debtor and began to choke him! Unreal! How could one who had been forgiven so much be so quick to condemn his fellow servants? Though the king had great reason to be angry at the large debt owed to him, he dealt in a dignified way with his debtor. Here, we see the forgiven servant deal in raw, vindictive emotion. A chokehold accompanied his demanding words.

Keeping up with the parable, may we ask ourselves, "Have we ever been there?" Have we felt justified in nastiness and brutality of the physical or verbal kind because of what a fellow human has done to us? Perhaps $12,000 was much to the forgiven servant . . . but it was not nearly as much as the very life and freedom that was given back to him! Perhaps the wrong we have suffered seems intolerable to us, but it is not. It is nothing compared to the sinfulness that has been forgiven us – and the very life from God with which it has been replaced!

The debtor in the chokehold begged the forgiven servant to have mercy, but none was granted. As the second servant lay in prison, the forgiven servant was called to give account to the king. Upon the servant's arrival, the king pronounced him wicked, saying, "I forgave you all that debt because you pleaded with me. And should not you have had mercy on your fellow servant, as I had mercy on you?" (Matthew 18:32b-33, ESV) Consequently, the unmerciful servant was thrown to jailers to pay all his debt. This certainly appears as a metaphor to eternal punishment for those who owe God and are not abiding by His way of forgiveness.

Jesus is quick to inform us that we, too, will be thrown to eternal punishment if we do not forgive our brothers and sisters in Christ . . . from the heart (Matthew 18:35). The phrase "from the heart" is critical, because when we have actually accepted and rightfully recognize the miracle of our king's forgiveness, we will certainly forgive others from the depths of our being. We will not reach out to choke them, for the magnanimous grace of God now abides in us. When we are saved, Christ comes to live in us. With God in us, we have available all the mercy necessary to forgive as we have been forgiven. If we cannot have mercy, we cannot have the God of all mercy living in us. If we can forgive, it is because the Spirit of forgiveness is really in us.

Now we go back to the original question, "Chokehold or mercy?" The answer reveals our eternal destiny.

The Weakness of God

*For the foolishness of God is wiser than man's wisdom,
and the weakness of God is stronger than man's strength.*

I Corinthians 1:25 (NIV)

The God of the Bible is both all-powerful and unchanging. He is not, therefore, weak. Having created the universe and every system within it, He upholds the same universe. Our God is strong, for sure. Why then does the apostle Paul clearly say, "The weakness of God is stronger than man's strength"? (I Corinthians 1:25, NIV)

Beginning at verse sixteen of the same passage, Paul begins to tell us the world system simply could not understand the death of Jesus Christ of Nazareth. While the Greeks saw the message of a god dying on a cross as foolishness, the Jews saw it as weakness. The Jews – as Paul points out – demanded miraculous signs, as they wanted their Messiah to come in power and take over the governments of the world to set His people free in the here and now. Therefore, Jesus was a "stumbling block to Jews" because they had their eyes fixed on an earthly ruler. While running after that kind of a deliverer, they tripped over the real Jesus who came the first time to earth to pay for our sins. The full redemption of the universe is yet to come. Priority at the first advent of Christ was His sacrifice for our sins, without which we are eternally lost. This mission was painful beyond imagination and was viewed by many as weakness, but – in reality – it was the most powerful thing ever done. Perfect God takes on human flesh to provide the way out of sin's curse for people. Eternal deliverance for those formerly hopeless is brought to the forefront; that is power!

Let us go back to that beautiful phrase, "The weakness of God is stronger than man's strength." God is not weak – not even close. However, His power appeared as weakness to the world. The crucifixion did not make sense to the masses of unbelievers. Even today, we are largely taught to work hard, to solve our own problems, to be self-sufficient, and to get all we can. Antithetical to the selfish mind is this concept of a God who purposefully allows Himself to take on flesh and die for the sake of the world. Also antithetical to the sinful mind is the idea that we as humans can be truly forgiven and released from our sins because of God's payment instead of our efforts. This kind of thinking – this amazing plan – appears to the world system as frailty. It is not – in fact – weakness, though many view it that way. It is – in reality – the ultimate power of a God both loving and holy.

What appears to be God's inadequacy is actually the thing that saves us! In other words, God's "weakness" is actually more powerful than the greatest strength of humans. People can accomplish many things, and our greatest efforts do contribute to the course of life. However, when it comes to the most essential areas of reality, our greatest strengths mean nothing. No person can save himself from sin. No person can overcome sin's power in her life. No person can escape the curse of sin. No person can overcome death. We are doomed – despite our greatest accomplishments – unless the "weakness" of God rushes in. What appeared to make no sense – the crucifixion of Jesus Christ – powerfully pays for our sin!

The weakness of God is stronger than man's strength. May we also remember this in everyday moments of life. Metaphorically speaking, God has more strength in His pinky finger than all the collective power of every human being who has ever lived. I need not worry about my life if He is my Lord. Furthermore, whatever part of God's plan appears powerless or foolish is actually stronger than anything I can imagine. What God is currently "up to" in my life may not make sense to me, but at the times He seems to make the least sense, He is up to something incomprehensibly effectual! "The weakness of God is stronger than man's strength."

Living in Awe!

When your strength seems gone, remember that the veritable weakness of God is more than enough for you. God works in paradoxes; He takes pleasure in turning things inside-out. The greatest story He has written is that of our salvation, and though it has often been interpreted as foolishness and weakness; it is the supreme work of an all-powerful God.

How will He now work when you feel weak and confused? We can only imagine!

The Vital Connection Between Learning and Humility

When pride comes, then comes dishonor, But with the humble is wisdom.

Proverbs 11:2

Our perpetually plugged in, multi-tasking culture poses some threats to deep thinking and learning. Barely able to focus for more than a brief period of time due to multiple technological interruptions and background noises, many people today lack the ability to explore and think critically about issues and texts. As Bauerlein (2011) states,

> An 18-year-old who has maintained a personal profile page for five years, created 10 cool videos, and issued 90 text messages a day may not be inclined to read 10 of the Federalist Papers and summarize each one objectively. He may be more inclined to say what he thinks of them than what each one actually says.
>
> Complex texts aren't so easily judged. Often they force adolescents to confront the inferiority of their learning, the narrowness of their experience, and they recoil when they should succumb. **Modesty is a precondition of education**, but the Web teaches them something else: the validity of their outlook and the sufficiency of their selves, a confidence ruinous to the growth of a mind. (p. 31, emphasis mine)

Read the last sentence of Bauerleins's quote again. Notice how he emphasizes the vital nature of modesty. Our world falsely portrays everyone as an expert in any area of his choosing. We are quick to speak, and slow to listen – let alone methodically and patiently digest deep thoughts and incredibly complex content. Ironically, God tells us to do the opposite. He says we are to be quick to listen and slow to speak (James 1:19).

Professor Bauerlein brings to light a biblical truth, even if this was not his intention. He reminds us that all truth is God's truth when he declares that "modesty is a precondition of education." God expressed this proverb in His Word, "When pride comes, then comes dishonor, But with the humble is wisdom" (Proverbs 11:2).

Furthermore, God directly expressed the heart of the matter when it comes to intelligence, wisdom, and learning. He says, "The fear of the LORD is the beginning of wisdom, And knowledge of the Holy One is understanding" (Proverbs 9:10). In other words, wisdom cannot even truly get started until a person honestly reverences God. The beginning point for wisdom is humility – an understanding that God is big and I am small. Wisdom starts when I realize I do not know it all; in fact, I know nothing compared to the infinite wisdom of God, from Whom all reality flows.

We humans need put in our proper place; it is befitting that we grapple with our need for God and His ways. My mind was created to relate to God, and only in the context of that relationship can I learn to full capacity. As long as I ridiculously attempt to stay as the center of my world, my pride prohibits considerable understanding. People's atheistic bents notwithstanding, the human mind was created in the image of God with a desire to learn, but only as it is rightly directed by God. It is part of human nature to be limited, and in need of the realization that it is in my best interest to admit the endless things I yet need to learn.

Though our culture promotes hyperindividualism, it is in our children's best interest to promote the vastness of God and His world, and to impress on them the necessity of a desire to learn deeply. As a corollary, we must relate to them that learning takes humility and time. First, we must admit we have things to learn. Second, we must treat that need with respect, investing uninterrupted time in reading and pondering. This requires the realization that my sent or received text messages will not change the world. My ego does not need fed by innumerable email responses, tweets, or snippets of entertainment from the television set or iPod. Humility declares that I need to sit down for quite awhile and absorb the expertise of respected others.

Proverbs 9:9 declares, "Give instruction to a wise man and he will be still wiser; Teach a righteous man and he will increase his learning." Truly wise people realize their need for instruction first from God, and secondarily from people God has gifted in areas of knowledge. Wise people will then persevere in wisdom, growing moment by moment. The righteous man is humble enough to seek learning no matter how smart others think him to be. He will become a person of insight, able to teach others.

God is a God of creation and discovery. He is the One who gave us the innate desire to learn, explore, and be creative. Our God created this world of fascinating things, from creatures of the deep to galaxies afar. He made us in His image to rule over this creation by knowing it and interacting with it (Genesis 1:26). The creativity we see in the natural order and the human mind is there because our God put it there. He intends us to enjoy learning.

True wisdom only comes when one rightfully fears the Lord. Though people of great intellect who ignore God may seem to accomplish much, their enjoyment of God's image in them will abruptly end at a particular point in time (Psalm 1:5-6, Psalm 37:38, I Peter 1:24). Only those who come to God for salvation through Jesus Christ will continue on into the unending beauty and exploration of the New Heavens and New Earth (John 5:24, John 14:2-3). We were originally destined to live and learn forever in a world of righteousness. And that will happen for those who make their goal God's glory and the righteousness that comes from Jesus.

Living in Awe!

Can you imagine entering our home of righteousness, where we will see Jesus face to face? Can you imagine learning and exploring and creating in a way unhindered by shortcomings and pain and time constraints? In God's presence – with cares all gone – we will walk with our God and enjoy all that He intended as we take in wonder after wonder . . . forever.

A New Song

Sing to Him a new song.

Psalm 33:3

We are to sing to God a new song. Yesterday's rejoicing will not do. Recalling only God's past work is insufficient. Being content to bask in the goodness of God at rare, pinnacle moments is not right. At all times, a new rejoicing is to be in our hearts. Why? Because "all His work is done in faithfulness" (Psalm 33:4).

God is never unfaithful to His children. At all times – and in all things – He remains singularly focused on His purpose. There can never exist a moment of time that our God is not steadfast, holding to His plan. Of course, moments and hours and months and years of time can feel senseless or haphazard to us, but "the counsel of the LORD stands forever" (Psalm 33:11).

Our desperate clinging to the Word of God is our salvation, for "the word of the LORD is upright" (Psalm 33:4). Circumstances are upside-down, and people's actions are unjust, but God's Word is upright. We must focus unwaveringly on the truth of the big picture. It is the enemy's sly plan to get us looking to the left and right, at every unnerving and changing circumstance. It is God's command that we gaze into the very heart of our Savior, whose plans will last throughout every generation (Psalm 33:11).

Yes, the plans of God's heart go on forever. For that reason, we must sing a new song. If we find no reason to love Him and thank Him in the newness of this hour, then our focus is misplaced. God has sustained us through yesterday, and His work in this last hour is just as faithful and loving as His work will ever be. Our short-sightedness does not negate His perfect working. The question is:

are we looking at His steadfast love, or are we looking frantically and randomly all about us?

Unrest and confusion abound for now, but only under the dominion of the God who made the heavens by His Word and the host of the heavens by His breath. He will – at a definitive point in the future – make sense of all He has permitted. He will finally and definitively overtake the world. His Word proclaims, "The LORD nullifies the counsel of the nations; He frustrates the plans of the peoples" (Psalm 33:10).

Knowing God's promises by knowing His Word, we are instructed to sing right now a fresh song – a song deriving from our observations of God's goodness at this very moment. If we cannot rejoice in God right now with new adoration and love in our hearts, we need to reexamine our beliefs. Without equivocation, the LORD tells us, "the earth is full of [my] lovingkindness" (Psalm 33:5). Can we see it? Or do we need to get on our knees and ask God for better vision?

What Do Swaddling Cloths Have to Do with Anything?

And she gave birth to her firstborn son and wrapped him in swaddling cloths and laid him in a manger, because there was no place for them in the inn.

Luke 2:7 (ESV)

Jesus, the Creator of all reality, invaded earth to be wrapped in swaddling cloths. This seems ridiculously ironic to me, for God is free to do as He pleases without answering to anyone. When He came to earth in human flesh, however, He purposefully restrains His own power and is relegated to the position of being swaddled. For a newborn in first century days to be swaddled meant that he was bound to prevent free movement. In an attempt to keep the child warm and his limbs' formation regular, mothers would wrap an infant tightly after the umbilical cord was cut and the baby had been washed and rubbed with salt. Can you picture the all-powerful God of the universe lying in a feeding trough bound completely with strips of cloth? How can the One who "stretches out the heavens like a tent," "makes the clouds his chariot," and "rides on the wings of the wind" now lie flat, arms and legs bound at the loving intent of his parents? (Psalm 104:2-3, NIV)

First, we must realize that though Jesus endured the reality of human nature, the Father and Spirit always loved Him. For an infant to be unwashed and unswaddled in biblical days was metaphorical for abandonment. Ezekiel 16:4-5 (NIV) makes clear in an allegory of Jerusalem, "On the day you were born your cord was not cut, nor were you rubbed with salt or wrapped in cloths. No one looked on you with pity or had compassion enough to do any of these things for you." We realize then, that God the Father did not abandon His Son, though the earthly road was difficult and

Living in Awe!

marked at the very beginning with a symbol of the sacrifice being made. To picture Jesus wrapped in cloths brings us to the edge of Philippians 2:6-8 (NIV), "Who, being in very nature God, did not consider equality with God something to be grasped, but made himself nothing . . . he humbled himself . . ." And though Jesus willingly assumed this lowly, limited position, his Father demonstrated care in Christ's swaddling. As any first century parent would know, Christ's swaddled little body proclaimed the care of his family.

We go back to the apparent incongruity of God bound in strips of fabric. The Almighty Lord – who gives the sea its boundary (Proverbs 8:29, NIV) – now rests with arms and legs secured. We sense a faint hint of what is to come years later. Matthew 27:1-2 (NIV) explains a binding far greater than what Jesus endured as a baby, "Early in the morning, all the chief priests and elders of the people came to the decision to put Jesus to death. They bound him, led him away and handed him over to Pilate, the governor." Yes, the early swaddling of Jesus was of a gentle and caring nature, while the later binding of Jesus was driven by malice, betrayal, and the enemy of our soul. Nonetheless, even this binding foreshadowed a constraint to come in which we need sincerely to rejoice! The first and second restraining of Jesus are not the end of the story.

Fast-forward to the close of time as we know it. Advancing onto the scene comes the "KING OF KINGS AND LORD OF LORDS" (Revelation 19:16, NIV). He is no longer tiny Jesus in a manger wrapped in swaddling cloths or grown Jesus offering Himself to His Father to be crucified for our sake. He is now the King, in full command of His angels and armies. "Binding" is now turned upside down as Revelation 20:1-2 (NIV) explains, "And I saw an angel coming down out of heaven, having the key to the Abyss and holding in his hand a great chain. He seized the dragon, that ancient serpent, who is the devil, or Satan, and bound him for a thousand years." Now we have it! Our greatest enemy is put in his proper place. No longer is Jesus willingly restrained; now Satan is unwillingly wrapped up. His fate is sealed. Revelation 20:10 (NIV) goes on to announce, "And the devil, who deceived them, was thrown into the lake of burning sulfur, where the beast and the false prophet had been thrown. They will be tormented day and night for ever and ever." God allows Himself to be bound in order to save us; but, at the great inversion of the sin curse, Satan and evil will be eternally vanquished that we may thrive in righteousness forever.

Meanwhile, as we stand between the binding of Jesus and the full restraint of Satan, each of us can access what Christ purchased with His humble sacrifice. Jesus was both swaddled at the outset and bound at His arrest for one purpose – to set us free from the enslaving power of sin. No more do we have to live in bondage to our wrong, selfish desires. No longer do we have to remain hopeless, as enemies of God. Clearly – from the very start – Jesus came for one, main purpose: "She will give birth to a son, and you are to give him the name Jesus, because he will save his people from their sins" (Matthew 1:21, NIV).

Just think, our God was swaddled when He came to us the first time, so that He could set us free! The most powerful One was willingly restrained so that the most pitiful ones can be gloriously unleashed to truly live . . . forever. "So if the Son sets you free, you will be free indeed" (John 8:36, NIV). Amen.

Spanning the Gap

I am the Alpha and the Omega, the first and the last, the beginning and the end.
Revelation 22:13

Tomorrow, I don't know you;
I'm only familiar with today.

The problem with tomorrow is,
From my vantage point, it's a chasm away.

Before I reach tomorrow,
Unknowns will proudly abound.

So clinging to the One who knows all
Is the glorious solace I have found.

The chasm between now and then
That threatens my sanity

Is obliterated by the One
Who defines eternity.

Oh, can't you see it, friend,
Although I don't know how,

My Savior calls to me from tomorrow,
Even as His arms embrace me now?

No gap for Him stands between
What is and what will be.

He is always eons ahead
Of what the keenest eye can see.

Living in Awe!

When I walk the road with Him beside,
Nothing shall surprise and be my undoing.

For Jesus always knew
The place my path was going.

And when I fear I shall be swallowed
By an ominous gap ahead,

Jesus reminds me that He bled and died
To remove my fear and dread.

That gap between now and then
Into which I think I'll tumble

Is spanned by the very Cross of Jesus,
A bridge to tomorrow for the helpless and humble.

And not only tomorrow
Can Jesus safely transport us to,

But He will even span the gap
When the end of earthly life's in view.

He is already in tomorrow,
Building a smooth bridge for me to travel from today.

He is already in eternity,
Ready to clasp my hand when I fly away.

He stands ready
In the next moment I shall endure.

No gap will I be lost in,
For He is my Bridge, my Way for sure!

Wait.For.It.
(Cognitive Wait Time in a Rapid-Fire World)

A time to keep silence and a time to speak.
Ecclesiastes 3:7 (ESV)

Wise Solomon related in the book of Ecclesiastes that there is "a time to keep silence and a time to speak" (Ecclesiastes 3:7b, ESV). Of course, God – the Creator of all life – inspired Solomon to pen these words. God knows that our minds require both input and output, and the timing of each is essential.

In the educational community, we now know that "wait time" is a critical part of learning in a classroom environment. Instead of reacting to the first hand that is raised and disrupting the thoughts of many, a teacher is wise to allow at least a few seconds of reflection before anyone responds aloud to a question. Marilee Sprenger (2005, 43) says, "Offering students the opportunity to have just a few seconds to respond can give them enough reflective time to access prior knowledge, evaluate what has been said, and formulate an appropriate response." In order for our brains to make meaningful connections and process new information, we need time. Students who do not receive enough time to mentally process are clearly at a disadvantage. In fact, all students will probably benefit from knowing they will not face unrealistic pressure to respond to a question. For, when we are nervous, we are less likely to think clearly.

Speaking of nervous, our Lord Jesus took time to instruct His disciples on the topic of unnecessary anxiety. When He did, He encouraged His followers to ponder. He said, "Consider the ravens: they neither sow nor reap, they have neither storehouse nor barn, and yet God feeds them. Of how much more value are you than the birds! And which of you by being anxious can add a single hour to his span of life? If then you are not able to do as small a thing as that, why are you anxious about the rest?" (Luke 12:24-26, ESV)

Notice above that Jesus told the disciples to consider the ravens. The Greek behind this word implies they were to observe, understand, consider attentively, or fix their mind upon the concept. He takes a familiar concept – the feeding of birds – and asks the people to pause and consider what this might have to do with God's provision for people. In other words, one thing Jesus was doing was prodding the disciples to connect prior knowledge to a new presentation. As Sprenger (2005, 40) notes, "Keep in mind that active working memory allows us to hold onto incoming information while our brains search long-term memory for patterns or connections that it recognizes." Jesus beautifully drives home a commandment not to worry with a tangible example of common birds (thereby incorporating the stimulating realm of emotion) and asks His listeners to take time to consider the connection.

We are further fascinated by the fact that Jesus – after encouraging a time to ponder – then asks three questions. He probably did not mean for these questions to be answered directly, as we have no record of a response. Nonetheless, he encourages the disciples to once again think. We cannot know for sure, but we can imagine that Jesus most likely paused after each question to give His frail, human learners time to digest. I know that my own mouth falls agape after reading each sacred question on the printed page as I realize the impact on my own life!

In a rather famous chapter, the Psalmist says, "I will meditate on your precepts and fix my eyes on your ways" (Psalm 119:15, ESV). The word meditate here denotes musing and pondering. We are to take the precepts of God and silently think on them in a meaningful way. Also wrapped up in the Hebrew word here is the idea of talking, singing, and speaking of the concept. Interestingly, God encourages time for meditation and rehearsal.

Finally, we see Jesus stimulate personal pause and consideration with His disciples when He outright asks them, "Who do people say that the Son of Man is?" (Matthew 16:13b, ESV). His friends have no problem reciting the thoughts of the crowds as they reply, "Some say John the Baptist, others say Elijah, and others Jeremiah or one of the prophets" (Matthew 16:14, ESV). Answering this question was easy, as it is a simple observation. However, Jesus – not allowing the disciples to be satisfied with the recitation of others' beliefs – asks a second, personal question, "But who do you say that I am?" (Matthew 16:15, ESV).

Notice the disciples are quick to answer the first question, and we are assured more than one of them did because of the plural pronoun used in verse 14. Then Jesus, the Master Teacher, caused His learners to do some deeper pondering by driving the question to a personal level. We see Jesus here as a patient Teacher, willing to do what is necessary to get to the heart of the matter. Classroom teachers ought to be encouraged to be patient as well, carefully employing wait time in order that students may consider, ponder, and muse. Just three or more seconds can make all the difference. Effective pausing is a wise use of time!

Following are just some of the ways wait time can have an impact, as outlined by Sprenger (2005, 43): "Responses change in length from a single word to whole statements, self-confidence increases, students 'piggyback' on each other's ideas, responses by 'slow' students increase, students ask more questions, students propose more investigations, and student achievement improves."

Is it not wonderful to see how all truth is God's truth? Time to pause and ponder is God's idea.

The Paradox of Life

> For whoever wishes to save his life will lose it, but whoever loses his life for My sake, he is the one who will save it.
>
> Luke 9:24

Even if you appear to be "losing" according to the standards of culture, you may – in fact – be gaining everything. If you sacrifice your time, your passion, your money, and your reputation for the sake of Jesus; you will be given back more than you can ever imagine.

It is the paradox of all paradoxes. This life inversion is one the world cannot wrap its collective mind around. Working contrary to everything this world system understands, the biblical principle of "losing to save" truly turns things upside down for the faithful follower of Jesus Christ. Although the general world philosophy under an antichrist mindset instructs us to do all we can for ourselves – looking out for the health and well-being of number one – God makes clear it is only in sacrificing me to His will that I gain anything at all. No wonder Darwinian survival-of-the-fittest and pantheistic "inner divinity" take root so easily. All of Hell stands against the truth of God, and Jesus Himself proclaimed how narrow and difficult is the way of truth and life (Matthew 7:13-14).

But Hell shall not triumph! God's truth – of which the ultimate end has not yet been seen – will prevail. This is what God has spoken in two contexts in one Gospel. First, Luke 9:24: "For whoever wishes to save his life will lose it, but whoever loses his life for My sake, he is the one who will save it." The Greek root for "save" has a rich meaning, including: keep safe and sound, rescue from danger, restore to health, and preserve from destruction. The root for "lose" is shamelessly direct: destroy, abolish, kill, render useless, perish, and be lost. Okay, so whoever seeks to preserve his own life for any reason at all will ultimately lose his life. Work, scrape, continue on in your futile attempt to preserve your life from destruction; but your end is determined. Building up a large reserve of cash, visiting the gym five days a week, stockpiling for nuclear disaster, accumulating a list of good deeds done, and sheer self-will cannot preserve your life. In the end, all will be lost.

Paradoxically, if we lose our life for one particular reason – for the sake of Jesus – we will save it! Right! If I abolish my own life for the cause of Christ, I save my life. Remember that "save" here is a wonderful and all-encompassing word. My life will be rescued from danger, I will be restored to wholeness and health, I will see no destruction come upon me, and I will be safe and sound! Amen! The fullness of the promise is not realized in a world awaiting full redemption, but this salvation will be completely released on me one glorious day!

The woman who loses her life for Christ is the one who yields her time and affection to her Savior. Perhaps she is the one willing to choose investment in proclamation of the Gospel over investment in things that glitter. Maybe she is the one taking time to love the forgotten instead of seeking ways to be admired. She chooses to pray instead of indulge, for Jesus bids her come. The man who allows his life to be lost for Jesus' sake is the one who dedicates His strength to things eternal. He does not grasp what he has with a tight fist, but He gives of himself that others might really know God's love through him. He values the Word of God more than the musings of man or the entertainment of the world.

We see Jesus' second declaration of the greatest paradox in Luke 17:33. The context here is the end of this age; Jesus is clearly speaking of the future and His return. He now says in a most straightforward manner, "Whoever seeks to keep his life will lose it, and whoever loses his life will preserve it." Here the selfish word is "keep," and it can mean "make to remain for oneself" or "get for one's self; purchase." In other words, the person who is clutching to all he can for selfish gain will find himself with nothing in the end – not even peace at death. However, the one who loses her life for Jesus will preserve it! The Greek for "preserve" is glorious . . . "to bring forth alive, to give life." Not even death can stop the power of God in the life of a person who has yielded his being, his possessions, his time – his everything – to Jesus. God will bring that person forth in vibrant, perfected life one day!

In mathematics, we call a function that "undoes" a given function an inverse function. The inverse literally produces the opposite effect of the original. The graphs of inverse functions are mirror images of one another about an axis. Picture this: giving your life away to Jesus will literally be "undone" by God. What you gave will be gained! What you lost will be found! If you are discouraged because all you now see is the loss you suffer for the cause of Christ, picture on the other side of the "axis" a point exactly opposite of where you are. Pain becomes joy. Loss of time becomes gain of eternity. Ridicule becomes honor. Poverty becomes riches. Weariness becomes strength. Clearly – oh, so clearly – he who loses will find!

Endure

> And you will be hated by all for my name's sake.
> But the one who endures to the end will be saved.
> Matthew 10:22 (ESV)

Reality check: Genuine followers of Jesus Christ will have a rough time of it in this lifetime, and endurance is required. Jesus was speaking to His hand-picked group of twelve apostles when He warns, "And you will be hated by all for my name's sake. But the one who endures to the end will be saved" (Matthew 10:22, ESV). Yes, God is brutally and lovingly honest with His own.

When Jesus alerted His followers of the persecution they would surely face because of their relationship to Him, Jesus had already been accused of blasphemy and of casting out demons by the power of Satan. The unbelieving world proved ferocious. The people were determined to discourage and destroy the Son of God, as they were fueled by their "father," the devil. Certainly, Jesus instructed His disciples that we who follow Him will also come under direct attack of the powers of darkness working through people and circumstances. What is the response we are to have in the middle of this fierce hatred? Persevere to the end, and God will take care of everything in ways unimaginable.

My heart is thrilled by the terms our Savior uses here, "The one who endures to the end will be saved." In other words, the end is not the end; it is essentially the beginning of a real and tangible salvation of our whole being. God saves us now from sin, then we endure through the persecution of the enemy during our brief lifetime, and finally God saves us completely and in all ways from every hint of destruction that sin promotes. As we have been saved from the power of sin, so we shall be saved from the possibility of sin's damning effects and given the promise of the redemption of the entire universe.

For now, the battle rages. For now, the devil tempts us at every turn. For now, the light in our hearts is scorned by those in darkness. For now, we hear the words of Jesus and realize we must continue to bear up under every evil plot; and we are not alone. When encouraging the disciples not to be fearful in the face of confrontation, Jesus promised that "it is not you who speak, but the Spirit of your Father speaking through you" (Matthew 10:20, ESV). Clearly, God's own Spirit residing in us provides the wisdom needed in what to say and the power needed to keep trekking forward through the forest of wickedness. With the Holy Spirit in us, where shall we find excuse to give in? With Jesus having given everything of Himself on our behalf, how shall we claim we are not loved deeply enough to go on? With the Father's plan prevailing and ready to be entirely revealed, why should we give up?

Endure to the end – to the end of this age, because the end is the beginning of the fullness of God's kingdom (Revelation 11:15). Persevere until the end – until death or His return. Can you see it? Can you feel it? Can you believe it? There it is, spoken by the Lord of All, "But the one who endures to the end will be saved."

Swordtails and God's Sleeve

> Who has believed our message?
> And to whom has the arm of the Lord been revealed?
> Isaiah 53:1

When I was in middle school, I had an aquarium full of tropical fish. One of my favorite types of fish was the orange swordtail. The difficult part of adoring these particular creatures is that their young are born live, and the adult fish eat them. In order to protect the precious little baby fish, I would have to separate the fry in a rectangular net on one corner of the tank. Catching the tiny, agile babies is not easy.

The fact is that I had to get personally involved in the protection of the new swordtails. When one of the females was pregnant, I knew I had to get off the school bus quickly and run into the house to check on the situation each afternoon. I certainly could not design an eye-catching poster to hold up in front of the aquarium that warned, "Swim behind the castle little fish . . . swim!" Fish cannot read. It was pointless to kneel down in front of the tank and yell loudly, "Hide behind the plant . . . hurry!" Fish cannot hear us. The only way to help the swordtail babies was for me to roll up my sleeve and dip my arm into the sometimes algae-ridden water full of slimy fish and all their waste. Yes, if I was to save the fry, I had to invade their world.

Similarly, God crashed into our world to save us. When we were overcome by our sin and had no way to escape the curse, our God entered this space-time continuum. We are helpless without His personal intervention. He rolled up His sleeves, and entered a world of pain, sorrow, and mess to rescue us by His own hand. He put on human flesh and endured all the discomfort and longing earthly life brings. Then – in one particular season of time

– He suffered more spiritual, emotional, and physical pain than we could ever imagine, as He willingly took on the sin of the world at the Cross. With His own body – with His own being – He saved us.

The great prophet Isaiah asked, "Who has believed our message? And to whom has the arm of the LORD been revealed?" (Isaiah 53:1) What poignant words! What critical consideration! All of life boils down to this . . . do we believe the message of the God who revealed His own arm in the mission of saving us? This question is paramount, for its answer differentiates biblical Christianity from all other religions and worldviews. Whereas the various religions of the world involve the work of humans to one degree or another in their salvation, true Christianity says that God saves – and the rolling up of our own sleeves is useless. His holy, strong arm is the one that redeems us from the pit of sin and hopelessness.

I can see the devil and the powers of Hell shaking in their boots as God Almighty begins to roll up His sleeve! Jesus, the God-Man, comes to redeem His people! As the tiny swordtails were placed safely in the net by my own hand, so we are drawn out of the kingdom of darkness and placed safely in the kingdom of God by God's own hand.

The question is, "Do you believe this message?" The Hebrew word for believe in Isaiah 53:1 is the root from which we get the widely used term, "Amen." Belief means that we truly agree. We stake our very life on it. We hear the message and we say, "So be it!" It is right! The arm of our strong and gracious Jesus has been revealed! When He rolls up His sleeve, I am safe!

Distracted to Death

> Let your eyes look directly forward, and your gaze be straight before you.
> Ponder the path of your feet, then all your ways will be sure.
> Proverbs 4:25-26 (ESV)

Choices abound. Distractions are pervasive. Our demise may very well be our decision to lend too much credence to choices and distractions. While I may feel good about standing in a cereal aisle at the grocery store with the freedom to choose from hundreds of quite similar options for an early morning feast, it may not be in my best interest to spend an inordinate amount of time differentiating between wheat and oat delights. Similarly, just because our current culture offers us countless options for filling our time, it is not necessarily in our best interest to allow limitless distraction for the sake of pleasure and entertainment. Where do so many options leave the soul?

"Let your eyes look directly forward, and your gaze be straight before you. Ponder the path of your feet, then all your ways will be sure," says Proverbs 4:25-26, ESV. God lets His people know that a direct approach to living is best. We ought to keep our focus forward and fixed on the path God has given to us. Looking constantly to the lives of other people can lead to envy, bitterness, or even idolatry. How much time do we waste speculating about others or adoring their lives as our lives pass us by? Looking frequently to potential activities rather than actually engaging in the one God has set before us leads to nonfulfillment, dissatisfaction, and wasted resources. Looking often to ways to escape the sometimes arduous task of committed work can lead to laziness and unrealized dreams.

God is clear: Look directly forward. Furthermore, He tells us to ponder the path of our feet. In other words, be intentional about what you are doing. Always take time to consider your actions and their alignment with the revelation of God. In this forward momentum of life to which the Lord has called us, be doubly sure to forsake all turns of your feet that run counter to God's heart. Keeping your eyes on your Savior, never hesitate to step over or step away from obstacles on the path that are contrary to biblical principles. Ponder that path beneath your feet, and God promises to make your way sure. Your life will be one of clear purpose and stability.

Finally, our Creator prefaced the two aforementioned verses with another that appears critically tied to the same notion. Verse 24 proclaims, "Put away from you crooked speech, and put devious talk far from you." One aspect of the direct gaze we are to have toward our Savior and His plan is a mind that determines to act and speak truthfully and beneficially. Do not waste time talking wrongly of others, and do not lie. Rather, let your speech be honest, springing from a heart genuinely desiring the best for others. At times talk will be easy and at times it will be difficult, but it must always be truthful and rightly motivated.

"Let your eyes look directly forward." This proverb reminds me of Hebrews 12:2 (NIV), "Let us fix our eyes on Jesus, the author and perfecter of our faith, who for the joy set before him endured the cross, scorning its shame, and sat down at the right hand of the throne of God." Stay focused for the sake of Jesus and His kingdom. The byproduct is a life of surety, rather than demise.

When the Walls Come Crumbling Down

> The unassailable fortifications of your walls He will bring down,
> Lay low and cast to the ground, even to the dust.
>
> Isaiah 25:12

Speaking about the enemies of God, Isaiah writes, "The unassailable fortifications of your walls He will bring down, Lay low and cast to the ground, even to the dust" (25:12). These words strike me as I read them, for how can "unassailable" fortifications be assailed? By God! His strength supersedes the combined forces of evil. No enemy of His stands a chance when God decides to bring vengeance and deliver His own people from tyranny and affliction.

Isaiah is writing prophetically during a time when godless Assyria is threatening Israel and Judah. Isaiah lived long enough to see the northern kingdom of Israel conquered by Assyria and taken captive. Isaiah continued to plead with Judah concerning their sin, knowing they, too, would suffer the same consequence if no change took place. Nonetheless, God prompted Isaiah to speak forth the ultimate victory of the Lord and His remnant of followers. Assured God would one day destroy Assyria and Babylon – and bring His people back to their land – Isaiah proclaims that God's enemies who have carefully built high strongholds would eventually come to ruin. Though they invested strength and wealth in their own protection, it would not prove to be enough when God Almighty steps into the action of His wrath.

Typical of Isaiah's style, he projects past the immediate future to the glorious hope we shall all witness at the close of history. Our God will utterly destroy every enemy. That which we struggled against so long – all the heinous work of the devil and his minions – will crumble before our eyes. As a very high wall tumbles and breaks into particles of dust, so will everyone and everything that held its veritable fist to the face of God and His children. No longer will sin's cruel outcomes be unassailable. Not high enough to avoid God's "bringing down" are the walls of injustice and evil. Back to the granules from which the strong walls were fashioned, they will return. Though evil men and hideous Satan work assiduously to build their bastions of sinister deeds, none shall stand a chance when the Maker of earth turns all this disgusting work back to dust. God will bring down evil and pulverize its effects to powder, so that His New Heaven and Earth stand rightly – springing forth at the end of time. And we, His people, shall tread this new land, trampling the bits and pieces of the evil that used to be.

What once loomed high and threatened our undoing will effectively be undone. We get glimpses of that ultimate victory each time the gracious Lord defeats sin's destructive power in our lives. In every single instance of God's divine protection from harm or demise, we peer into the mysterious realm of the grand future yet to be revealed. He is with us now, though many of the "unassailable" citadels yet stand. Just remember, "unassailable" is a relative term to God when it comes to the evil we battle. He turns things inside out. The high fortifications will be brought low – even to the dust. Our God wins.

So, when you look up and see that incredible wall that threatens your well-being and your future, say with Isaiah to the enemy, "The unassailable fortifications of your walls He will bring down, lay low and cast to the ground, even to the dust"!

Living in Awe!

The End of the World as We Know It

> Since everything will be destroyed in this way,
> what kind of people ought you to be?
>
> II Peter 3:11 (NIV)

A definite, predetermined, cataclysmic event awaits us. It is not far off, as understood in the context of God's plan. The world knows it will happen; though people may refer to vague and remote catastrophes such as the earth falling into the expanding sun after a few billion years, or a massive asteroid impact, or dreaded and deadly nuclear war, or a black hole disaster, or any other number of proposed life-ending episodes. No matter what people propose as the method, something in human nature points to a general feeling of the temporary nature of this world as we currently know it. In their suspicion of final destruction, humans are right. However, the circumstances and the ultimate result are critical.

The infallible Word of God reports to us the glaring and glorious reality: everything of this earth as we know it will be destroyed. Peter is specific, "The heavens will disappear with a roar; the elements will be destroyed by fire, and the earth and everything in it will be laid bare" (II Peter 3:10, NIV). As straightforward as this message is and as threatening as it sounds, God tells us to look forward to this earth's end (II Peter 3:12). Why? Because the dissolution of what is imperfect and painful means a rebuilding into what is perfect and delightful. Jesus must clear the old to make room for the perpetually new!

Getting back to the heartbeat of Peter's theme of introspection here, we listen to him say once again, "Since everything will be destroyed in this way, what kind of people ought you to be?" Wow. This is one serious, life-altering question. Everything of this earth and heavens is going to be consumed by fire – absolutely everything. What, then, should be my focus? What should my life look like? What should constitute the moments of my days, the thoughts of my mind, and the affections of my heart?

My life would be quite radical in comparison to the average life if I honestly lived by the proposition that this current world system is headed for a colossal undoing. Does the constant redecorating of my house just to keep up with current trends really matter? Does a scratch on my new car bother me more than the sin in my own heart? Is my investment in another vacation or summer home important compared to my investment in the seeking of lost souls in this life? Are hours of television viewing a worthy endeavor compared to the saturation of my mind with the living Word of God? To put it another way, what am I doing? What kind of person am I?

A temptation of the enemy is to get us to live moments in light of the here and now, rather than in light of the immense change just on the horizon. Hebrews 10:37 (NIV) describes it this way, "For in just a very little while, 'He who is coming will come and will not delay.'" He will come in just a very little while. Though the end of this current world seems so far away, it comes upon us quickly. Our timeless God does not view events as we do. He knows Jesus will be coming back soon. We need to listen to God's truth and prepare ourselves in light of what He knows – not what our opinion or feeling is. We may not sense the return of the Lord while we brush our teeth in the morning, but the truth remains. Though I do not always feel the reality of the impending eradication of the world, I need to operate according to that truth.

The entire Bible is God's Word. Everything will be destroyed. Then righteousness will reign in the Person of Jesus Christ. So, what kind of person should I be?

A Deep Greeting

> Paul and Timothy, bond-servants of Christ Jesus, to all the saints in Christ Jesus who are in Philippi, including the overseers and deacons.
>
> Philippians 1:1

The New Testament book of Philippians is known as a letter of encouragement and joy. Ironically, the apostle Paul wrote this letter while imprisoned in Rome. He opens the book by addressing his listeners as "the saints in Christ Jesus who are in Philippi" (Philippians 1:1).

Before we delve into the beautiful depths of that greeting, consider the memory Paul had of his founding of the church at Philippi. We read of Paul's first visit there in Acts 16. After sharing the Gospel and casting an evil spirit out of a young girl, Paul and Silas were persecuted by the authorities and thrown into jail. (Yes, in doing the will of God we can find ourselves in challenging circumstances!) During their ordeal in prison, Paul and Silas chose to worship the God who is bigger than our trials. They sang and praised God after having been beaten with rods and placed in stocks. Our very real God chose to shake the foundation of the prison house and set His servants free. (And yes, God intervenes in the tangible circumstances of life!)

The city of Philippi, then, no doubt brought to the surface many emotions for Paul. He remembered severe and physical persecution on the heels of service to the Lord. He remembered, too, an irrepressible joy that pervaded the very place of pain in which he had resided. Paul surely smiled as he recalled singing to Jesus with a bruised back and restrained in a dark place. The smile arose from a heart that had come to understand the inexplicable joy that erupts when a person chooses to place his life in the protection of Jesus Christ. Chains or no chains – discomfort or comfort

– Paul and Silas were shielded by the Savior who lives in their hearts. Defying what circumstantial evidence dictates, the Holy Spirit delivers protection incomprehensible. Trust bubbles over. Joy outruns pain.

Fast forward ten years to the early AD 60's. Now Paul is imprisoned in Rome under the general persecution of Nero. As a prisoner, he is writing to the church of Philippi where he was ten years ago. Armed with the memory of God's faithfulness in that Philippian jail a decade earlier, Paul greets his friends this way, "To all the saints in Christ Jesus who are in Philippi." A deep salutation it is! We Christians today need to claim it as our own. Though we do not live in Philippi, we are the saints in Christ Jesus who are in (insert your own town).

What exactly is a saint? The Greek word behind "saint" here is a word that could be alternately rendered "holy one." We are saints because we are "set apart for God's purposes" (the essential meaning of holy). In other words, we are different – and not simply for the sake of being different. We are peculiar because we have been forgiven and made new by the death and life of Christ Jesus. We operate counter to the dark ways of the world. We take the path largely untrod. Our very countenance is noticeably and beautifully strange to the unredeemed, as the light of Jesus Christ shines in us. We operate with different motivation, out of gratefulness and adoration for a merciful God. We are saints, and no one can make a saint but Jesus! Hence, Paul proclaims, "To all the saints in Christ Jesus."

This point cannot be overemphasized. I am not holy because of what I do; I am set apart because of Him to Whom I belong! Since I am "in Christ Jesus," I am different. I am in Him; He surrounds me with His presence. As a child in His arms, I rest. As a warrior with Him as my shield, I enter battle. Wherever I am, Christ Jesus is with me, encircling me with His power, and encompassing me with His faithful love.

Living in Awe!

Since I am "in Christ Jesus," nothing can touch my life that does not first touch Him! Why were Paul and Silas okay in the Philippian jail? They were surrounded by Jesus! Paul knew nothing invaded His life without first passing through the plan and love of Jesus. Jesus knows our limits and knows the ways in which we need refined. If we are in Him, we have nothing to fear.

Notice, too, these are the "saints in Christ Jesus who are in Philippi." Is God really with you in the home in which you live? On the road where you walk? In the office where you work? In the hospital where you recover? In the town in which you dwell? Yes! You are in Christ Jesus, and He is quite literally with you geographically. Christ surrounds you, and He also surrounds the place where you are. He is Lord of all locations! (Psalm 24:1)

We are safe no matter where we are or how we are. We are set apart for God's purposes as we live in Christ Jesus. We must – like Paul – proceed forward in the high calling of God. Experiences and memories of imprisonment did not thwart Paul. Hard times did not dissuade him. As he sat imprisoned in Rome, he wrote those precious words to us, the saints in Christ Jesus who are in (insert town here).

Will Christians Have Knowledge of the Great White Throne Judgment?

> Then I saw a great white throne and him who was seated on it. Earth and sky fled from his presence, and there was no place for them. And I saw the dead, great and small, standing before the throne, and books were opened. Another book was opened, which is the book of life. The dead were judged according to what they had done as recorded in the books. The sea gave up the dead that were in it, and death and Hades gave up the dead that were in them, and each person was judged according to what he had done. Then death and Hades were thrown into the lake of fire. The lake of fire is the second death. If anyone's name was not found written in the book of life, he was thrown into the lake of fire.
>
> Revelation 20:11-15 (NIV)

First, we must understand that God's judgment of people is right. Unlike human judicial systems which can make mistakes or include corruption, God's judgment is pure and altogether fitting. We humans know amazingly little compared to God whose understanding is without limit (Isaiah 40:28). And when God takes any action of wrath, that action is centered on His holiness. His anger is right anger, unlike ours. As the Definer of all terms and Creator of all workings, God has the authority to proceed based on truth. Because He offered Himself – in Jesus – as the object of His own wrath, He is altogether right in judging those people who do not accept His sacrifice and choose to carry their guilt on their own (I Corinthians 5:21).

When God carried out the unimaginable deed of having His Son bear our sin on the Cross, the act was public. Both the unbelievers and the believers could witness the divine judgment of God that day, as Jesus took our rightful place. Three days later, Jesus rose from the grave – victorious over sin and death – and walked the earth for forty days in the presence of many. God did His work of judgment and salvation publicly on this earth. Similarly, God tells us to confess our own salvation as we believe (Romans 10:9-10).

God never has reason to be ashamed. In fact, God's final act of judgment against Satan and those who follow him is a day of victory for righteousness. While God loves all people, He must once-and-for-all rid the heavens and earth of sinfulness. If He did not, we would forever suffer in this broken world. Our hope is a place of rightness, where God is truly and fully worshipped. Honoring His creation with dignity, God will give to unbelievers their choice – to be separated from God's reign and plan.

With all this in mind, I am prone to think that believers will be aware of the Great White Throne Judgment as outlined in Revelation 20:11-15. Justice will be served as all of death and hell – and those whose names are not recorded in the book of life – are thrown into the lake of fire. No more will those opposed to the perfect plan of God be allowed to bring sin to the scene. Satan will have already been deposited in the lake of fire by the time of the final judgment of humans (Revelation 20:10). This ultimate judgment is what allows God to fully usher in the New Heaven and New Earth; wherein is no sadness, pain, or death (Revelation 21:1-4). Why? Because the source of sadness, pain, and death – sin against God – is consummately removed. For this day, we are thankful. Our true grief over this day ought to be grappled with now. We should be proclaiming the grand, overarching plan of God to every person we can. We need to make known redemption through Jesus Christ.

When we are tempted to believe God's end plan is unfair, let us fix our perspective. Guilty humans being held accountable for the sin they commit and refuse to place by faith on Jesus is not unfair. Mind-boggling is Jesus, the God-Man, bearing the sin of others even though He had no sin! Jesus faced the wrath of God though He deserved no wrath. His punishment for us sinful people is the experience we should meet with amazement, not the punishment of humans for their own guilt.

Living in Awe!

Every person has the choice to place his sin on Jesus, rather than to be punished eternally for what we deserve. Our infinite God was able to absorb the payment for all sin in one, finite moment; while finite humans would have to go on forever in punishment for sin against a boundless God. We have the beautiful choice to bear our sin or place our sin on Jesus Christ.

All choices will be honored as God keeps His Word to provide a perfect place for His people one day. That glorious existence requires both the separation of sin and all its adherents from Heaven and justice to be served. Our witness of this will be eclipsed by what comes next, as God wipes our tears away and commences an existence for us so grand we simply cannot imagine.

Living in Awe!

My King Is In the Pit

> My God sent His angel and shut the lions' mouths
> and they have not harmed me.
>
> Daniel 6:22

When I'm in the pit,
I look the lion in the face;
And I see Jesus' mighty hand
Close tightly the beast's firm jaw.

The lion that once roared
And threatened unknown dread
Stands helpless now before me,
As on the Creator's strength I draw.

The pit is very deep;
While on its upper edge I wondered
How I could ever quite survive
The hungry brutes below.

But I found that if I walk
Up above or down so deep,
The God who promised care
Is the one whose mercies always flow.

That compassion can't be hidden
By the darkness of the pit.
That compassion can't be trampled by the enemy,
Though he be fierce and wild.

For the God who called me to Himself
Promised to stay with me,
And protect me,

Living in Awe!

Whether times be troubled or times be mild.

Oh, lion, you are hungry,
And your den is very dark;
But my King is so much greater
And to His power His creatures must submit.

So roar as you can
And threaten my undoing;
Your jaw will never know my flesh,
For my King is in the pit.

Counting Trials as Joy

Consider it pure joy, my brothers, whenever you face trials of many kinds . . .
James 1:2 (NIV)

Sometimes we mistakenly assume that joy will come to us on a silver platter, plain and understandable. We think joy looks like worldly happiness. However, circumstances we deem favorable are not the source of true joy. Godly joy is not so thin as to come only when "good" things happen. Godly joy is deep, abiding no matter what things happen. In fact, difficulty may cause joy to erupt to the surface of our soul.

God did not tell us to rejoice when all is going our way. We are designed to rejoice when all is going His way, for He alone defines reality and satisfaction. If I limit my rejoicing to the confines of superficial circumstances, I am to be pitied. Conversely, if I expand my rejoicing to the bigness of God's transcendent plan, I am blessed beyond human measure.

James tells us to take action when times of testing come. He proclaims, "Consider it pure joy, my brothers, whenever you face trials of many kinds" (James 1:2, NIV). We are to consider – or "reckon" – or "count" – as joy the trials that pervade our comfort zone. To reckon one reality as a completely different concept takes will and action. Times of testing come and I am to count them as pure joy; this is unnatural to me. It goes against the grain for me to not only find hope somewhere in the midst of many trials, but to actually consider my endurance of testing actual joy. I guess this is why so few Christians seem to be joyful. We are not rightly applying the biblical, mathematical equation: Facing trials of many kinds = joy.

Living in Awe!

And exactly why should we radically equate the endurance of all kinds of trials with joy? God gives a very direct answer, "... because you know that the testing of your faith develops perseverance. Perseverance must finish its work so that you may be mature and complete, not lacking anything" (James 1:3-4, NIV). Are you familiar with the word "fulfillment"? The entire world seems to be chasing the elusive feeling of fulfillment in life. Actual fulfillment comes at the end of perseverance's work in our lives. We will "lack nothing" when we have grown to completion in God by enduring many tests that draw us closer to the only One who can make us who we are supposed to be. I am to count the trials as joy because they strip me of all self-dependence and force me to acknowledge the only One who harnesses all of life and time for His purposes (Ephesians 1:11). Joy is the freedom that comes in recognizing God is in control; I don't have to fear any person, power, or circumstance because God reigns supreme over all of them. As I come to the end of myself through trials and testing, I come to the beginning of God's true reign in me.

The word perseverance in this passage comes from the root, "to remain under." God allows the testing of difficult circumstances to develop in me an ability to bear up under pressing problems with the knowledge that Jesus is completing me. He is whittling away at me, so that I become like Him. He is preparing me for my ultimate destiny – an abiding in righteousness in a place God prepares that delivers us from this broken world. When we endure with a faith in God, we demonstrate our trust in His loving and righteous hand. We show we believe not just in word – but in action – that God delivers on His promises. We trust that being completed by the Perfector of Everything is worth the difficulty. In the accounting system of God's kingdom, perseverance is highly valued. Remember the words of Jesus to His disciples as He explained the persecution they would encounter, "All men will hate you because of me, but he who stands firm to the end will be saved" (Matthew 10:22, NIV).

Living in Awe!

    When trials come, be reminded that we are on the road to perseverance, and the ultimate end of godly endurance is completion. Therefore, trials ought to be reckoned as joy. God is working in us! He cares enough to continue the process of refining us and making us who we ought to be. Only in being who God designed me to be will I be fulfilled in any real sense. Happiness is defined by the world as favorable circumstances; joy is defined by the Lord as His work of completion in me. Let Him work, and let the trials come. All the while, use right mathematics and count the tests as joy.

A Good Captivity

...we are taking every thought captive to the obedience of Christ.

II Corinthians 10:5

How serious is God about the way we think? He is determined enough to inspire the Apostle Paul to proclaim, "We are taking every thought captive to the obedience of Christ" (II Corinthians 10:5). Captive? Yes, captive. We are to take our thoughts and bring them under the full control of Jesus. Actual obedience does not just automatically happen. We Christians are commanded to be proactive, by forcing our thoughts into submission to Christ.

Let's be real. Our thoughts can sometimes tend to run wildly. Flashing into my mind like strikes of lightning come angry, fearful, greedy, and selfish thoughts. By the power of God's Spirit in me, I have the ability to grab those lightning bolts and tell them to submit to Jesus before they ignite a fire of disobedience lived out in the flesh. This is my responsibility – to get deliberate about apprehending my brainwork. My outward actions are a direct result of either my obedience or disobedience to this very command. Our behavior is rooted in the life of our minds. Hence, Jesus needs first to be Lord of my mind in order to be the real Master of my behavior.

"What is God's will for my life?" people often ask. The answer is found not just somewhere down the road, but in each approaching moment. God's will comes to fruition as we take every thought – one by one – and ensure its submission to Christ. As the day proceeds, this captivity brings results. Allow me to give tangible examples of questions we should be asking in the moments of our hours and days:

What is God's will for the words that proceed from my mouth immediately following an attack on my character?
What is God's will for my participation in Thursday's staff meeting?
What is God's will for the look on my face when I pass in the hallway the person I like the least?
What is God's will for how I spend the hour of 7-8 pm this evening?
What is God's will for my paycheck?
What is God's will for my conversation at lunch today?
What is God's will for my reaction to the neighbor I find most annoying?
What is God's will for the way I conduct myself while standing in line at the grocery store?
What is God's will for my prayer life today?
What is God's will for my attitude in this very moment as I read this devotion?

Okay, how do our answers to the aforementioned questions look in light of God's command to "take every thought captive to the obedience of Christ"? Do you see how this works? It is not simply an ethereal directive. The decree has to do with all of life – at each incremental level.

How different could our lives turn out five years down the road if we obeyed this "thought command" each moment until then? Finding God's will for your life is not as complicated as it seems. It is the outcome of a life lived according to I Corinthians 10:5. If every thought is under the authority of Jesus, then so, too, will the whole life be.

Blown Out of the Water

> Let all the inhabitants of the world stand in awe of Him.
> For He spoke, and it was done; He commanded, and it stood fast.
> Psalm 33:8-9

One day long ago, Jesus told His disciples to travel with Him to the other side of the Sea of Galilee. They did. They left the crowd and got into a boat with Jesus Christ.

Since the disciples were directly following the will of Jesus, one might anticipate "smooth sailing" on the sea. Instead, a fierce storm arose, and their boat began to fill with the water of the vicious waves. Christ slept while all this ruckus took place. Imagine, omniscient Jesus had told His followers to go out to sea, and then He snoozed as they began to fear for their lives in a terrible storm!

Our God was up to something; He had a purpose for the squall. Our God is up to something in our lives, too, when He sends us into tumultuous waters. As Jesus demonstrated while napping in the stern of a boat, God is never unnerved by trouble surrounding us. He is in control, ready to use what appears as chaos to accomplish a vital work of the soul.

What happened next for the disciples was a dramatic, necessary shift in their understanding of Jesus Christ. As those men began to fear their demise in the storm, they awoke Jesus and said, "Teacher do You not care that we are perishing?" (Mark 4:38b). Notice how they addressed Christ; they called Him Teacher.

To be sure, Jesus is a Teacher; but He is infinitely more! If Jesus is only a religious instructor, we are hopeless. Following only a moral teacher means trying to be saved by doing all the things

Living in Awe!

prescribed in the body of teaching. Our problem is that "doing good" does not help us because we are dead inside. Spiritual death requires the prescription of a miracle – new life. New life comes because Jesus is God. His death pays for the sin of all who believe in Him, and His resurrected life enables us to live. I count His death as the payment for my sin, and I count His life as my Way to live (Romans 6:10-11).

The disciples needed desperately to realize that Jesus was more than their Teacher. When they cried out to Him in that storm, He told the sea to be still, and the sea listened! A complete calm ensued. Staring into the face of the new situation Jesus had wrought by His own power; the disciples "became very much afraid and said to one another, 'Who then is this, that even the wind and the sea obey Him?'" (Mark 4:41). His followers' notion of Him as simply "Good Teacher" was blown out of the water, if you will.

A new-found, vital reverence swept over the men as they became awakened to the true nature of Jesus. They must have thought to themselves, "This Jesus tells creation what to do!" I wonder if any of the disciples ever looked back to the Psalms to find what is spoken in chapter 33, verses 8-9, "Let all the inhabitants of the world stand in awe of Him. For He spoke, and it was done; He commanded, and it stood fast."

Jesus is God. He is more than my Teacher. I have hope because He commands all of creation. I have hope because He gives me life when I can only offer death. I have hope because He can tell the swirling circumstances of my life to come to calm perfection when He sees fit.

Rather than appearing too dignified and declaring only, "Jesus is my Teacher," I will stand with my mouth agape and proclaim, "This Jesus amazes me!"

Living in Awe!

Pondering Stephen Hawking's Statements

> He has made everything beautiful in its time. He has also set eternity in the hearts of men; yet they cannot fathom what God has done from beginning to end.
>
> Ecclesiastes 3:11 (NIV)

I am pondering the profoundly sad conclusions of Stephen Hawking, the brilliant physicist. Although God has given to him a valuable brain, Mr. Hawking has chosen to disregard his Creator and, therefore, His Creator's unfathomable plan.

As reported by Liz Goodwin on May 16, 2011, at "The Lookout," a Yahoo News Blog, Stephen Hawking said, "I regard the brain as a computer which will stop working when its components fail. There is no heaven or afterlife for broken down computers; that is a fairy story for people afraid of the dark." Given all of his scientific musing, I cannot understand why Hawking does not recognize that computers are always the result of design, and so the metaphorical "computer brain" must also be the consummation of design. Humans contrive computers and build them of earth's content, and the devices stand devoid of soul or consciousness. God created people and the universe out of nothing, and He deposits in His grand creatures, humans, a living soul. A computer shows similarities to a brain (although it is far less superior than the human organ) precisely because the CPU is designed by people whose minds are made in the image of God. God created human minds, and His creatures make computers. Hence, we trace God's hand in the technology. Computers being the obvious result of intricate human planning, why cannot Hawking see that human brains must also be the result of intricate divine planning?

Of course there is not an afterlife for broken down computers . . . because there is no "now" life for computers. Mankind alone received at creation the "breath of life" from God. The "human computer," as Hawking may like to refer to it, has life now. People (and their minds) were made to live. God has prepared for them continuing life. Evidenced throughout history is man's innate desire to live. Always, people have generally had a great aversion to death. Carlos Eire (2010) quotes Pierre Chaunu,

> The death of any human being is an outrage; it is the outrage par excellence, and all attempts to diminish this outrage are contemptible, no more than opium for the masses . . . Death is the unacceptable. The annihilation of one memory cannot be compensated for by the existence of the universe and the continuance of life. The death of Mozart, despite the preservation of his work, is an utterly evil thing. (p. 1)

Even the atheist philosopher, Bertrand Russell, admitted to a need for "safety" regarding annihilation. As Eire (2010) also quotes Russell, "Brief and powerless is Man's life; on him and all his race the slow, sure doom falls pitiless and dark. Only within the scaffolding of these truths, only on the firm foundation of unyielding despair, can the soul's habitation henceforth be safely built" (p. 14). Eire then adds his own thought, "Safety in despair: if that is not a leap of faith, nothing else is" (p. 14).

We humans long for eternity because we were made by an eternal, transcendent God. The Bible declares, "[God] has made everything beautiful in its time. He has also set eternity in the hearts of men; yet they cannot fathom what God has done from beginning to end" (Ecclesiastes 3:11, NIV). Having been made in God's image (Genesis 1:26), we have a slight grasp on eternity – we sense it and we long for it. When we call on the God of the Bible for salvation, He grants to us eternal life. While we cannot yet know the experiential reality of that fact in its fullness, we begin to operate in a hope that "blows our mind." One day, when we stand in the presence of our Creator, the perfect will come, and the partial will be done away (I Corinthians 13:10). We will begin to see clearly the amazing, true nature of eternity. For now, we trust the "imperishable seed" that has been planted in us through the Word of God (I Peter 1:23).

As far as heaven being a "fairy story for people afraid of the dark," I am not so much scared into Heaven, as I crave what I know is the greater reality. Just because the idea of everlasting life in a perfect place seems too good to be true does not make it untrue. In this life we often say, "[This or that] is too good to be true" because this world is, in fact, a sinful mess. We find ourselves held within a realm of brokenness and incompletion because of sin. We must believe in and live for a home of righteousness that is infinitely greater than the present universe in its collective state of rebellion against God in order to realize what is actually "not too good to be true"! Ironically, genuine fear should come into the picture only when dealing in damning reality, not made-up tales. What should justly haunt humans is the very real existence of Hell, a place of complete separation from God and all that is right. Heaven is not a fairy tale, and Hell is to be feared.

When Stephen Hawking was asked what humans should do to lend meaning to their lives since we are all destined to power-down like computers, Hawking said, "We should seek the greatest value of our action." This is the point that confuses me the most. If, as Hawking posits, nothing of our existence survives the death of the body, the value at its highest point evaporates. For, no matter what earthly good someone achieves – whether medical advances for the sick, accruement of great wealth for family, the provision of more entertainment for bored masses, the enhancement of personal rights, or any other earthly thing – all of this comes to naught quickly for both the one who acts and the one who receives. The paradigm of the atheistic person leaves no room for anything lasting in the case of any individual person. The "greatest value" of any action amounts to nothing in just moments, hours, days, or years.

On the other hand, the simplest of obedient acts for the sake of Jesus Christ and His kingdom leads to the proliferation of

Living in Awe!

eternal things. When I deal in eternal investments – prayer, human conversations, study of the Bible, kindness to others, generosity reflecting God, teaching others of His Truth, etc. – I get a return on my action that is currently unimaginable to me. The greatest value is not any finite amount, but rather an infinite reality. Matthew 6:19-20, II Corinthians 4:16-18, and I Peter 1:4 are just a few of the places in God's Word where the reality of eternal investment is made clear.

Stephen Hawking has great knowledge of math and science. Sadly, he has suppressed the truth. I say this standing on the authority of the Word of God. Romans 1:18 makes clear that those who reject God and His Gospel are those who actively "suppress" or "hold back" the Truth. Truth is in front of us, revealed generally, through all God has made (Romans 1:20); and it is available especially to all who cry out for it, as Jesus is the Truth (John 14:6). He stands ready with His Word to answer those who will quit pushing back, with tired arms, the obvious Truth. I pray even Stephen Hawking responds to His Holy Creator and is made new by Jesus and fit for Heaven – the place that is not too good to be true (II Corinthians 5:17 and Revelation 21:1-5).

What About Your Legs?

> He does not delight in the strength of the horse;
> He does not take pleasure in the legs of a man.
>
> Psalm 147:10

God made both horses and humans. In fact, after creating this celestial orb and its creatures, God commanded humans to "Be fruitful and multiply, and fill the earth, and subdue it; and rule over the fish of the sea and over the birds of the sky and over every living thing that moves on the earth" (Genesis 1:28). Our Lord delights in His own creativity, and He is watching the crown of His creation – people – employ their intelligence and strength in harnessing the creation for God's purposes and enjoying it to His glory, just as He dictated.

I take pleasure in watching colorful birds fly through my yard, and I know many people who marvel at the beauty of horses. Once I was captivated by the vibrant patterns of a simple caterpillar. No doubt, God is pleased with His myriad, marvelous works. After all, He boldly declared, "It is good" after each step of His creation act.

So what does the Psalmist mean when He informs us that "[God] does not delight in the strength of the horse; He does not take pleasure in the legs of a man"? (Psalm 147:10) The context makes clear that our Lord finds no joy in any part of His creation that is not properly yielded to Him; for as His creatures align rightfully under His sovereignty, then they find favor with their Maker. In other words, though God made both the horse and the man, neither can delight God while opposed to God's will. Man was made to obey God, and horses (for example) were made for man's enjoyment and use, in alignment with righteousness. When a man or woman depends on the strength of a horse, or the size of a 401(k), or the results of blood work, or the influence of a career promotion, or the measure of an IQ, or the strength of his or her own body/will; that man or woman is out of line with God's heart. God Himself takes no pleasure in the strength of the horse or the legs of a man.

Rather, the Psalmist goes on to say, "The LORD favors those who fear Him, those who wait for His lovingkindness" (Psalm 147:11). Although I exercise quite regularly, I cannot give in to the cultural tide. A fit body does not the woman of God make. Although a man may climb far up the career ladder, a powerful position does not the man of God make. A human being is favored by the Mover and Shaker of the universe when he fears the Lord and patiently places all his hope on the mercy of God. No matter how strong the horse we ride or the legs that carry us, our only hope is that God has everlasting pity on us when we honestly recognize Him for who He is. When we reverence God, He will show us His kindness – first in the sacrifice of Jesus for our sin, and second in the expectation of all good things according to His grace. (Romans 8:31-32)

It is certainly wise, as long as we are able, to treat rightly the body God has given us; for it is His temple (I Corinthians 3:16). However, the temple is made for worship! The heart inside the temple needs to be in proper posture, one of reverence and hope in God's kindness. Our feeble attempts to outrun tragedy or speed ahead of troubles are most certainly in vain. It is God alone whose favor compels the world and all its powers to work on our behalf as He sees fit. If my Lord wants me out of the pit, it is His power that shall lift me! My contribution is my genuine gaze into His eyes as my heart cries out, "I am waiting for your kindness, God!"

We know that God can delight in not only the legs of man, but the very feet of him. The prophet Isaiah declared, "How lovely on the mountains are the feet of him who brings good news, who announces peace and brings good news of happiness, who announces salvation, and says to Zion, 'Your God reigns!'" (Isaiah

52:7) Though our feet may be tired, dirty, and lowly depending on where we are in the journey, our feet are beautiful in the sight of God when we bring the good news of salvation to a dark and dying world.

What about your legs? And your "horse"? Is God delighted or disappointed? Are we depending on our strength or God's kindness? Are we running to win for the sake of pride, or are we standing on the mountain of life proclaiming God's plan for the sake of His glory?

As I write, I am now thinking of those among us who may have diseased feet, weakened legs, or no limbs at all. Remember that God favors the heart's position, not physical or intellectual drive. Even if you have no legs, God pours His kindness on you as you look to Him. One day, you will have a right body because of His mercy! Amen!

Truly Wonderful

Look, Teacher, what wonderful stones and what wonderful buildings!
Mark 13:1 (ESV)

Jesus had just finished teaching in the temple about His lordship over all creation, when the disciples exited the grand structure with Him. The temple in the first century was of a quality that is said to have exceeded that of the Seven Wonders of the World. Its stones measured 37' X 12' X 18' and the perimeter of the whole area was nearly one mile. The historian, Josephus, described its magnificence, "The front was all of polished stone, in so much that its fitness, to such as had not seen it, was incredible, and to such as had seen it, was greatly amazing." The temple was built of white marble – with plates of gold in the front – and its courts were a succession of terraces. Herod the Great had expanded this temple to twice the size of Solomon's temple. What an overwhelming edifice it surely was!

With the magnificent nature of the physical structure in mind, we read of the disciples' reaction as they leave the temple with Jesus, "Look, Teacher, what wonderful stones and what wonderful buildings!" (Mark 13:1, ESV) The disciples were focused on what their eyes beheld – to the neglect of what their spirits should have homed in on. The disciples' recognition of the beauty of the structure is not wrong, but surely Jesus at this particular time desired their hearts be preoccupied with the greater reality.

How quick we are to notice what is outwardly pleasing. How apt we are to acknowledge stylish clothes, beautiful houses, expensive decor, and pretty faces. All the while, the Lord wants us to be quick to focus on inward beauty – the reality of His ultimate reign in every facet of life. What constitutes true excellence is an unbroken connection to Jesus, and acknowledgement of Him – the

Living in Awe!

Maker of all things beautiful. God wants us to see that the pre-eminence of Jesus in anything is what makes that thing fitting and grand. A homely face or a crippled body is beautiful when Jesus is Lord to the people who view it – when the physical structures and bodies are seen as temporary, yet Jesus is exalted as the eternal Hope of Glory!

The disciples called attention to the stones and building by calling them wonderful, a term with a Greek root meaning, "of what sort or quality." In other words, they were exclaiming, "What manner of building is this!" The same Greek term is used in Matthew 8:27 (ESV) of Jesus after His disciples had experienced His miraculous calming of the Sea of Galilee when their ship was about to sink. They marveled at Him and said, "What sort of man is this, that even winds and sea obey Him?" How appropriate to marvel at Jesus, who made the wind and sea and, therefore, controls it completely. How fitting to be amazed at Jesus, who is the center of our worship. But does it take a storm to marvel at His power? When surrounded by all that allures, why do we lose our way?

Our Lord was quick to set the disciples straight in drawing their attention away from the temple structure and to a bigger plan. He responded, "Do you see these great buildings? There will not be left here one stone upon another that will not be thrown down" (Mark 13:2, ESV). The destruction of earthly Jerusalem and the temple would surely come in A.D. 70 under Titus, son of Roman emperor Vespasian. Jesus longed for His disciples to base their lives on the eternal reality of God's unshakeable kingdom. Temple rituals could not save. All the sacrifices offered through the years only pointed to the ultimate, saving sacrifice of Jesus Himself. He is the temple! He is the center of our worship and adoration! In Him, we enter God's presence!

Remember Jesus cleansing the temple of the money-changers and all their items? After exhibiting such zeal, the Jews asked Jesus, "What sign do you show us for doing these things?"

Living in Awe!

(John 2:18, ESV). His response was, "Destroy this temple, and in three days I will raise it up" (John 2:19, ESV). The Jews became confused and could not understand how Jesus could restore a temple in three days that took half a century to build. But, the Bible is clear: Jesus was speaking about the temple of His body. (John 2:21) A group of religious people were fixated on tradition, ornate things, and what the eyes could see. Jesus' focus is salvation – the offering of Himself for sin and His doubtless victory over death. We ought to concentrate on Him and not all that glitters or appears religious or outwardly pleasing.

The culmination of the temple's purpose is seen unequivocally in the amazing book of Revelation. We gain from this unbelievable future event a clearer understanding of why Jesus is intent on pushing our focus to true, spiritual majesty. The apostle John was given a vision by God of the New Jerusalem, and we rejoice in this truth of Revelation 21:1-4:

> Then I saw a new heaven and a new earth; for the first heaven and the first earth passed away, and there is no longer any sea. And I saw the holy city, new Jerusalem, coming down out of heaven from God, made ready as a bride adorned for her husband. And I heard a loud voice from the throne, saying, "Behold, the tabernacle of God is among men, and He will dwell among them, and they shall be His people, and God Himself will be among them, and He will wipe away every tear from their eyes; and there will no longer be any death; there will no longer by any mourning, or crying, or pain; the first things have passed away."

John then goes on to describe specifics of the city, the New Jerusalem, in Revelation 21:10-11,22 (emphasis mine):

> And he carried me away in the Spirit to a great and high mountain, and showed me the holy city, Jerusalem, coming down out of heaven from God, having the glory of God.

> Her brilliance was like a very costly stone, as a stone of crystal-clear jasper . . . I saw no temple in [the city], for the **Lord God the Almighty and the Lamb are its temple**.

Did you see it? Eternally, the physical temple is replaced by the One it was pointing to all along, our Jesus! How He must have longed for His dear disciples to be obsessed with His beauty and love instead of the outward appeal of costly structures and rituals. Let us walk with Jesus – and as we do – let us say to Him, "What a wonderful Savior and what a wonderful hope!" Let us fix our eyes on spiritual loveliness – that of a heart fully yielded to the Savior. He is the magnificent temple!

Rescue from the Wrath to Come

> Jesus, who rescues us from the wrath to come.
> I Thessalonians 1:10

There is a wrath to come. Oddly enough, I affirm that statement with both grief and gratefulness. God does not delight in the pouring forth of His wrath (II Peter 3:9). In fact, He delights in the demonstration of mercy (Micah 7:18). As one of His children, I also do not take joy in God's wrath, but I imperfectly grasp its necessity.

I am aware of horrible things in this current world system: children starve to death, dictators wield unjust power, people suffer with a myriad of debilitating diseases, parents neglect and abuse little ones, angry people kill other humans, desperate people give up on themselves, natural disasters destroy homes and lives, people speak hateful words, humans die in loneliness, entire groups wage war on nations, and some orphans never find homes. In light of these observations, I thank God that one day He will set things right and refuse to allow sin to influence anymore. The Bible makes clear that the sinfulness of human beings has brought a curse to this world. All who choose to follow the sinful nature will have to be dealt with in order for God to bring to reality a right world. All who choose to follow Jesus and accept His righteousness in exchange for their sinfulness will abide eternally in that right world (John 3:36).

At the helm of sinful choices stands Satan. He leads those who want to follow him in rebellion against God and God's ways. He leads the march against all that is right. Satan leads the march toward destruction, because God must pour out His holy wrath on sin and all its horror. Revelation 20:10 declares, "And the devil who deceived them was thrown into the lake of fire and brimstone,

Living in Awe!

where the beast and the false prophet are also; and they will be tormented day and night forever and ever." The greatest tormentor will be tormented so that horror will finally be confined. Atrocity and pain will be imprisoned with sinful rebellion in a place of God's making. Justice will be served so that Heaven can flourish. There is wrath to come.

Following the ultimate demise of Satan, Revelation 20:14-15 proclaims, "Then death and Hades were thrown into the lake of fire. This is the second death, the lake of fire. And if anyone's name was not found written in the book of life, he was thrown into the lake of fire." And there we have it. All people who have chosen death instead of life by choosing sin instead of Jesus (Romans 6:23) will be confined to the same place of torment in which their leader will exist. The wrath of God Almighty will be poured forth on all the sinfulness that has perpetuated the horrible things of which I spoke earlier. God hates sin, and God hates what sin does. God also dignifies His human creatures. We are made in His image, with the freedom to choose. Sin, therefore, originates in the human heart (James 1:13-15). Unless Jesus is asked to stop it, sin continues to reign in the souls of those who choose it to be so. Therefore, the wrath of God must extend to those souls. In His mercy, God must one day eliminate sin and its indescribable damage.

Let us now focus on our hope found in the Scripture we are studying. I Thessalonians 1:10 (emphasis mine) describes our hope as **"Jesus, who rescues us** from the wrath to come." Jesus Christ, the Son of God, can rescue us from this wrath. He is our Way to the right world God is preparing (John 14:1-6). We have no chance of escaping God's wrath but by divine rescue. Ours simply cannot be a mission of self-help. There is nothing we can do to change the bent of our heart from sinfulness to righteousness; for us, only one answer exists – rescue by Jesus Christ! He alone can make our whole being brand new – apt to love and serve Him (II Corinthians 5:17).

Living in Awe!

Two millennia ago, Jesus died on the cross of Calvary to suffer the wrath of God on behalf of humans He loves. The infinite, holy God bore the wrath of the infinite, holy God so that finite, failing humans who believe in Him may enjoy eternal life rather than suffer eternal wrath. God's holiness demands justice. Jesus offered to meet the just requirement of payment for sin on our behalf by shedding His own blood. We must now run to Him and yield our hearts and lives to Him.

I have asked Him to save me from the wrath to come by re-making me so that I am fit for righteousness through Him. His sacrifice is my only hope. Please turn to Him this moment and ask Him to save you from the wrath to come. The divine rescue of Jesus – and the needed wrath of God – work together to give us the eternal hope that we will one day suffer no more!

What Does It Mean to Live, and What Does It Mean to Die?

For to me, to live is Christ and to die is gain.

Philippians 1:21

In my observation of discussing death and entrance to the next life with various people, most are apt to give the same type of answer to the question, "Why are you not ready to die (or be taken to Heaven) at this particular time?" The vast majority give a reply something like this: "I want to live on earth at least a little longer because I have not yet _____." (Insert into the blank space any number of various experiences, e.g., travelled to a foreign country, gotten married, earned my doctoral degree, held my first grandchild, owned my own home, etc.) Even though most of the people I have spoken with are Christians, the basic response remains unchanged. People are not ready to die because some desired earthly experience has yet eluded them. If the people with which I have interacted through the years are truly representative of Christian feeling on the subject, we would be tempted to conclude that the Apostle Paul was out of his mind when he wrote the letter to the Philippians.

Under Roman house arrest and the shadow of his own execution, Paul penned these stunning words, "For to me, to live is Christ and to die is gain" (Philippians 1:21). My mathematical mind forms succinct equations: Living = Christ and Dying = Gain. The strong and intellectual apostle boldly proclaimed a truth so simple, yet so antithetical to our regular way of thinking. Paul believed – and was inspired by God to record – that to die is actual gain. No matter what Paul had or had not experienced to date in his life, he knew that his death would result in a tangible gain that far surpassed any unrealized goal. No matter what supposed earthly pleasure or experience Paul might not have had, he knew that the reward of Heaven wiped out the loss by infinite measure.

Many Christians today believe our best life is this life – within a broken universe. Wrong. Our best life is the one to come – in the presence of God. The recreated heavens and earth, the restored bodies, the whole minds, the healed relationships, the contented hearts basking in the uninterrupted blessing of God, the everlasting adventures in the universe that is then made right, and an unbroken relationship with God will more than make up for anything we perceive ourselves as "losing" here. Paul stood firm in the reality – the unequivocally substantial nature – of Heaven. Thus, he could declare without doubt that his death is really gain . . . solid, true gain.

Let us go back to the other equation, "To live = Christ." How many of us can proclaim that equation without reservation? How do I view living? Is life for my enjoyment? For my happiness? For my fulfillment? From a biblical perspective, the answer is "No." My life should be defined in one beautifully simple way, "Christ." I am always amazed and inspired by Paul's firm grasp of God's truth. This apostle actually believed and lived the equation, "To live = Christ." Paul was not in the business of the Gospel for himself. He did not seek glory, admiration, or pleasure. He resolutely sought to make Christ known through both the everyday moments and the pinnacle experiences of his life. Paul would not have said, "Let me live on earth a little longer so I can take a dream vacation or complete a five-year plan of mine." Paul would only say, "Let me live on this broken planet longer only if it means people will see Jesus in me."

I fear we have negated God's life and death equations in our lives by adding or subtracting our own ideas. The equations are simple: Living = Christ and Dying = Gain.

Living in Awe!

Rest, Not Religion

Come to me, all who labor and are heavy laden, and I will give you rest. Take my yoke upon you, and learn from me, for I am gentle and lowly in heart, and you will find rest for your souls.
Matthew 11:28-29 (ESV)

Salvation is rescue
- not reward.

Heaven is given
- not earned.

Obedience is reaction
- not action.

God's burden is easy
- not oppressive.

Worship is natural
- not forced.

Joy is relational -
- not conditional.

Forgiveness is real
- not fairy tale.

Jesus died for all your sin
- not just some of it.

He asks for all your heart
- not just most of it.
God gives rest

Living in Awe!

- not religion.

Talk to Him today
- not tomorrow . . . before it is too late.

What if the Sun Went Dark?

> Immediately after the tribulation of those days the sun will be darkened, and the moon will not give its light, and the stars will fall from heaven, and the powers of the heavens will be shaken.
>
> Matthew 24:29 (ESV)

We count on the rising of the sun. We take for granted that the moon will shine at night. We expect the stars to stay in place, twinkling through the darkness. Though humans may never ponder exactly why we hold these assumptions, the clear answer is the created order of our God. The Creator "gives the sun for light by day and the fixed order of the moon and the stars for light by night . . . the LORD of hosts is his name" (Jeremiah 31:35, ESV). Yes, He is the Lord of hosts! He is the Master of that which goes forth, including angelic beings and heavenly bodies.

Precisely because the order of the heavens is so regular and very much taken for granted, the words of Matthew 24:29 (ESV) ring forebodingly in our ears, "Immediately after the tribulation of those days the sun will be darkened, and the moon will not give its light, and the stars will fall from heaven, and the powers of the heavens will be shaken." Imagine it. Whether we take these words of Jesus literally, figuratively, or as a combination of the two, Christ means for us to know that He is going to shake things up in a way as never before. The natural ordinances on which we had depended will suddenly evaporate, as God Almighty displays His power for judgment, accountability, and newness. The Boss of the sun and stars will demand the heavenly bodies change their course and usher in a cataclysmic shift to a new order. As radically as Jesus Christ can make a person's spirit new by the power of His blood, so will he radically recreate the cosmos.

Living in Awe!

Make no mistake about it; the beginning of the miraculous change is marked by fundamental, unexpected feats and by a judgment that will shock unbelievers at their core. Matthew 24:30 (ESV) goes on to instruct, "Then will appear in heaven the sign of the Son of Man, and then all the tribes of the earth will mourn, and they will see the Son of Man coming on the clouds of heaven with power and great glory." Notice the word "mourn." People from every part of the earth will wail as they realize – once and for all – that Jesus changes everything. Sadly, unbelievers will then know that God will be recognized for who He is, whether willingly in the present, or by mandate in the future. All the world will ultimately realize what believers now know – Jesus is in charge!

On that day, the clouds of heaven will not float peacefully against a blue sky. Rather, the clouds will escort the very Son of Man to the earth He has created. With power and glory untold, Jesus will begin the necessary task of judging wrong and rewarding right. He will return to do what He has promised – deliver His people from a twisted existence to enjoy Him forever.

Are you ready for the essential, inexplicable change about to occur in the heavens? When you see Jesus, will you grieve because you have not responded to His forgiveness, or will you rejoice in that power and great glory which will materialize just as He promised? The shakeup is coming. The next time you stand in the light of that old sun, or dream upon a star, or delight in the moon's glow; think about the words of Jesus Christ. He means what He says.

Equipped

~~~

> Bezalel and Oholiab and every craftsman in whom the LORD
> has put skill and intelligence to know how to do any work in the construction
> of the sanctuary shall work in accordance with all that the LORD has
> commanded. And Moses called Bazalel and Oholiab and every
> craftsman in whose mind the LORD had put skill,
> everyone whose heart stirred him up to come to do the work.
> Exodus 36:1-2 (ESV)

Does God give us what we need to fulfill our calling? Most Christians answer, "Yes." However, would you like a very precise passage of Scripture to build your godly confidence? Oddly enough, we find the unique and inspiring verses in the Old Testament book of Exodus. The setting is God's directive to the Israelites to build the tabernacle and make all its furniture. Recall the serious nature and glory of this task. Each craftsman and builder is charged with the construction of God's dwelling place! Exodus 36:1-2 (ESV) says, "Bezalel and Oholiab and every craftsman in whom the LORD has put skill and intelligence to know how to do any work in the construction of the sanctuary shall work in accordance with all that the LORD has commanded. And Moses called Bazalel and Oholiab and every craftsman in whose mind the LORD had put skill, everyone whose heart stirred him up to come to do the work."

May I promptly call to your attention two phrases? The first is "in whom the LORD has put skill and intelligence," and the second is "in whose mind the LORD put skill." Way back in the Old Testament era – more than 3,500 years ago – we see God interacting directly with the minds of men to equip them for the specific task at hand. I simply marvel at the fact that the Creator of this universe cares enough for His servants to touch our minds with His Spirit in order that we may work skillfully and intelligently. When it comes to the work of your hands and – simultaneously – the work of your mind, never allow the enemy to steal from you confidence that is found in your relationship with God. Similarly, never allow the enemy to tempt you toward the sin of conceit, believing your skill comes from anywhere or anyone other than God.

On a broad level, God intended humans to harness the creation He made in order to fill and subdue the earth (Genesis 1:28). He, of course, meant for this to happen in accordance with His will as people walked in right relationship with Him. Though sin has complicated things, God's will continues to prevail. In this day of grace, the Lord allows people to carry on in the moment-by-moment work of interacting with and taking dominion over creation. Though some human beings refuse even to acknowledge their Creator, still God permits them to function, providing their minds and their lives to them.

As we examine Exodus 36:1-2 again, we notice that true success is found as God's people determine to "work in accordance with all that the LORD has commanded" (verse 1). The tabernacle was a most elaborate and beautiful edifice. A brief study of it provokes thoughts of color, detail, majesty, and care. God ordained the details of the construction, as this work would be the location for the heart of worship. The skilled men and women who labored at the task committed to follow God's plan down to the minutest of details.

Additionally, we realize that each of God's people worked precisely because his "heart stirred him up to come to do the work" (Exodus 36:2, ESV). In other words, the Lord is pleased to provide the intelligence and skill necessary for our labor as we rejoice deep inside to serve Him. The stirring of the human heart to work for God is a treasured concept. How overjoyed the Lord must be to see a heart that wants to serve and to equip that same heart, mind, and body with all things necessary to go forward.

God is your Maker. No matter your IQ or socioeconomic status, He can give to you the skill and intelligence necessary to do what He has called you to do. The keys are obedience and a willing heart. We see obedience reiterated in II Timothy 3:17 (ESV), where Paul instructs us to immerse ourselves in the Scripture so that we may be "competent [and] equipped for every good work." Whereas God commanded specifics in the building of His tabernacle in the aforementioned part of the book of Exodus, His commands for all of life are found throughout the Bible. Every word of it is critical for faith and obedience. We observe a willing heart emphasized at the close of God's revelation: "whoever wishes, let him take the free gift of the water of life" (Revelation 22:17, NIV).

My friends, your equipping by your Creator is both free and nearly unbelievable. His grace gives you all you need to do all He asks, and His own Spirit touches your mind and your hands. Go to it!

Are You Drained?

> When I kept silent about my sin, my body wasted away through my groaning all day long. For day and night Your hand was heavy upon me; my vitality was drained away as with the fever heat of summer.
> Psalm 32:3-4

Unconfessed sin drains our strength. When our thoughts, words, or actions displease God – and we do not run to Him for forgiveness – we will sense a spiritual drain that, if ignored long enough, saps us of physical and emotional vigor. David noted a critically important concept when he penned these words of God, "When I kept silent about my sin, my body wasted away through my groaning all day long. For day and night Your hand was heavy upon me; my vitality was drained away as with the fever heat of summer" (Psalm 32:3-4).

I wonder how many times our low points – periods when we just cannot seem to "rise above" – are the direct result of refusing to deal with an area of our life in which we know God is not being honored. God Himself knows how arduous it can be to humbly go to Him and confess our wretched disposition; for when we go to Him confessing shameful ways, we are brought low. However, our loving God "regards the lowly," while "the haughty He knows from afar" (Psalm 138:6). In other words, the painful act of confession and realization of our wrong causes God to look our direction and react with His mercy.

Oftentimes, I pray aloud to God when I need to admit sin. If acknowledging bitterness, for example, I dread the sound of the words describing my nasty heart attitude. Afterward, though, I sense God's nearness and cleansing because I have been real with Him. God is asking that we demonstrate our knowledge of the great cost of sin. If my transgression is difficult to speak aloud, I know it grieves the heart of God. I begin to realize how ugly sin is – to God and to others. In my honest confession, I reckon with the crushing, serious nature of rebellion against God Almighty.

David proclaims, "How blessed is he whose transgression is forgiven, whose sin is covered! How blessed is the man to whom the LORD does not impute iniquity, and in whose spirit there is no deceit!" (Psalm 32:1-2) To be people of complete joy and stability, we must be people who confess sin and do not hide from God or ourselves. How often we may have deceit in our own spirit because we are not honest about our sin. We need to run constantly to the Bible and pray consistently in order that God's Spirit keeps our heart tender and able to discern sinfulness. Once discerned, we must be quick to confess. In this way, God will not have to impute the iniquity to us, but He will allow the death of His Son to cover the penalty. The righteousness of Jesus Christ gets credited to us (I Corinthians 1:30).

Notice how David tells us that unconfessed sin led to his human vitality being drained away as with the fever heat of summer (Psalm 32:4). How amazingly we see the work of Jesus on our behalf in a parallel verse found in Psalm 22:15, "My strength is dried up like a potsherd, and my tongue cleaves to my jaws; and You lay me in the dust of death." This prophetic passage alludes to Jesus on the cross – sapped of strength, thirsty, and dying. Can you see it? Jesus endured for us the depletion of vitality we should have to face. He took the brunt of sin's penalty and its damning, draining effects! He lay in the dust of death that we might stand in the light of life!

Please do not allow your life to be depleted of strength and joy because of unconfessed sin. Run to the God who emptied Himself for the sake of our filling. Be blessed – filled with the stability of joy and peace – by having your sins forgiven through Jesus Christ. In a broken world, there may exist other physical or emotional reasons for a lack of vitality; but do not allow unconfessed sin to drain away your life. Be truly blessed!

Dendrites and Deuteronomy: The Alignment of Brain Research with the Timeless Word of God

> Love the LORD your God with all your heart and with all your soul and with all your strength. These commandments that I give you today are to be upon your hearts. Impress them on your children. Talk about them when you sit at home and when you walk along the road, when you lie down and when you get up. Tie them as symbols on your hands and bind them on your foreheads. Write them on the doorframes of your houses and on your gates.
> Deuteronomy 6:5-9 (NIV)

Current brain research is invigorating, as it inspires us to acknowledge the amazing circuitry of our minds. The neuronal pathways spanning the various parts of the brain are employed tirelessly by the God that made them. It is estimated that the human brain contains as many as one hundred billion neurons, each neuron sprouting delicate dendrites, and transmitting impulses through appendages called axons. Jesus is Lord over all this gray and white matter. As Christ holds together all created things (Colossians 1:17), so He allows and ensures each synaptic connection.

Incredibly, God had full understanding of brain function in mind when He instructed His people in the Old Testament. The people to whom He spoke were most likely not pondering at the time the inner functions of the brain, but their Creator spoke to them with dignity – holding reality in the palm of His hand. The Bible is not archaic; it is accurate. Its words were spoken and recorded in the context of the existing culture. Looking back, we can see that the ultimate Author of the Bible is truly the Maker of the brain. Thankfully, the Hebrews took God at His Word, no matter what they did or did not understand of the mind's inner

Living in Awe!

workings. We should also immediately trust God's Word, knowing science will always "catch up" with the timeless truth of the Bible.

Let us explore the fascinating intricacies of Deuteronomy 6:5-9 in light of current brain analysis. First, we recall the passage: "Love the Lord your God with all your heart and with all your soul and with all your strength. These commandments that I give you today are to be upon your hearts. Impress them on your children. Talk about them when you sit at home and when you walk along the road, when you lie down and when you get up. Tie them as symbols on your hands and bind them on your foreheads. Write them on the doorframes of your houses and on your gates." (NIV)

God first proclaims that He intends we love Him "with everything we've got"! I call to your attention particularly the phrase, "with all your strength." The Hebrew root implies that we ought to love our Lord to the highest degree, with force, with abundance, and exceedingly so. Following on the heels of this great commandment is its corollary: all the precepts God gives to us are to be upon our hearts. In other words, our love for Him will come to fruition as we actually treasure God's Word at our core. The Hebrew term to designate our heart in this instance is a concept implying that God's commandments are to reside in our inner being, our mind, or our soul. The nuance tells us that the Word of God should be part of our thinking and our memory; it becomes fluid in our conscience and is present at the seat of our emotions. When His Word inculcates our minds at this level, it becomes natural, for example, to speak of Isaiah 40:26 when looking into the night sky. Instead of simply seeing stars, we are now pondering the mighty God who sustains each one with precision and intention.

In fact, the flow of God's Word in my conscience prompted a wonderful conversation about Isaiah 40:26 with my eleven-year-old nephew as we sat casually under a starry sky in the summertime. Verses that had become a fluid part of my mind through memorization, study, rehearsal, and application, suddenly cascaded into the moment at hand. This is as it should be, for God

Living in Awe!

is the Lord of everything. The natural points to the supernatural (Romans 1:20), and proper training of the mind is obedience, and can lead to yet more obedience. In this case, the human interaction and discussion of God's power and care for the stars led to an opportunity to express the even more unbelievable care of God for people made in His very own image. My nephew loved looking at stars, and this was a perfect opportunity for God's Spirit to work through what had become a part of my mind's wiring.

As the Lord continues His directives, we realize that we are to impress His Word on our children and talk about His commandments continually – while rising, walking, sitting at home, and lying down. Could God have made His intention of repetition and discussion of His Word any more clear? In effect, He declares, "Keep doing this. Talk about Me always, in many contexts and in many ways. Over and over and over again I want you to rehearse and discuss My Word – especially with the younger ones."

Guess what brain research has revealed? Brain growth continues past birth! When we actively rehearse and learn in different ways – stimulating various regions of the brain – we can expand and strengthen neuronal pathways. We can make it easier to recall information readily. As Willis (2006) noted, "The brain pathways and connections that are used regularly are maintained and 'hard-wired,' while others are eliminated, or pruned."

It seems God would desire His law to be the hard-wiring of our brains. For my actions and reactions to be healthy, the very Word of God needs to be part of the structure of my mind. Willis (2006) informs, "New connecting cells, called dendrites, can be formed throughout life . . . after repeated practice, working memories are set down as permanent neuronal circuits of axons and dendrites ready to be activated when the information is needed."

God rightly requires us to "impress [the commandments] on [our] children." The word "impress" here means to sharpen or whet, as a knife. One nuance implies a wounding or piercing through. Our children and all young ones under our influence ought to feel the emotional, deep piercing of God's Word. This is not simply an intellectual experience. His Word – when practiced – pricks our soul in ways unimaginable. I will never forget the penetration of my heart while watching my grandmother die. The summary of those final days in her bed could be, "She drew unbelievably close to Jesus as her outer shell fell away." I observed a woman of God as all her belief and obedience culminated in glorious moments.

I was pierced through in a simpler moment when the practice of genuine forgiveness led to a feeling of victory and love. The bottom line is that reinforcement of God's Word as gained in the practice of the principles that have been purposefully hard-wired in our minds leads to deeper understanding and easier retrieval. Current research refers to this as episodic memory and experiential learning. Willis (2006) asserts, "With strategies that engage the senses, students 'become' the knowledge by interacting with it. As a result, a new memory that might otherwise be forgotten is linked to a sensation, a movement, or an emotion, and therefore it travels into the memory storage in more than one pathway. This redundancy of pathways means greater memory retention and recall."

It is no wonder that the Lord demands we ponder His Word in the daily experiences of life. When my mind is fresh in the morning and the world is new, when the quietness of the evening settles in, when walking through the events and relationships of the day, and all times; my musing on His commandments must mix with the occurrences of my life. I need to observe His Word as it relates to all the circumstances I encounter. Behind the scenes, my Creator-God is firing neurons in all the lobes of my brain, hard-wiring me for increased focus on Him.

God adds that His people ought to "write [the commandments] on the doorframes of [their] houses and on [their] gates." I will here focus on the fact that the people ought to manually write God's Word. In our brains, the occipital lobe is involved with reading and visual perception; the parietal lobe relates to tactile perception and academic skills; and the frontal lobe is involved with consciousness and attention. Since the Hebrews had a largely oral culture of communication (directly involving the temporal lobe), it is of note that God directed His people to engage all four lobes of the brain in regard to His Word. He obviously desires that all our mind engages. Interestingly, when referring to students' study of electrons orbiting a nucleus, Willis (2006) recommends, "If they then draw a sketch of their visualizations and verbally communicate them to partners, or write about them in their own words, multiple brain pathways will be stimulated to enter long-term memory."

Whether taken literally or symbolically, God clearly advises the Hebrews to "tie [the commandments] as symbols on [their] hands and bind them on [their] foreheads." The root for the term "forehead" is "frontal." The frontal lobe of our brains is the epicenter of attention, motivation, guidance of social behavior, judgment, and decision-making. The Lord means for His Word to be right there at the headquarters of our motivation. Let everything be driven by Him.

As we begin to contemplate current brain research, we notice that God is never "behind the times." He stands omniscient and outside of time and space. Though God inspired the writing of Deuteronomy approximately 3,500 years ago, its words are accurate and align with the latest brain discoveries. At the risk of sounding simplistic, I must say that the Creator best knows the creation. Imagine, when God first created man, He did so giving us the most intricate and organized of bodies and organs. God knew all about branching dendrites and invaluable synapses, for He brought them into existence. We must always trust His Word, because our timeless God has given it to us freely from His unfathomable wisdom.

As we function, using the minds God has given us, may we always cling to John 14:26, for the Creator transcends the creation. Although the design and workings of the human brain point to the One who made them, the Lord is infinitely greater than us. His work cannot be fully captured in the study of created things. In John 14:26, Jesus says, "But the Counselor, the Holy Spirit, whom the Father will send in my name, will teach you all things and will remind you of everything I have said to you." (NIV)

The Creator of our minds is infinitely greater than our minds. God sent His Holy Spirit to be our Teacher. God's Spirit superintends the workings of my brain. The genuinely Christian perspective is one that makes a personal God central. God made me more than the sum of the neurons and cells of my body. God Himself is working in my heart and mind as I yield myself to Him. His Holy Spirit works through and above the astounding, intricate brains God has given to us. God chooses to work in us profoundly when we obey His Word, which naturally both aligns with and transcends the created world.

Thank you, Jesus, for giving Your life that the Holy Spirit might live in me so that I can obey God's Word, using the brain He has given me!

Living in Awe!

Most Bosses Don't Listen, But . . .

> The LORD is high above all nations, and his glory above the heavens! Who is like the LORD our God, who is seated on high, who looks far down on the heavens and the earth? He raises the poor from the dust and lifts the needy from the ash heap, to make them sit with princes, with the princes of his people.
> Psalm 113:4-8 (ESV)

If you had a general suspicion that bosses tend not to listen, your suspicion was confirmed by a recent study reported by Good Morning America on September 19, 2011. It seems the more power someone gains in an organization, the less likely they are to listen to the people under them. While this is, of course, a generalization (for we can cite great exceptions, e.g., my boss), we sense the frustration of the study's main point.

In our ordinary experience, we often find that people with the most power, resources, and ability to effect change are those who are least likely to care about "average" people. Those among us who are hurting many times feel abandoned. The inflated confidence of bosses, the blatant disregard of less influential people by those with fame and fortune, and the sheer inability of the powerful to connect with the ordinary person all present obstacles to genuine help for regular people. The problem is that the recent study of bosses who don't listen is limited to the realm of the natural. What about God? Can He – does He – intervene?

Read the beautiful, comforting words of Psalm 113:4-8 (ESV):

> "The LORD is high above all nations, and his glory above the heavens! Who is like the LORD our God, who is seated on high, who looks far down on the heavens and the earth?

He raises the poor from the dust and lifts the needy from the ash heap to make them sit with princes, with the princes of his people."

The irony of this passage is that the most powerful being who exists is the One who reaches down the lowest to lift up the helpless and heartbroken. Influential humans tend to ignore the needy. The most exalted Lord of the universe fixes His eye upon the disadvantaged. I especially enjoy verses 5 and 6; God is seated on high, but He is looking far down to see who wants to be rescued. His majesty does not deter Him from helping; He is the God who "raises the poor from the dust" and "lifts the needy to sit with princes."

Flying in the face of corrupt human nature to grow bigger and care less, God's promise is to lift us up with His own hand – though he is in charge of everything and owns everything. I fear that many people cannot conceptualize of a God like that because we are so accustomed to human failure. Remember, God stands outside the universe; He is transcendent. He is not simply the biggest or most powerful among us; He is completely other than we are. He is not the most compassionate human you have ever known; He defines compassion. We cannot allow our experiences with humans to taint our understanding of God. We must take Him at His Word.

Psalm 138:6 (ESV) succinctly proclaims, "For though the LORD is high, he regards the lowly." Will you believe that today? God alone stands as the power over all things, and He is also the One who cares about those who are brought low by life, sin, and circumstance. Unlike the human tendency to care less as we become more elevated, God cares the most even though He is the holy, exalted Creator. Please call out to Him now, and picture His mighty hand reaching down to hold you and lift you up. Do not allow human failure to cloud your view of God. Take Him at His Word.

Earlier in this article I spoke of the possible "sheer inability of the powerful to connect with the ordinary person." Jesus Christ

Living in Awe!

shattered that obstacle! Jesus is God, and in Him God put on the flesh of an ordinary human in order to connect with us for salvation and eternal life. God is the highest and actually became the lowest two thousand years ago in order to bring the lowly to the highest place! Through Jesus, we are lifted to God. Our voice is heard. Our heart is observed. Our need is met. Our future is secured. The Highest reaches to the lowest, defying the recent study bosses!

Living in Heavenly Places

Blessed be the God and Father of our Lord Jesus Christ, who has blessed us with every spiritual blessing in the heavenly places in Christ.
Ephesians 1:3

A recent, sweet conversation with my nephew reminded me of our access to all spiritual blessings of the heavenly places (Ephesians 1:3). My nephew assured me that he remembered vividly a ten minute period of time that occurred eight years ago. He recalled the place we were during a moment of emotional distress and the words I spoke from the Bible concerning the New Heavens and New Earth. That precious boy's eyes lit up as he listened to me review that conversation of long ago and my counsel that Jesus will keep His promise to make things right so that one day people who love each other will no longer have to be separated. As we remembered together, I could see the wheels of his mind turning furiously. He had held onto the truth of God's Word all this time. For him, the book of Revelation and II Peter had been sealed as reality.

What struck me the evening of our recollection is the power of spiritual blessings. When we focus on and access the stuff of God's Word and kingdom, eternal and life-changing phenomena occur. Though much of the time the drudgery of everyday living can mask the workings in the spiritual realm, God moves through us when we choose to think and act in the heavenly arena. For example, I just encouraged a friend of mine who uses the text message medium to send Bible verses to others. In a world of technological overuse and abuse, I wanted her to know that often the Lord confirms His leading through her "heavenly thinking" when it comes to such a common thing as text messaging. This woman accesses the spiritual blessings of God's Word, chooses to think about her Savior during the course of ordinary days,

Living in Awe!

and then positively affects another person's walk with the Lord. Eternal differences are made rather than just the proliferation of more gibberish so common to texting.

Paul instructs in Ephesians 1:3, "Blessed be the God and Father of our Lord Jesus Christ, who has blessed us with every spiritual blessing in the heavenly places in Christ." How many times do we miss those spiritual blessings simply because we do not recognize our position in the heavenly places? A dinner table in a restaurant, for example, can be a heavenly site when food and laughter are shared and savored to the glory of God. Our Lord made us to enjoy the earth He has created, and we reflect His image in holy fellowship with one another. The location on the map is one thing, but children of God are seated in heavenly places (Ephesians 2:6) and allow God to transform the ordinary into the extraordinary.

A year or so ago, one of my young relatives expressed the need for some school clothes that fit well. I went to a department store and a drug store and stocked up on clothes and supplies for him. I felt the glory of God in those stores, because the act of obedience was in the spiritual realm. The clothing became a tool for Heaven. I wrote a letter to go with the supplies and outfits, and I explained that all of our needs are ultimately supplied by Jesus. He is the reason and the source of all we receive. Clothing a loved one became sacred.

How often do we waste our time stuck in the ordinary? God has blessed us with every spiritual blessing! He tells us these blessings are in heavenly places in Christ. Make no mistake about it, a New Age type of spirituality is not what is mentioned here. We have access to the blessings because of – and in – Jesus Christ! We used to be dead to spiritual things, but the sacrifice of Jesus made us alive! (Ephesians 2:4-5) Now we ought to live – and live abundantly! A bird flying through the yard now reminds us of the freedom from sin we have in Jesus. The simple acts of reading and thinking now remind us of the creativity and orderliness of our great God, who has things yet unimaginable in store for us.

A drink of iced tea reminds us of His faithfulness to quench our spiritual thirst and bring contentment even now. A look at the tall trees stretching toward the sky, growing more intricate with each expanding branch, hints of our approach toward Heaven and the New Jerusalem.

    Please live in heavenly places in Christ. Be always communing with Him and ponder His Word (Psalm 1:1-2). Be perpetually giving Him glory as we stand amazed at all He has given and all he does. Make moments and experiences count for eternity. We have been blessed with all spiritual blessings; we have to live in heavenly places in Christ.

Plunging Up Through a Mound of Dirt

> And he said, "The kingdom of God is as if a man should scatter seed on the ground. He sleeps and rises night and day, and the seed sprouts and grows; he knows not how."
>
> Mark 4:26-27(ESV)

The kingdom of God is both unstoppable and mysterious. Jesus likened it to seeds scattered on the ground that slowly, methodically, and automatically grow.

Have you ever actually watched a plant grow (without the benefit of time lapse photography)? We could sit with eyes fixed steadily upon the seed for hours, days, and weeks to observe any progress – and still our human eyes could not catch the "movement." Rather, we plant a seed and go about our days. We do what we can to water and fertilize, but the earth itself does the work. God has programmed this planet to make plants grow; and the Lord consistently sustains all the energy, processes, and products necessary for the curious work of cultivation and harvest.

We humans plant a seed and do exactly as Jesus said, "[We] sleep and rise night and day" (Mark 4:27, ESV). In other words, we persevere through the stuff of life. We lay our heads down on the pillow at night and arise to a new day. We live out that day, and the next, and the next . . . all the while "the seed sprouts and grows," though we "know not how" (Mark 4:27, ESV).

This parable of the growing seed is a comforting one to us. God is at work behind the scenes, even as we continue on through the regularity of life! His kingdom is growing, even if the naked eye cannot grasp its movement. The seed we faithfully planted is sprouting and getting larger, even if we go on sleeping and rising.

Be faithful to spread the Word of God. Be faithful to plant the news of Jesus wherever God has asked. Though your days may seem ordinary, God is growing the seed. How He actually works in a human heart is as incomprehensible as the earth's toiling with a little seed. Against the force of gravity and plunging up through a mound of dirt comes the sprout. So comes the beginning of God's kingdom in a human heart once the seed of Truth is planted. Through seasons of sun, rain, cold, and heat grows the plant until the fruit appears. Likewise, the fruit of our investment in the proclamation of the Gospel arises despite obstacles and discouragement. Count on God to grow the kingdom as you plant the seed. Sleep at night knowing He is on the move. Wake in the morning assured growth is taking place. Scatter seed and let God work.

As Jesus promised, one day "when the grain is ripe, at once he puts in the sickle, because the harvest has come" (Mark 4:29, ESV). The final gathering of all that's been planted and grown will take place and bring to light that which developed in such an unfathomable way. Suddenly, we shall realize just how majestic and impenetrable is this kingdom of God. The mysterious working of God in souls we touched with his Word will shine forth.

Keep scattering seed. Continue letting God work – faithfully and in an often unseen manner – as we go about our days in obedience.

Life-Building: Will You Crash or Stand?

> Therefore everyone who hears these words of mine and puts them into practice is like a wise man who built his house on the rock. The rain came down, the streams rose, and the winds blew and beat against that house; yet it did not fall, because it had its foundation on the rock. But everyone who hears these words of mine and does not put them into practice is like a foolish man who built his house on sand. The rain came down, the streams rose, and the winds blew and beat against that house, and it fell with a great crash.
>
> Matthew 7:24-27 (NIV)

What do followers of Jesus have in common with those who do not follow Jesus? Two things are for sure: we both invest in our lives and we both suffer. Jesus directly addressed these two issues when He taught the Parable of the Wise and Foolish Builders. He also clearly expresses the one thing the wise and foolish builders do not have in common – the end result of life as a whole. At the surface – and from a bird's-eye view – much can appear similar when it comes to working through life and enduring all the nasty things the world can bring. However, a marked difference exists. For one person, the result is everlasting endurance; for the other, it is final destruction.

Keep in mind that Jesus is not simply a storyteller or a kindly teacher. Jesus is God . . . and the Creator and Designer of reality. When He speaks to the issues of life, He knows what He is talking about! This parable is not just an inspirational speech; this teaching is Truth. Do you want to be hit square between the eyes with what matters? Do you want to face actuality head-on? Do you want to take the blinders off and be real about your soul and destiny? Then listen to the words of Jesus Christ in Matthew 7:24-27 (NIV):

> Therefore everyone who hears these words of mine and puts them into practice is like a wise man who built his

Living in Awe!

house on the rock. The rain came down, the streams rose, and the winds blew and beat against that house; yet it did not fall, because it had its foundation on the rock. But everyone who hears these words of mine and does not put them into practice is like a foolish man who built his house on sand. The rain came down, the streams rose, and the winds blew and beat against that house, and it fell with a great crash.

My mathematical mind so prone to symmetry immediately notices the similarities and differences between the two types of "life builders":

1. Both types of people hear the words of Jesus. So, hearing or reading or even knowing God's Word is not the answer to a secure life.

2. While one group hears and does not put the words into practice, the other type actually lives out the Word of God. This is no little thing. The wise builders do not simply read the Bible in order to feel good about themselves or to appease church-going onlookers. The wise builders actually apply God's Word to the inner workings of their minds and the outer working of their lives. They do not just hear Jesus say, "Take up your cross and follow Me," (Luke 9:23) or scan publicly that sobering statement in the Bible, they really rise in the morning with a consciousness of death to self and life to Christ! They lay aside their selfish desires to obey God's voice in the big and small stuff of everyday living.

3. Both types build. Both are at least spending minutes, hours, days, and years doing what is necessary to survive. Both must toil, eat, relate, and plan for the future. Both are occupied. One, however, is immersed in his own desires. The other is going about the business of living according to authentic biblical principles.

Living in Awe!

4. Both experience hardship. Notice the careful wording of Jesus here. The wise and the foolish builders each experience the same three difficulties: rain coming down, streams rising up, and winds blowing and beating against what they have built. Building a life wisely on the Word of God is no guarantee of a carefree life. This world system is broken by sin, and everyone in it experiences adversity. Do not think God has abandoned you because distress arises. No, think rather that – for now – you are stuck in a broken world.

5. The major difference between the two groups emphasized here is the ultimate outcome of life-building. Living out God's Word is likened to erecting the house of your life on a solid, rock foundation. The rain, streams, and wind cannot destroy such a life; for the foundation is the Rock Himself, Jesus! The Maker of weather is greater than weather's effects. So, too, Jesus is the Maker of life. He is certainly greater than life's effects. When we build according to Him, no tragedy can annihilate us and no annoyance can dissuade us. Our lives will stand! In great contrast, the life of one who hears but does not actually obey will fall; and the crash, says Jesus, will be great. That final demise is assured because any foundation other than Jesus is likened to sand. Sand subsides in the end. As the rains come down, sand begins to shift. The house built without adherence to the Word of God gives way; it is not able to withstand the accumulation of blasts from this broken world. In the end, its crash is great; its demise is sealed. How great is the disintegration of a life completely lost because of the refusal to walk in alignment with the God who made everything and defines the parameters for true and successful living!

Which kind of builder will you be? Wise or foolish? Both hear the Word of God. Both build and endure hardship. Only one kind actually lives out the Word, and only the same survives.

What the Stars CAN Tell Us

Lift your eyes and look to the heavens: who created all these? He who brings out the starry host one by one, and calls them each by name. Because of his great power and mighty strength, not one of them is missing.

Isaiah 40:26 (NIV)

God is asking you, "To whom will you compare me? Or who is my equal?" (Isaiah 40:25, NIV) God provokes us to consider just how influential we deem to be situations, people, and powers. God lovingly but firmly confronts us with the possibility that we are living as though He has a rival.

Do we fear an employer's attitude or decision? Do we stay awake at night wondering how a financial situation will affect us? Are we uncomfortable because we think some power of Satan is intending to wreak havoc in our life? Are we debilitated by dread of how a health issue will impact our existence? Do we spend an inordinate amount of time wondering what an unknown circumstance may bring? If so, then we are living as though that situation, person, or power can go to battle against God's will for our lives and perhaps win! In other words, we are affirming that God Almighty has an equal – at the very least. Maybe we are living as though He has a superior.

In fact, God stands sovereign over all creation. Every human, every power, and every state of affairs is dependent on Him for existence. Nothing stands a chance against God. When we live in fear or distress of situations, authorities, or people; we are living in idolatry. The first commandment God gave to Moses on Mount Sinai is "You shall have no other gods before me" (Exodus 20:3). Although a well-known requirement, I sadly believe many of us transgress this law in our intellect and heart rather regularly. When we dedicate time, thoughts, and passion to the dread of anything in life – rather than to an honest reverence to God – we are designing an equivalent for God in our own mind. We are committing idolatry.

The antithesis to this sinful, destructive line of thinking is a focus on both the greatness and intimacy of God. Isaiah 40:26 (NIV) goes on to say, "Lift your eyes and look to the heavens: who created all these? He who brings out the starry host one by one, and calls them each by name. Because of his great power and mighty strength, not one of them is missing." He is grand enough to have created the billions and billions of stars and the vast expanse in which they reside, but tender enough to know each one by name and ensure each is sustained on a moment-by-moment basis just as it should. If God does this for giant, burning balls of hydrogen and helium; what does He do for living people with souls, made in His own image? On this illustration given in God's Word we ought to depend in order to avoid the sin of idolatry.

God is transcendent – above and beyond us and our understanding, and wholly self-sustaining. However, God is also immanent – very close to His creation. His greatness does not preclude His intimate care! Hallelujah! The most wonderful, infinite, inexplicable, and Creator God knows my name and every circumstance that touches my life. For that reason, I should make none His equal.

Let us aim to obey God by putting Him above all else in thought, devotion, time, and respect. May we realize He is to have no competitor when it comes to that about which we ponder, obsess, believe, treasure, work toward, dream, and expend time and energy; for, the answer to the question, "Who is like Him?" is "No one!"

*For more reading about God's transcendence and immanence, see Acts 17:24-28.

The Operative Word

> Now He was telling them a parable to show that at all times
> they ought to pray and not to lose heart.
>
> Luke 18:1

Christian, do you pray as much as you should? Are there situations left untouched and quandaries floating about because you refuse to pray as God desires? Prayer is necessary. God works mightily through prayer. For the child of God, prayer is not an option or a task to which we resort when things look bleak. Prayer is powerful, delivering answers derived in a world currently unseen to us.

Luke, the disciple, was a physician in his day. He clearly understood, however, that health of spirit, emotion, and body come ultimately through God. In Luke 18:1, he instructs, "Now [Jesus] was telling them a parable to show that at all times they ought to pray and not to lose heart." Luke reminds us that God is unequivocal in His demand that we pray. In a culture of "quick fixes," shallow relationships, and mitigated perseverance; God desires that we press into His heart by prayer. How does that sit with you? Does your heart respond, "Yes! I know the experience and wonder of pouring myself into prayer!" Or, does your heart answer, "No. I am not there. My prayer life is quite flat, and I realize my need to heed the call."

The apostle James proclaims in James 5:16, "The effective prayer of a righteous man can accomplish much." The Greek root here behind the words effective and accomplish is a word that means "to be operative." It is the same Greek root behind the word works in this glorious verse, "Also we have obtained an inheritance, having been predestined according to His purpose who works all things after the counsel of His will" (Ephesians

1:11). Imagine, the power of God working in our prayer life is related to the power of God working everything in the universe for His purpose! When we truly pour ourselves into seeking and petitioning our Lord, God operates on our behalf. He accomplishes things. No longer dormant lie the possibilities. Prayer is the "operative word"!

Unique about prayer is the inherent relationship between the physical and spiritual realms. When I speak to God with my voice (using the physical body and brain He has given me), I am functioning in the spiritual realm with God. He, in turn, may produce results back in the physical world. It is the intersection of Heaven and Earth, if you will. Prayer is the place where we are instructed to lay hold of heavenly things and blessed to see outcomes both spiritual and material.

Shadrach, Meshach, and Abednego prayed to God in Heaven, and God answered by protecting their physical bodies from seemingly inevitable consumption by fire. Prayer wrought tangible results. Of course! This is God's will – that His children pray! Do you set aside with marked intention minutes and hours of your days for intense seeking of your God? Is your heart rising to Him on a regular, deliberate, and serious basis? Is He hearing your petitions? There is no shortcut to the effects only prayer can bring. It is God's will. We must pray.

Living in Awe!

Like Water Through My Fingers

For whoever wants to save his life will lose it,
but whoever loses his life for me and for the gospel will save it.
What good is it for a man to gain the whole world, yet forfeit his soul?
Mark 8:35-36 (NIV)

Like water through my fingers
Slips the promise of satisfaction
In any other source but Christ.

Spent rapidly and uselessly
Are the myriad moments
Of craving and seeking to no avail.

As dark as a midnight sky
Is the feeling in the heart
When worldly things become our aim.

Pounding as hail on the rooftop
Is the pressure to give in -
To live a life stuck in the temporal.

Pressing in on every side
Are the messages of concealed defeat
Beckoning us to waste our days.

Like a bridge built on false calculations
Crumbling to the water below
Is a life lived for material things.

As a rock falls to the bottom of a stream
Drops the meaning of a life
Squandered on selfish indulgence.

Living in Awe!

Sorrowful one, call to Jesus.
Broken one, live for Him.

As the promise of spring follows winter
Is the assurance of joy in the soul
For those who go against the flow.

As God will not be mocked
So He shall surely give
Very real, heavenly treasure.

As God will not be mocked
So He shall surely return to earth
For those who love Him more than life.

As God's Word stands true forever
His heart has been made known
And the cost is everything.

Prayer or television?

Trivial conversation or discussion of things eternal?

Another movie or a chapter of the Bible?

Shopping trip or memorizing God's Word?

Ipod and texts or sitting quietly with Jesus?

Sporting event or gathering with His people?

Investment in a bigger house or investment in the kingdom of God?

Time spent taking care of more and more material things or time to be thankful for what matters?

Living in Awe!

A schedule so hectic our head spins or a day built with time to adore the Savior?

The easy road or the difficult walk of the Cross?

A life of the temporary or the present infused with the everlasting?

"Yes" to the world or "Yes" to Jesus?

Like water through my fingers
Goes the world.

But tightly shall I grasp
The cross of my Jesus.

And more firmly still shall I be held
By the One who holds forever.

The Real You and the Plans of God

How great are Your works, O Lord! Your thoughts are very deep.
Psalm 92:5

There is a distinct and strong comfort in the ability to be oneself. Transparency's enemy is the mask so many people wear in order to appear to be who they think they ought to be in any given situation. Freedom and peace are stolen by these masks. We crave to jump headlong into life, unhindered by the pressures of appearances. Why this longing? It is how God designed us.

Transparency was assaulted in the Garden of Eden. Human rebellion against God caused people to run – from their Creator and from each other. Sin brings shame and separation. Jesus shed His own blood to bridge the gap between us and God –and between us and everyone else.

The problem so many people face is our reluctance to run to God. Too proud to admit we are a mess, we try to hide the "real us" while the facade continues. Have you ever – like me – convinced yourself you were doing something for God when, in fact, it was mostly for you? Have you ever engaged in church activity or pious practices when your heart was full of self-righteousness or pride? Have you ever acted out the life of a Christian when your heart was so much more about you than about Jesus? Have you ever convinced yourself that you were doing something right even though you knew it was wrong – simply because you wanted your preferred results?

The prophet Isaiah is very clear when he proclaims, "Then the Lord said, 'Because this people draw near with their words and honor Me with their lip service, but they remove their hearts far from Me' . . . Woe to those who deeply hide their plans from the

LORD, And whose deeds are done in a dark place, And they say, 'Who sees us?' or 'Who knows us?'" (Isaiah 29:13,15). Notice the phrase about people who are surely doomed; they "deeply hide their plans from the LORD." How foolish we can be! We actually convince ourselves that if we hide our plans deeply enough, God will not know our inner musings. We ridiculously come to believe that we can act and say things that do not align with the thoughts and truth of our inner being and get away with it in the sight of the Almighty. We cannot!

For as deeply as we try to hide our core, the God of the universe digs deeper still! I cannot hide my soul from the very One who breathed the breath of life into the dust that is my body. He knows the atoms of my exterior and He knows the invisible intentions of my interior. Therefore, I want to run to Him with honesty for the work that only He can do in me.

I sing with the Psalmist, "For You, O LORD, have made me glad by what You have done, I will sing for joy at the works of Your hands. How great are Your works, O LORD! Your thoughts are very deep" (Psalm 92:4-5). Deeper than the vainly hidden plans of the unrighteous are the thoughts of our righteous God. The blessed cure for the unrighteous is to run to the God who is deeper than elaborate, useless plans to cover sin. God's deep thoughts are thoughts of cleansing and rebuilding. Since eternity past, He planned the sacrifice of His own Son for the redemption of those who – without vain attempts to cover their hearts – will run into His arms.

Psalm 92:5 tells us that God's thoughts are very deep. The Hebrew root for the word "thoughts" is amazing. It implies that God is thinking, planning, calculating, inventing, and imagining. In other words, God is working to build our lives into what He desires. We are a great workmanship – a wonderful edifice! My God has made the Heavens and the Earth, and now He wants to make us into people who reflect His heart, His love, His wonder, and His creativity. God's planning and calculating and inventing and imagining is so deep! We cannot even begin to ponder how great a design we could be if we would truly yield our hearts to Him without reservation and bring praise to Him for the work of His hands and His thoughts!

The same Hebrew root for the deep thoughts of God in Psalm 92 is used in other passages that give us the flavor of what a wonderful thing God longs to do with us. When God instructs Moses how to build the tabernacle, He says, "Make the tabernacle with ten curtains of finely twisted linen and blue, purple and scarlet yarn, with cherubim worked into them by a skilled craftsman" (Exodus 26:1, NIV). This curtain of colorful, elaborate beauty is the result of the plan and imagination of God. What a gorgeous curtain came to be from the thoughts of God.

In II Chronicles 26:15 (NIV), the same root word is used to describe the inventions of King Uzziah, "In Jerusalem he made machines designed by skillful men for use on the towers and on the corner defenses to shoot arrows and hurl large stones." The plan and invention here is that of Uzziah and skillful men, who reflect the infinite wisdom of their Creator. Interestingly, God can build into our lives the weapons we need to thwart the enemy of our souls. As God gave these men of old the mathematical and scientific skill to build physical weapons, so God gives to us spiritual skill to fight with spiritual weapons the battles in which we stand.

The same Hebrew root is obviously meant to imply precision, as we see it used in Leviticus 27:18, "If he consecrates his field after the jubilee, however, then the priest shall calculate the price for him proportionate to the years that are left until the year of jubilee; and it shall be deducted from your valuation." The exact mathematical evaluations of this verse solidify our assuredness that God is building us to precise specifications. He knows exactly what we ought to be like in the end, and He has calculated accurately the plans necessary to get us there. A trial here, a success there, an answered prayer here, a time of persevering there, a season of difficulty here, a season of rejoicing there – all of these are definitely working together to make me who I ought to be.

    Will you now say with me, "How great are Your works, O LORD! Your thoughts are very deep" (Psalm 92:5)? Will you now run to Him, instead of hiding?

Actually Finding Life

> For whoever wishes to save his life will lose it;
> but whoever loses his life for My sake will find it.
> Matthew 16:25

The majority of humans, no doubt, wish to save their lives – to hold onto what we deem so precious. Most people hope to retain their souls – to continue to enjoy that which is enjoyable. Recent research reported in Putnam & Campbell's book, American Grace (2010), says that "Sixty percent of Americans are absolutely sure there is a heaven" (p. 7). Largely, people from all walks of life want to believe that a good life awaits us after this earthly life is finished.

Desiring to hold onto our lives is no guarantee that we will. In fact, Jesus Christ boldly declared, "For whoever wishes to save his life will lose it; but whoever loses his life for My sake will find it" (Matthew 16:25). Notice keenly Jesus' use of the word "wishes." People who wish to save their lives, in fact, lose them. On the other hand (and quite amazingly, I might add) people who actually lose their lives for the sake of God will actually find life!

There we have it . . . the great paradox. Attempting to grasp at life by our own methods ends in utter loss, whereas, forthrightly giving up our lives for the particular sake of God culminates in gain. Here we have spelled out before us an undeniable truth from the very mouth of the Son of God. It is a sure thing that any attempt to cling to life and any of its "treasures" is a mistake of inexplicable cost. Accordingly, it is also an indisputable thing that the sacrifice of all we hold dear for the cause of Christ results in finding life that both never ends and never lets us down.

Living in Awe!

Please allow me to expound upon the hope at the near horizon. Jesus went on to say, "For the Son of Man is going to come in the glory of His Father with His angels, and will then repay every man according to his deeds" (Matthew 16:27). Clearly, then, Jesus will return a second time with glory as the Judge; this visitation stands in stark contrast to His first coming with humility as a Servant. No, when Jesus returns to His earth again, it will not be to offer salvation, but to enact judgment. Christ will grant to His followers great reward, and He will deliver to the rest wrath and indignation (Romans 2:8).

The decision to follow Jesus is a decision to deny self. It is a determination to count earthly desires as nothing compared to the work of building God's kingdom. Self-indulgence comes in countless forms: buying what we do not need, gorging simply because we crave, mindlessly absorbing entertainment for hours upon end, envying what we do not own, allowing laziness a regular place, blocking from our vision the needs of others, ignoring the eternal to pursue the temporal, and . . . the list goes on ad infinitum. Self-indulgence will one day meet its bitter end: loss of soul and life. In the same way, self-denial for the sake of Jesus Christ and the fame of His name will one day meet its glorious result: eternal reward and life unending.

The determination of the judgment is not arbitrary, but precise. Jesus Christ will repay every person in exact accordance with his or her deeds. Am I saved by Jesus' death and resurrection? Then my life – and all its content and moments – belongs to Him! My actions each and every day of living ought to emit a resounding declaration that Jesus is the reason I exist!

I know that as we await the return of Jesus, the prevalence of good and bad in human lives seems random and unfair. Hold on, for one day the Savior and Judge of the universe will repay every man according to his deeds.

Living in Awe!

Dingy Socks

> And his clothes became radiant, intensely white,
> as no one on earth could bleach them.
>
> Mark 9:3 (ESV)

Sometimes I read statements in the Bible that strike me as particularly odd and make me smile. So was the case when I recently read Mark 9:3 (ESV), "And [Jesus'] clothes became radiant, intensely white, as no one on earth could bleach them."

The longstanding market for laundry bleach testifies to the fact that we humans like things clean and bright. If socks are meant to be white, then – generally speaking – we would like them to stay white and new-looking as long as possible. Something about white "whites" makes us feel good. That sounds fitting, for God made us with both a desire to be right and a hope for newness.

How down to earth Mark is when he pens Peter's observation of the transfiguration of Jesus. Mark tells us in straightforward fashion that the clothes of Jesus became whiter than any launderer could possibly bleach them. We are told the clothes glistened in a way no human product or effort could ever make them sparkle.

And so it is with God! No human product or effort can produce the results only God alone can bring about. Our innate desire to shine and remain new is answered only in the work of Jesus. How wonderful it is for God to assure us of our hope in simple fashion. On an ordinary day in Israel two thousand years ago, Jesus was transfigured before the eyes of His closest friends: Peter, James, and John. Jesus chose to have His clothes gleam exceedingly, and we are gently reminded of His supernatural power to accomplish effortlessly what we struggle to do. The brilliance of Jesus is our comfort. I have no majesty of my own; I am fading, and I am sinful. Worse yet, I cannot muster any radiance for myself. I, instead, look to my Jesus.

Strange as it may seem, dingy socks may be a great reminder for us that only Jesus can bring the righteousness and newness for which we long. His blood cleanses us when nothing else can. His resurrected life gives us new life that will one day be completed with a new body that never grows old or worn.

Dingy socks and the smell of bleach will never be the same to me.

Living in Awe!

Far Beyond Gasoline Prices

So we fix our eyes not on what is seen, but on what is unseen.
For what is seen is temporary, but what is unseen is eternal.
II Corinthians 4:18 (NIV)

The devastation in Japan that took place in March 2011 was heartbreaking, to say the least. I spent time praying that God would intervene as He sees fit, especially in the area of the human soul. I have prayed that this disaster will turn people to God, rather than away from Him. I have asked the Lord that people who feel helpless and hopeless will find their ultimate help and hope in the salvation of the God of the Bible. As many of us know in a familiar way, the Lord often gets an honest hold of us through tragedy. Since, "even the darkness is not dark to [God], and the night is as bright as the day" (Psalm 139:12), we know that the Lord can use even the most horrible of situations to accomplish His greatest work – the salvation of a human being.

One day, I heard a radio commentator connect the Japan catastrophe to a jittery stock market and even greater rises in the cost of gasoline. Not anything close to an economist, I do not understand completely the fragile relationships behind the economic changes. I do, however, realize the effect of the changes on many people. Some of us focus mainly on the tsunami's effects on our own, material lives. We are frustrated to pay two or three more dollars to fill our tanks. For those struggling financially, this can have a profound effect on the household. However, in a broad sense, we need to get hold of our reactions and trace the problem back to what really matters.

Instead of focusing on the higher gas price or lowered portfolio value, realize what the devastation in Japan truly represents. The tragedy reminds us human beings just how amazingly close we are to the end of earthly life. We are on the precipice. We are so fragile. In a moment – in a heartbeat – we may cross from life to death. Though myriad people try desperately to forget the reality of death – and they push it away with any number of meaningless distractions – death will still come. We are one tsunami, one accident, one affliction, or one calamity away from our standing before the God and Judge of existence.

As I drove by a gas station soon after the disaster and noted the ten cent increase per gallon of fuel, I refused to let it frustrate me. Instead, I allowed it to remind me of what thousands upon thousands of people are facing. They are recognizing the brevity of human, earthly life. They are apprehending the vital nature of spiritual truth. They are contending with the deep questions only a real God can answer.

We who are relatively safe and content (for now) ought to allow the calamity in Japan to spur us to prayer for others and to a dynamic change in our thinking. Disaster and death are strange friends, reminding us that the status of our soul in relation to God is at the forefront of reality. Our mundane preoccupations notwithstanding, a brief life will end, and we will face God to receive the eternity He grants according to His will and His Word.

Genuine Christians need to remember two truths during these difficult days: 1) Our mission is clear and critical, and we only have limited time. Jesus said, "As long as it is day, we must do the work of Him who sent me. Night is coming, when no one can work" (John 9:4, NIV). Friends, direct your energy to the work of God. Live the Gospel. Preach the Gospel. 2) Our focus is essential. The apostle Paul proclaimed, "So we fix our eyes not on what is seen, but on what is unseen. For what is seen is temporary, but what is unseen is eternal" (II Corinthians 4:18, NIV). We must shed the non-essential and live for what lasts. Think eternal. Live for the everlasting.

Living in Awe!

When We Almost Can't Believe God Would Still Love Us

˜

The Lord will fulfill his purpose for me; your love, O Lord, endures forever –
do not abandon the work of your hands.

Psalm 138:8 (NIV)

Have you ever had jumbled emotions? Have you ever known a fact to be true from a rational perspective, but your heart could not wrap itself around the concept? Have you ever hoped for something, but were unable to completely believe it could happen? Have you ever been caught between belief and disbelief? If so, then you fit right in with the human race, including Christians throughout the millennia.

So how does God deal with these lackluster emotions of ours? In His perfection – His holiness – does He understand our wavering and our doubts? Let us go to a Psalm of David to investigate. Since every word of the Bible is God's Word, we shall see from His heart how He reacts to our raw emotion.

Remember that David is in the lineage of Jesus. In fact, the very first verse of the book of Matthew proclaims, "A record of the genealogy of Jesus Christ the son of David, . . ." God spoke of David early in his life and said that he was, "a man after [God's] own heart" (I Samuel 13:14, NIV). David slew Goliath with a motivation to defend the name of the Lord. As king, David denounced idolatry. His overall being exuded a love for God and a trust in His providence.

However, David allowed his own fleshly desires to get the best of him at one point in his life, and he committed adultery with Bathsheba. In a futile attempt to dismiss his sin, David then had

Bathsheba's husband murdered. To what depths the man of God sank! Had he not grasped the grace of God, how could he have survived the horror of his sin? Yet, we find David to be a man fully repentant, crying out to God in Psalm 51 as he confesses his sin and trusts God for his future hope and restoration.

Keeping all this in mind, we move to Psalm 138, a song David wrote in affirmation and adoration of his Lord. It is the last verse, however, on which I want to focus. Psalm 138:8 (NIV) says, "The LORD will fulfill his purpose for me; your love, O LORD, endures forever – do not abandon the work of your hands." What a beautiful and strange statement. It seems just a bit paradoxical that David would both affirm God's providence in his life and beg God not to desert him. The shepherd boy-turned-king seems to have some juxtaposed emotions here. He boldly declares that the Lord will fulfill His purpose for David's life. He reminds us that God's love never fails. Then, in the very next phrase, David pitifully asks God to not abandon him – since David is the work of God's own hands.

Have you ever felt this way? Have you ever proclaimed God's truth to yourself, but then turned around and asked God if He would really stay? Have you ever wanted to believe, but then you needed to express your weakness in believing? By including this passage in His inspired Word, I think that God wants us to know that He understands our mixed-up emotions. He hears our human hearts. He is allowing us to see – through David – that our Lord is faithful to even wavering people. Of course, David knew God and put his ultimate hope in the Lord; but David also knew the pangs of unworthy feelings.

Surely, as David penned the words, "The LORD will fulfill his purpose for me," he recalled his terrible sin. Perhaps tears welled up in David's eyes as he declared God's unfathomable love to make sense of the life of a man who failed so miserably. Just to know that God had a divine purpose for a sinner could have driven David – as us – to a fountain of cleansing tears. And so, David continues by reminding himself that God's love "endures forever." The

Living in Awe!

Lord's love continues through failure, heartache, rebellion, hopelessness, attack, instability, and disbelief. Despite everything that would seem to push back its tide, God's love rolls on.

Finally, the frailty of David's sweetly broken heart comes through as He asks God to not abandon him. How Jesus longed to wrap His arms around David at that point and assure Him that He died to recreate David. Jesus gave His life to make David a beautiful creation – despite his weakness. How fitting it is that one of Jesus' titles is "The Son of David." What grace God has to identify with someone such as David. God is declaring that He does not give up on us. Even when we cannot quite grasp His grace – even when we waver between emotions – God is there holding us. I can just hear Jesus saying, "No, David, I will not abandon you." Similarly, the Lord reminds us in Hebrews 13:5 (NIV), "Never will I leave you; never will I forsake you."

In this verse tucked away at the end of Psalm 138, it's as if David could hardly believe in the love of God to continue with him. It seemed too good to be true. But, we know that David did "get it" way down deep inside. We, too, know that God understands His love's almost unbelievable nature. God is patient with us, and He allows us to express our need. He loves us over all the range of emotion that His grace produces.

Living in Awe!

Do My Eyes Deceive Me?

All the ways of a man are pure in his own eyes, but the Lord weighs the spirit.
Proverbs 16:2 (ESV)

Dependence on God goes far deeper than trusting Him for physical sustenance. Dependence on God is continual and necessary at the level of the unseen motives of the heart. We mortals are inclined to think we are doing right when, in fact, we may be wrongly motivated. Made in the image of God, but seriously falling short of His glory (Romans 6:23), humans depend on God to weigh the spirit within.

Our eyes can be funny things. They can deceive us into thinking that a particular selection is good simply because of its "appropriate" appearance. Recall the Lord instructing Samuel when the priest was tempted to choose the strongest looking brother in David's family, "Do not look on his appearance or on the height of his stature, because I have rejected him. For the Lord sees not as man sees: man looks on the outward appearance, but the Lord looks on the heart" (I Samuel 16:7, ESV). Recall Eve in the Garden of Eden on the brink of rebelling against God, "So when the woman saw that the tree was good for food, and that it was a delight to the eyes, . . . she took of its fruit and ate, . . ." (Genesis 3:6, ESV). In both historical accounts, a person's eyes saw something that the heart interpreted as good. However, what was seen needed to be filtered by the Lord. Whether the man looked tall and strong or the fruit looked delightful was not the real issue. The vital component was the Lord's view of the choices. As Proverbs 16:2 proclaims, "All the ways of a man are pure in his own eyes, but the Lord weighs the spirit."

Recently I had to reject some options that mere eyes may view as good and prosperous. However, God made clear to me

Living in Awe!

that what "looked right" was not His will. For many years, I have prayed for God to weigh the motivations of my heart. I have asked Him to never let me be led astray – even sincerely so. Though we fail Him, He will be faithful to show us the "measurement" of our spirit after He carefully weighs our motivations. At that moment, we must make a critical decision to abide by God's assessment rather than what, at first, appears pure to our eyes.

Please take time today to pray this proverb. We ought to request that God weigh our spirit and show us the truth beyond what the eyes observe at first glance. Quite purposefully, God's admonition to check our heart before responding with our eyes is followed directly by a favorite verse of many Christians, "Commit your work to the LORD, and your plans will be established" (Proverbs 16:3, ESV). The first step in committing any plan to the LORD is to be sure it is His plan. What our physical or emotional eyes may see notwithstanding, it is God's will that matters. He establishes our plans when we trust Him above our own – often failing – instinct. We are not animals living solely by our inclinations, we are God's image-bearers, living by His direction, for which we plead each step of the way.

Dear Lord, please get out the scale and weigh my spirit!

Living in Awe!

Seasons and Changes UNDER Heaven

*There is an appointed time for everything.
And there is a time for every event under heaven.*

Ecclesiastes 3:1

One day I sat at my desk with my Bible and pondered some deep issues. This is not an unusual occurrence for me, but the thought God brought to me that day stands out in my memory. My face was not turned toward my desk, as I sat with my chair facing a bookshelf. My forearms rested on my knees as I grasped my Bible in both hands. I wanted God to speak directly to my heart, for I was feeling a rush of emotions. After gazing generally at the open pages of my Bible, I bowed my head and whispered a prayer to God. My head just hung there, and my body was bent over, waiting to sense God's presence. Just then, I decided to look up and out the window. As I did, my eye caught a poster hanging on my office wall. A bright butterfly was pictured beside the words of Ecclesiastes 3:1, "There is an appointed time for everything. And there is a time for every event under heaven." The words of the poster held my gaze for more than a few moments. My spirit focused on two words, under heaven. A rush of profound relief came over my mind as I sensed God impress on me this thought, "Shelli, everything under heaven changes and goes through seasons, and I [God] am in control all the while."

My attempted description of God's working in my heart that day simply cannot adequately relate how the Lord did a miracle for my thinking through His Word. I pray He will radically infiltrate your heart with the truth too. Under heaven – on this earth – we will experience the ebb and flow of life. Some seasons and changes are the direct result of God's mandate for the natural world: morning follows night, autumn follows summer, and a harvest follows planting. Some seasons and changes are the results

Living in Awe!

of man's will, whether his will is aimed at God or is in rebellion to God. A man may choose to shun embracing when true agreement over critical issues can no longer be reached. A woman may begin a season of laughter after a long struggle to emerge from grief. A man may embark on a season of dancing while blessings flow. A woman may choose to try to sew together various pieces of her life. A nation may declare war. A man may begin a time of searching for lost family relationships. Another may choose to embrace a season of loss rather than to continue a search. As these innumerable events continue under the canopy of heaven, God sits on His throne, carefully ensuring that "all things [work] after the counsel of His will" (Ephesians 1:11b). This is our assurance. Seasons come, and seasons go; but all events are appointed by a God with a plan.

The Hebrew root word implies that "there is a time for every 'delight or pleasure' under heaven." In other words, while we remain in this world, times of delight will come in spurts. A time of birth is amazing, but times of death come too. Even though we experience wonderful seasons of love, hate is close by. We rejoice in seasons of building up, and we mourn in seasons of tearing down. In this life, things are volatile. Pleasure and delight are limited, held to their seasons by the damning nature of sin.

However, our wonderful God assures us that His limitation of delight only happens under heaven. One day, we shall be in Heaven with God! Psalm 16:11 shall come to pass for us, "In Your [God's] presence is fullness of joy; In Your right hand there are pleasures forever." Praise to our God! No more will there be only seasons of pleasure; but we shall then experience the absolute, all-pervasive nature of God's joy, untainted by sin.

The apostle John's testimony resonates with the book of Ecclesiastes. In Heaven, there will be no more death or mourning (Revelation 21:4). Those seasons (as outlined in Ecclesiastes 3:2, 4) will be gone, and the fullness of life and joy will have entered in. In

Heaven, all will come together. All will love and experience blessed peace. All will be healed.

Until that day, I remember that the changes I now experience are seasons in the hands of a mighty God who stands above the earth, above the universe, and above every changing circumstance. Somehow, He has appointed every time and season. He not only sees what I am facing, He is in charge of it. I will trust the God who is over all, even as I wait for fullness of joy.

What Fallen Bridges Tell Us About God

And this I pray, that your love may abound still more and more in real knowledge and all discernment . . .
Philippians 1:9

On August 1, 2007, the I-35W bridge in Minnesota collapsed into the Mississippi River, killing thirteen people and injuring 145 others. This human tragedy is devastating, with consequences of death. Research points to miscalculation of gusset plate width as the reason the bridge collapsed.

Gusset plates are thick sheets of steel that provide strength at the intersection of beams. Apparently, the gusset plates used on the I-35W Bridge were not thick enough to support the added weight of construction vehicles and concrete that would come with time and use. It is essential for engineers to use exact calculations and mathematical formulas when building bridges. The physical universe only accepts true and accurate work; otherwise, disaster ensues. In medicine as well as construction, precision is necessary. Diabetics suffer physically and may die with a miscalculation of insulin dose, for example. The Creator of the universe has chosen to have the physical world operate according to mathematical and physical laws; this situation reflects His unchanging, reliable disposition.

Supernatural God runs the natural world with serious precision. Proper functioning requires uncompromised accuracy. If God has made this true of the natural realm, how much more is it true of the supernatural realm; for, the supernatural is more real than the physical! God Himself is supernatural, and the One from Whom all reality flows. His spiritual working requires exactitude to the same or greater degree than His tangible working. Certainly, the consequences of spiritual errors are infinitely graver than even the catastrophe of inaccuracy in the physical world. Injury and death are horrors, for sure; but the calamity of a lost soul in eternity trumps all earthly afflictions.

And so, with an urgent heart, the Apostle Paul calls to us in Philippians 1:9, "And this I pray, that your love may abound still more and more in real knowledge and all discernment." Do you see the connection here between love and knowledge? To Paul – and to God – love is not a feeling. Love grows in real knowledge. The building of a spiritual life requires unequivocal accuracy. If we think bridge building requires right engineering processes, how much more does soul building require right spiritual processes?

Our relationship to God must be built on truth! We need to study His Word as an engineer studies math and science to ensure design and construction according to reality. Our spiritual lives must be built on right knowledge. This will require sacrifice of time and effort. The risk is not physical injury or death, but spiritual injury and eternal death. The stakes are high, and it is time for Christians to take seriously the call for our love to abound in real knowledge and all discernment.

The church of Jesus Christ seems to be missing the call to methodical, intentional, and precise training in spiritual knowledge. Dean (2010) comments on the problems presented in the National Study of Youth and Religion,

> We "teach" young people baseball, but we "expose" them to faith. We provide coaching and opportunities for youth to develop and improve their pitches and SAT scores, but we blithely assume that religious identity will happen by osmosis, emerging "when youth are ready" (a confidence we generally lack when it comes to, say, algebra). (15)

We would not allow our loved ones to drive over bridges that we knew were designed without proper knowledge of or regard for mathematical principles. We trust that bridges are designed by professionals who have invested much time and effort into a solid education in the field of engineering. Here are some pivotal questions: Are we allowing our loved ones to drive over spiritual bridges designed and built on patchwork theology? Are we truly investing in a serious understanding of God as revealed in His Word? How much time do we spend intentionally growing in real knowledge? Do our children know sports better than the revelation of God Almighty? Do we require they know algebra well, but settle for a haphazard understanding of the things of God?

Jesus once said to an earnest inquirer named Nicodemus, "If I told you earthly things and you do not believe, how will you believe if I tell you heavenly things?" (John 3:12) In other words, the earthly points to the heavenly, which is far deeper and greater. Think bridges – fallen bridges. What is God saying to us through the physical, mathematical knowledge required for safety? He is telling us to get serious about biblical knowledge. Fallen souls are far more costly than fallen bridges.

Greater than a Fairy Tale

*For if while we were enemies we were reconciled to God
through the death of His Son, much more,
having been reconciled, we shall be saved by His life.*

Romans 5:10

If God brings us to Himself through the death of His Son, can you imagine what He does through the life of His Son, now that we are near? If God loved us enough to reconcile us to Himself while we were still in rebellious sin against Him, can you imagine what He will do for us now that we are on His side?

The questions above reflect the heart of God's Word found in Romans 5:10, "For if while we were enemies we were reconciled to God through the death of His Son, much more, having been reconciled, we shall be saved by His life." The words of this passage have penetrated my mind and soul at least three times in the past few months.

Perhaps at times fearful that we will be functioning in fairy-tale land if we hope too much, I believe followers of Jesus sometimes live far beneath His blessing because we do not digest His truth as He intended. The message is right there in Paul's letter to the Romans: God saved us from His wrath by Jesus' death, and He shall surely deliver us in all ways imaginable by Jesus' life. We need not be afraid that this verse is too good to be true. After all, fairy tales are the result of human imagination flowing from a mind given by a God who has an unbelievable "end" to this "story" of life. In other words, we can only dream of great endings because we were made in the image of the all-creative God who has planned from the foundation of the earth a real and tangible culmination to history that defies the highest expectation of limited, human reasoning. Fairy tales do not discourage me, but rather remind me that we were originally intended to "think big." The momentous point to remember is that the God behind our creation is actually able to complete His plan for reality! Human fairytales are feeble, short-sighted shadows pointing to an Almighty God who works in the stuff of actuality and truth.

Friends, stand on the promise that "we shall be saved by His life." Jesus' death was so powerful it brings sinners close to a holy God. How much more powerful is the life of Jesus! For one, we know that as He lives, He intercedes for us. Hebrews 7:25 proclaims, "Therefore He is able also to save forever those who draw near to God through Him, since He always lives to make intercession for them." The sacrifice of Jesus' life and blood paid the cost for our nearness to God, and now that we love our King, Jesus is so pleased to present us continually to the Father for help and deliverance.

We also know that the resurrection of Jesus has caused us to be "born again to a living hope" (I Peter 1:3). As a child comes out of a mother's womb and is surrounded by air he must now breathe, so Christians emerge from sinful darkness and are now enveloped by the hope of God they must now take in.

Do we face difficulty and disappointment? Certainly we do. However, do we have God's promise for ultimate deliverance? Absolutely, we do! As surely as spring follows winter – and as surely as Jesus' resurrection followed His death – that is how surely our deliverance will follow difficulty and disappointment.

If God loved us when we were rotten and staunchly turned against Him, will He not love us now that we have run into His arms? If God thought us valuable enough to send His Son to die, does He not count us valuable enough to benefit from His Son's life? This metanarrative – this overarching plan of God for the universe – turns out greater for followers of Jesus Christ than our minds can comprehend.

Actually, it does not just "turn out" that way; it exceeds what we can imagine in this present moment, because not one circumstance is lost in the working of God. Jesus, the Son of God, is all-knowing. He lives and intercedes for us. He does not miss one thing. Not one. As He goes to the Father on our behalf for every great and infinitesimal circumstance of our lives, the Holy Spirit moves in ways sometimes obvious and often mysterious to save us completely. We are being shaped into who we need to be for God's glory and to shine in that beautiful Heaven of His. This is no fairy tale, but a true account of the God in charge of reality.

A Warning with an Astonishing Promise

> Seek the LORD while he may be found; call upon him while he is near . . .
> Isaiah 55:6 (ESV)

We simply do not have forever to seek and find God. The implication of His straightforward message is clear, "Seek the LORD while he may be found; call upon him while he is near" (Isaiah 55:6, ESV). Obviously, then, there is a time that He may be found; but that time has an end point. Likewise, He remains near in His willingness to receive sorrowful people repenting of sin; but He stays close in this way for only a season. Two future time frames appear on every human horizon: 1) a person's own death, and 2) God's full revelation of His final wrath. Since we can escape neither event, we must be prepared for them. The only and glorious provision for safety is seeking God while He is ready to be found. If we need to cry out in repentance, now is the time to call. More important than clean dishes, a televised sports event, completed homework, a dusted dining room, dinner out with friends, a brisk walk, or any other impending task is the responsibility of calling out to our God who – for this moment at least – can still be encountered as One ready to receive us.

And do not be afraid to seek Him now. For this is His promise, "let the wicked forsake his way, and the unrighteous man his thoughts; let him return to the LORD, that he may have compassion on him, and to our God, for he will abundantly pardon" (Isaiah 55:7, ESV). How beautifully the words ring out that a wicked person – one who is guilty of sin – and an unrighteous person – one who is troubled by his vain pursuit of sinful ways – can both return to the Lord to find compassion! We expect our treachery has no cure, and we fear the reaction we so commonly find in other humans. But, no! When we forsake sin and turn toward God, He covers us with mercy and tender affection.

Living in Awe!

Moreover, He welcomes us back in such a manner that the Bible describes as "abundant pardon." The Hebrew root of the word pardon is forgiveness backed by the idea of "lightness" or "lifting up." The burden of guilt is removed, and we are once again raised up by God. We can walk freely with a spiritual and emotional spring in our step, for God has forgiven us.

He pardons us abundantly, not sparingly or with a grudge. The same word used here for "abundantly" is used in Genesis 1:22 to describe the multiplication of sea creatures in the ocean and birds in the sky following God's initial creation. Can you imagine? Can you picture the innumerable fish in the depths of the sea? The untold amount of microscopic plankton filling the waters? The countless little birds and butterflies in the skies above us? Those realities are to remind us of the amount of forgiveness – enough to cover every sin – which God offers to those who cry out now.

Does the compassion of God seem incomprehensible to us sinful people? It surely may be to us, but this does not negate its reality. When you think it's too good to be true, you need to read God's reminder to us, "For my thoughts are not your thoughts, neither are your ways my ways, declares the Lord. For as the heavens are higher than the earth, so are my ways higher than your ways and my thoughts than your thoughts" (Isaiah 55:8-9, ESV). Yes – it is true – I do not understand the depth of His forgiveness. My mind cannot wrap itself around such an offer of hope. Yet, there it is. The reason I don't quite "get it" is that God's thoughts and ways are infinitely higher than mine. He is altogether perfect, the Definer of what is. I will trust that what I cannot understand remains real, for the Maker of human reasoning capacity is greater than human reasoning.

Seek Him now; call upon Him while He is near, because the opportunity will not last forever. He will abundantly pardon. It seems too good to be true, but it is not. It is the way of God.

Integrity, the Second Law of Thermodynamics, and Jesus

> Blessed is the man who does not walk in the counsel of the wicked
> or stand in the way of sinners or sit in the seat of mockers. But his delight
> is in the law of the Lord, and on his law he meditates day and night.
> He is like a tree planted by streams of water, which yields its fruit in season
> and whose leaf does not wither.
>
> Psalm 1:1-3 (NIV)

Integrity is not a boring word. In fact, integrity encapsulates much of that for which we humans long. Integrity is not a fluffy concept; it is a very real and rich component of God's world. Integrity and the second law of thermodynamics have an all-important, inverse relationship. The importance of integrity is observed in mathematics as well as science, in relationships as well as language. Integrity hints of Heaven, a very real place where all will be as it ought to be.

Consider the phrase, "My world is falling apart." When spoken, we realize these words imply something ominous. A common response to the phrase might be, "Pull yourself together." Note that "falling apart" is associated with something bad and "pulling together" is associated with something good. Why? Even our language reflects the inner desire for integrity – wholeness or the state of being unbroken. Consider simple arithmetic. Would you rather add five whole numbers or five fractions? We like to deal with whole numbers or integers because we can easily wrap our minds around these. Fractions are messy and confusing; they take time to digest.

In much the same way, a human being without integrity is hard to figure. His life is confusing because he is broken. The essence of him is one way in one situation and another way in a different situation. Your mind cannot wrap itself around who the person truly is. This is precisely because we desire integrity; we desire to know people for who they truly are. A person without integrity becomes untrustworthy and easily shaken.

Lack of integrity – or disintegration – pops up not only in people and mathematics, it is embedded in the fallen universe. Scientific laws reflect disintegration's reality and, therefore, reflect the very real necessity of integrity. The first law of thermodynamics pronounces that our universe is a closed system; the amount of matter and energy in our world is constant. The second law of thermodynamics proclaims that, although the amount of energy in the universe is constant, the amount of useful energy is running down. As energy is converted, waste is produced. The world – for all practical purposes – is falling apart and disintegrating.

We note the effects of the second law of thermodynamics all around us. Our bodies are wearing out and winding down. Atrophy sets into the muscles unless we act upon them with force and energy. A room left to itself for very long will no doubt become disorganized unless energy is applied to its cleaning. Metal objects begin to rust. Erosion takes place. Everything is winding down and wearing out in its natural state. The second law of thermodynamics was set into motion by the sin curse. When mankind gave into sin and rebelled against God's way, God cursed man and woman, the serpent who deceived them, and the earth. To this very day, we suffer the effects of that curse in our hearts, our minds, our bodies, and in our universe.

Directly related to the physical effects of sin in this world is the very real effect of brokenness of heart. The curse of sin on us as people who have rebelled against God has produced a state of disintegration in our spiritual lives. For this reason, we tend not to keep our word, we tend to think one way and act another, we tend to portray ourselves one way to others and find ourselves quite another in the quietness of solitude. We are broken people

Living in Awe!

in a broken world. Disintegration and the second law of thermodynamics are related – they both reflect a rebellious state of things. We have failed God. Only God maintains a standard which produces perfection.

Is there hope? Hope is found only in Jesus Christ, the God-Man. As fully God, Jesus is holy. As fully man, Jesus is able to pay the price for human sin. When a man or woman comes to Jesus and trusts Him as the sacrifice for his or her sinfulness, that man or woman is made right with holy God. At that moment, a person becomes a new creation, fully re-made in his spirit (II Corinthians 5:17). This person is now in right-standing with God because Jesus has settled the sin factor between man and God. As relationship with Jesus Christ is maintained, a person continues to grow in righteousness. Righteousness is simply the state of "being as we ought to be" or being as God originally intended. While on this sin-cursed earth, perfection will never be complete. However, the spirit in the new man or woman desires righteousness and knows that Heaven holds the answer to disintegration of the mind, body, emotions, and universe.

Psalm 1:1-3a (NIV) says, "Blessed is the man who does not walk in the counsel of the wicked or stand in the way of sinners or sit in the seat of mockers. But his delight is in the law of the LORD, and on his law he meditates day and night. He is like a tree planted by streams of water, which yields its fruit in season and whose leaf does not wither." The withering leaf is a part of the second law of thermodynamics. Death and destruction are built into a fallen, rebellious world. It is quite natural for leaves to wither. What God promises, however, is that the law of nature can be overridden in the human heart when we love His Word and apply it to our lives in the midst of this broken world! A person who makes the law of the Lord his focus in the everyday moments of life will defy the sin curse. The inner man – the essence of who we are – will stand strong. Although disintegration produces confusion and destruction, the person following the Lord will be a person of integrity. We will be clearly understood for who we are, we will bring life and healing as opposed to death and hurt, we will reflect the place to which we are ultimately called – Heaven.

Remember that Jesus will come back one day to this world in which we live, and after He has brought judgment to those who have rejected Him, He will re-make this world. He will forever destroy the second law of thermodynamics and every kind of disintegration. Wholeness and life will finally prevail.

Regular Miracles

> Therefore you shall do my statutes and keep my rules and perform them, and then you will dwell in the land securely. The land will yield its fruit, and you will eat your fill and dwell in it securely. And if you say, 'What shall we eat in the seventh year, if we may not sow or gather in our crop?' I will command my blessing on you in the sixth year, so that it will produce a crop sufficient for three years.
> Leviticus 25:18-21 (ESV)

God clearly directed His people to acknowledge Him as the Provider and to allow the land to rest every seventh year. Though an agricultural people – depending on the field and the vine for sustenance – the Israelites were to cease from sowing and pruning every seven years (Leviticus 25:1-5). The continual cycle of six years of work followed by one year of rest demonstrated at the most basic level of life that God's will is the number one priority.

Knowing some of the Israelites would ask the same question I would ask, God preempts their doubt with this stunning statement, "And if you say, 'What shall we eat in the seventh year, if we may not sow or gather in our crop?' I will command my blessing on you in the sixth year, so that it will produce a crop sufficient for three years. When you sow in the eighth year, you will be eating some of the old crop; you shall eat the old until the ninth year, when its crop arrives" (Leviticus 25:20-22, ESV). Yes, God knew many of His people would question the practicality of the plan. How would they have enough to eat if no planting or harvesting happens for an entire twelve months? (Remember, the Israelites had no Wal-Mart!) The resounding answer comes back, "God is both the Giver of the harvest and the Grower of the crops."

Living for the Lord is not for the faint of heart – for those who do not grasp God's sovereignty over the very essence

Living in Awe!

of reality. Psalm 24:1 (ESV) comes to mind, "The earth is the Lord's and the fullness thereof, the world and those who dwell therein." If we believe this basic premise of God's rightful ownership of all creation, the corollary follows that He can, therefore, dictate creation's path. In other words, the Lord is fully able to require the land to yield three years of crop for one year of planting. He made the earth, and He sustains it. The land must follow the voice of God.

The question becomes, "Why?" Why would God require the land to yield a supernatural crop in the sixth year? Why would He faithfully provide sustenance during a season when no sowing occurred? This continual, rhythmic cycle of provision for the seventh year took place because of the continual, rhythmic obedience of those who love God. Leviticus 25:18 (ESV) makes clear, "Therefore you shall do my statutes and keep my rules and perform them, and then you will dwell in the land securely."

God reveals to us a right and productive way to operate. He knows "the land" best. He knows our lives best. He understands the way things ought to function. Moreover, He has the power to interject regular miracles into the flow of life. With obedience comes the consistent provision of God. As we trust the Lord enough to obey Him – even when it does not appear to make sense – God persistently offers His miraculous intervention in the daily stuff of our lives. To the Israelites, food and drink were basic and necessary (as they are with us!) The Lord consistently provided – even in the seventh year following a season without planting. The rational man without belief in God cannot see how this would naturally happen. However, the man of faith and rationality who trusts in God can see this as a reaction of God to His child's obedience. God moves heaven and earth for His people!

We may not always realize this rather rhythmic provision, but the Lord is giving us breath, food, love, sanity, and hope. Even in the Old Testament, God promises consistent miracles with consistent obedience. Can you imagine His provision fully realized in Jesus Christ? I am given opportunity to be God's child through Jesus, and I am given the strength to obey by His Spirit. Let us seek to regularly obey and regularly watch God work supernaturally!

Living in Awe!

The Cup and this Pitiful Creature

I tell you I will not drink again of this fruit of the vine until that day when I drink it new with you in my Father's kingdom.

Matthew 26:29 (ESV)

After sharing the Passover meal, Jesus instituted with His disciples the Lord's Supper. Toward the end of that event – after sharing the cup – Jesus proclaimed, "I tell you I will not drink again of this fruit of the vine until that day when I drink it new with you in my Father's kingdom" (Matthew 26:29, ESV). The following poem is based on that profound and comforting statement of Jesus Christ.

> Your promise to them
> Is Your promise to me;
> We will dine together
> When my sorrow does flee.
>
> Though burdened so greatly
> With the task just ahead,
> You demonstrated by simple cup
> I have nothing to dread.
>
> The fruit of the vine
> You drank on that day
> Is a weighty reminder -
> God gets His way.
>
> For though you would leave
> Soon after the cup,
> You said you'd come back
> As I keep looking up.

Living in Awe!

And Your loving heart realized
What I needed to know:
This special communion
Would not end, but grow.

So as you started down
Your dark road to Calvary,
You spoke words I treasure
In the deepest part of me:

"I won't drink again
Of this fruit of the vine
Until the day we sup together
And your hand is in mine."

Jesus, how I love you
For saving the purest wine
For the day without suffering
When together we dine.

In the Father's kingdom
So exceeding mortal comprehension,
We will talk and share together
When of sin there is no mention.

Surely we will have joy and life
And eating and friendship beyond the veil,
For your promises are true
And your plan can never fail.

The banquet of the Messiah;
How I long for that day!
When I will get to hug you
For the life you gave away.

Living in Awe!

Why are you waiting
To drink again the cup with me?
Oh, how special to you, Jesus,
This pitiful creature must be!

Embarrassed?

For whoever is ashamed of me and of my words in this adulterous and sinful generation, of him will the Son of Man also be ashamed when he comes in the glory of his Father with the holy angels.
Mark 8:38 (ESV)

Have you ever been embarrassed to talk about Jesus? Have you ever felt funny about including Bible verses in regular conversation? Let's now take this up a notch . . . Have you ever felt weird about including Jesus or His words in a get-together with another Christian? I have been in all three situations.

The world in general is largely opposed to Jesus Christ but comfortable with religion. The culture may even accept the idea of the Bible's existence, but the world certainly deems it odd to ponder the Bible's contents over coffee. And what about the church in general? Even among Christians, conversation and activity often swells around topics of little eternal significance. A person can find himself frowned upon for making Jesus or the Word of God a central part of thought and interaction. This should not be, my friends. But so it is.

Our own sin in this area should sicken us. Here is the straightforward deal spoken by Jesus Himself, "For whoever is ashamed of me and of my words in this adulterous and sinful generation, of him will the Son of Man also be ashamed when he comes in the glory of his Father with the holy angels" (Mark 8:38, ESV). This truth is both hard-hitting and not difficult to comprehend. If we are ashamed of Him and His Bible, He will be ashamed of us. But, take notice of the details. Jesus makes no excuses for our embarrassment just because the world is "so wicked." He tells us we are not to be ashamed even in the midst of sinfulness and adultery. The adultery He seems to speak of here is people's spiritual unfaithfulness to their Creator. The unsaved world is very sinful, and the church is often unfaithful. Still, the lover of Jesus is to proudly speak of Him and His Word. We are to allow no hostile situation or the lukewarm attitudes of friends or family stop us from centering our thoughts, words, and actions on the Person of Jesus Christ and the Bible.

If we choose to continue in the sin of being ashamed as we walk this difficult path in a sinful world, then Jesus will be ashamed of us in the light of His glory – surrounded by angels. Yes, I am called to stand firm and love Him and promote Him as my very life – no matter what. If some Christians think I am crazy for obsessing over Jesus and His Word, so be it. If unbelievers become malicious in word or deed, so be it. One day – if we remain faithful – our Jesus will be proud to call us His own when everything is finally made right. Stand up for Him and His words in a harsh and evil world, and He will stand up for you in a new and glorious world! The other option . . . well, I don't even want to think about that.

Living in Awe!

God on Good and Bad Days

~~~

> They will perish, but You remain; and they all will become old like a garment, and like a mantle You will roll them up; like a garment they will also be changed. But You are the same, and Your years will not come to an end.
> Hebrews 1:11-12

While cleaning our house recently, I was keenly reminded of a vital spiritual truth: God never changes, though my emotions do. Have you ever had a bad day? A good day? A mediocre day? What does it imply for us to qualify any given day by a description that is usually tied closely to our emotional state? For example, while enduring an incredibly minor inconvenience, I realized how quickly I can become irritated by circumstances. In that very moment, God brought to mind James 1:2-4 (NIV), "Consider it pure joy, my brothers, whenever you face trials of many kinds, because you know that the testing of your faith develops perseverance. Perseverance must finish its work so that you may be mature and complete, not lacking anything." The very thing that Satan would like to use to harass me is actually something God employs to help make me complete. God does not have "good" or "bad" days; He has created the whole concept of days and is continually in charge of them – with His glory as the end in mind.

Often we need to step back and realize that God's plan for us never changes. He is in no way caught off guard by any component of our lives. In fact, He superintends all of our joys and trials to make us who we are supposed to be – "conformed to the likeness of His Son" (Romans 8:29, NIV).

We experience moments, hours, and days when we do not feel the presence or goodness of God, but this in no way changes the fact of His abiding love. We humans are fleeting, changeable, easily-confused, moody, and limited in our understanding. In fact, when compared to God, even the heavens and earth "will perish, but You [God] remain; and they all will become old like a garment, and like a mantle You will roll them up; like a garment they will also be changed. But You are the same, and Your years will not come to an end" (Hebrews 1:11-12).

Everything changes except God, who stands above all reality and takes control as He sees fit. His unchanging nature – His immutability – is our hope on "good" and "bad" days. Though we may be feeling discouraged, God is never thwarted. He is not downtrodden, because He is perfect and knows the supremacy of His plan; and even though He reigns, He has compassion on us in times of disappointment and grief. Psalm 103:13-14 (NIV) declares, "As a father has compassion on his children, so the LORD has compassion on those who fear him; for he knows how we are formed, he remembers that we are dust."

What spectacular news! God's plan goes on no matter how dark the day or inconvenient the circumstances. We need not be overcome by the flood of emotions we experience as created beings. Instead, we need to remind ourselves of the eternal Word of God which boldly proclaims, "God is our refuge and strength, a very present help in trouble. Therefore we will not fear, though the earth should change and though the mountains slip into the heart of the sea; though its waters roar and foam, though the mountains quake at its swelling pride. There is a river whose streams make glad the city of God, the holy dwelling places of the Most High. God is in the midst of her, she will not be moved; God will help her when the morning dawns" (Psalm 46:1-5).

Did you catch that phrase above, "though its waters roar and foam"? Sometimes that is how we imagine the flood of feelings that come against us – they roar and foam and threaten our demise. No way, however, will they be our undoing! God is always present and in the midst of our emotions; He cannot be moved. Cling to God, stand on His truth, and remember Who He is. Our

Living in Awe!

God is both unchanging and unchangeable. He cannot change and He will not be changed by anyone or anything. On good days and bad days and every moment in between, our God stands ready to roll up the heavens and earth like a garment in order to usher in His perfect kingdom where we will finally see that He had it under control all along.

Living in Awe!

Enduring and Moving

> By faith Moses, when he had grown up, refused to be called the son of Pharaoh's daughter, choosing rather to endure ill-treatment with the people of God than to enjoy the passing pleasures of sin, considering the reproach of Christ greater riches than the treasures of Egypt; for he was looking to the reward. By faith he left Egypt, not fearing the wrath of the king; for he endured, as seeing Him who is unseen.
>
> Hebrews 11:24-27

At times it is necessary to move. When the status quo is against God's plan, the status quo must be left behind. Of course, it feels comfortable to stay with what is familiar, for – as disappointing as the familiar can be – at least we know we are surviving there. Exiting a place or circumstance with which we are accustomed can potentially be scary. Only one thing is to be feared more – God's displeasure.

When Moses left Egypt, he had worldly reason to fear the king. The powerful pharaoh would not be pleased with this Hebrew's renunciation of Egypt. Even though Moses was a Hebrew by blood, he had grown up in and been educated by this mighty nation. Though he had benefitted greatly from Egypt's riches, he now felt called by His God to leave. Yes, it had been God's will for Moses to be in the heart of Egypt, for we know he was found by the pharaoh's daughter on the Nile River in that basket of reeds his mother had so prayerfully prepared and sent. And now, it was also God's will for Moses to exit – in preparation for the furthering of God's kingdom. God may put us somewhere, and then carefully draw us away . . . all for the best of His kingdom.

The Hebrews were enslaved to the Egyptians, and Moses could no longer stand idly by and watch God's people be wrongly mistreated. He felt God tug on His heart to become part of God's next move on behalf of His beloved Hebrews. However, becoming part of God's plan would require Moses to now "endure ill-treatment with the people of God [rather] than to enjoy the passing pleasures of sin" (Hebrews 11:25). On the one side stands ill treatment, and on the other stands sin's temporary pleasure and ease. To leave Egypt now will mean Moses' life will become difficult. He will be persecuted by the enemy. He will give up riches and ease and familiarity. Wisely, Moses takes the long-term view. He understands that ill treatment now is infinitely better than temporary pleasure coupled with eternal regret.

Moses determines to persevere by moving. The Bible records, "By faith [Moses] left Egypt, not fearing the wrath of the king; for he endured, as seeing Him who is unseen" (Hebrews 11:27). Do you observe that word "endured"? The root of the word is "steadfast," and here is the only place this particular Greek word is used in the Bible. Moses stayed faithful to God by doing two things: 1) not fearing the power he was leaving behind, and 2) enduring by keeping his heart fixed on an invisible God.

Our Lord who is now invisible is greater than any power we might be inclined to fear when we press forward in God's will. Though we cannot yet see our God, He is the "King eternal, immortal, invisible, the only God" (I Timothy 1:17). Moses did not fear the wrath of the king of Egypt because He revered the true King who – while now invisible – is eternally the Boss of everything!

We, too, can endure as we keep the eyes of our heart fixed on the unseen Ruler of the universe. We need not look behind, or over our shoulder, fearfully wondering how the enemy might pursue us. Not only is the pleasure of sin temporary, so is the terror of sinners and Satan.

Soon after Moses' obedience, he and the Hebrews passed through the Red Sea on dry land. But, "the Egyptians, when they attempted it, were drowned" (Hebrews 11:29). My friends, we need to move when God says to move, no matter how difficult the road ahead appears. To stay would be sin when God says to go. The ill treatment we suffer will not last forever, and our future deliverance is a sure thing. God will make the way for us no matter how ominous the sea in front. All who stand in opposition to the Lord will eventually drown in despair.

"We shall endure." What an all-encompassing phrase! We shall endure because we have our sights fixed on the invisible, eternal God who has His perfect plan. We shall endure . . . as we move.

Imperishable Seed Beyond the Boundary of Science

For you have been born again, not of perishable seed, but of imperishable, through the living and enduring word of God. For 'All men are like grass, and all their glory is like the flowers of the field; the grass withers and the flowers fall, but the word of the Lord stands forever.' And this is the word that was preached to you.

I Peter 1:23-25 (NIV)

My recent trip to the local library led to my finding a new non-fiction book, "Long for this World," by Jonathan Weiner (2010). I have not read the volume, only its inside front cover. The book's subtitle is "The Strange Science of Immortality," and the last sentences of its main description are "could we live forever? And if we could . . . would we want to?"

The pursuit of immortality has always intrigued mortals precisely because we are just that – mortal. Created by an eternal God, we long for the everlasting. Having had death introduced to us with the commencement of human sinfulness, we most naturally long to regain what has been lost – eternal life. Those of an atheistic bent seek immortality by walking the path of science, hoping for continued advancements right up to the point of deathlessness. The problem is that science can only investigate the natural world, which – for the astute Christian – hints persistently at the attributes of the biblical God (Romans 1:20). However, the natural world alone contains not the solution for death. For the obliteration of ultimate human demise, we must turn to the supernatural. Science is limited by God; its boundaries are set in such a way that it cannot fix the human spirit. Only the Maker of both natural and supernatural things can reach into the depths of the unseen spirit of men and women, and only He can do work there. Death comes to the natural body because death has come to the spirit. The spirit must be fixed for the body to live.

Enter the glorious words of I Peter 1:23-25 (NIV), "For you have been born again, not of perishable seed, but of imperishable, through the living and enduring word of God. For 'All men are like grass, and all their glory is like the flowers of the field; the grass withers and the flowers fall, but the word of the Lord stands forever.' And this is the word that was preached to you." As God's Word proclaims, not only are we as fleeting as the grass in the field, but our glory is as transitory as the flower's blossom. One day we see it, and the next day it is withered. In stark contrast stands the mighty Word of God that literally endures forever.

The key for our help comes from verse twenty-three, which declares that we can be born again of a seed that never perishes. Inside a person, an eternal seed of life can be planted through the Word of God that has the power to carry a mortal over the chasm of earthly death into the astonishing reality of life everlasting. Moreover, this precious, indescribable Word is very close. Peter declares that this living and enduring Word of God "is the word which was preached to you" (I Peter 1:25, NIV). The Word that enables a sinful, dead spirit to be reborn into a righteous, living spirit is the Word about which you are reading right now! God has not kept this Word from us, but He has sent it to us!

The Bible is God's written Word, and Jesus Christ is God's living Word. At this very moment, He has come to you to deliver the incorruptible seed of life. A human spirit is dead because of sin; it needs a living seed planted in it in order to live and last forever. No string of scientific breakthroughs can ever blast through the impenetrable wall of mortality; only the eternal Word of God, Jesus, can carry a mortal past death to life.

Jesus said, "I am the Living One; I was dead, and behold I am alive for ever and ever!" (Revelation 1:18, NIV). Jesus begins alive.

Living in Awe!

We begin dead. We are born into corruption by our very nature. Jesus is God, and so "Before the mountains were born or [He] gave birth to the earth and the world, even from everlasting to everlasting, [He] is God" (Psalm 90:2). Jesus was alive before He came to earth, and He rose from death after bearing the penalty for our sin. Notice God's Word says Jesus is the Living One, that He was physically dead for a brief period, and that He is presently alive forever and ever.

Jesus can plant the imperishable seed of His salvation in us. Then, we can follow Him in this world. Ultimately, we can follow Him in His pattern of life after death. One amazing day, we will be able to stand with Him in Heaven and say, "I was dead, but now I am alive forever because of Jesus!"

Back to the inside cover description of "Long for this World." The last question is, "And if we could [live forever] . . . would we want to?" In a world that is itself crying out for redemption and restoration (Romans 8:20-23), I believe we realize we would not want to live forever in the present state of things; with disaster, disease, and disappointment abounding in every direction. "This world" needs changed, just as we do. We long to be immortal, but in a perfect world. The flawless world is coming, my friends. In the same way that we are made imperishable – by the Word of God – this creation will be rendered right. II Peter 3:5, 7, 12-13 (NIV) tells us, "Long ago by God's word the heavens existed and the earth was formed out of water and by water . . . By the same word the present heavens and earth are reserved for fire, being kept for the day of judgment and destruction of ungodly men . . . That day will bring about the destruction of the heavens by fire, and the elements will melt in the heat. But in keeping with his promise we are looking forward to a new heaven and a new earth, the home of righteousness."

There it is . . . crystal clear. The Word of God brings an imperishable seed to humans and to the universe. Immortality is not so much a "strange science" as it is the loving work of a redeeming

God. Our supernatural God blasts through the natural to deliver to us immortality and an unbroken cosmos, something science can never do. Though you may have enjoyed or endured many science classes, know also that the Word of God has come to you this day, offering an imperishable seed!

Upsetting the World

~~~

> These men who have upset the world have come here also.
>
> Acts 17:6

After being imprisoned in Philippi for sharing the Good News of Jesus, Paul and Silas proceeded to Thessalonica and were accused of something most peculiar. A mob gathered to come against Paul and Silas and said of them, "These men who have upset the world have come here also" (Acts 17:6).

What a wonderful accusation! The apostles were guilty of upsetting the world. Oh, that we would be known for the same, as this world certainly needs shaken. The world system is inside-out and headed in the wrong direction. It is on a fleeting, selfish, and deceptive course toward destruction. We need men and women who will follow God in swimming upstream, against the flow of sin and confusion.

Ads of all kinds attempt to convince people that more things and expensive things are necessary to be respectable. This notion flows from the false assumption that the respect or envy of other people won through materialistic efforts holds the potential to bring real joy. The glitz of fancier modes of entertainment pushes people to believe contentment is found when we have more time and ability to laugh mindlessly and to avoid reality as we deny the core questions of the heart. Recently, a television commercial portrayed a grown woman as amazingly excited to discover seven people were searching for her online. Does it really change our lives to know a handful of other mortals is looking for us? Can self-centered living bring peace?

When Jesus saves people, He turns them inside-out; He makes them new (II Corinthians 5:17). On this earth, Jesus begins to prepare His people for the new world He is someday making. Jesus begins to shape individuals who are no longer content to waste hours, days, and years accumulating things that distract us from the pursuit of God. Jesus molds men and women who radically race toward what is broken in order to bring healing. Jesus transforms people into those who embrace the greatest paradox – that in giving our lives away to God, we gain everything (John 12:25).

As a Christian, I ought to feel the friction of my travels in a direction opposite the flow of the current, unrighteous world system. When I undergo new birth in Jesus, every fiber of my being ought now to sense that sin is to be battled vehemently.

Our Jesus is coming back to make a home of righteousness (II Peter 3:13). In other words, He will invade again the space-time continuum to make a world that is as it ought to be. Obviously, right now this world is far from being as it ought to be. The earth is broken (as seen in natural disasters and the second law of thermodynamics), bodies are broken (by disease, disability, and aging), relationships are broken (by selfishness, impatience, and unrealistic expectations), and hearts are broken (in ways innumerable). But, the Maker of the universe will miraculously remake the universe. Only the God who made everything from nothing can make wholeness out of brokenness. The fixing of this world will come by no human endeavor. It will take the invasion into history of our God . . . and He will do it!

Meanwhile, Jesus remakes people one at a time as He redeems us from sin. And then He calls us to "upset the world" – to live radically different from this vanishing, sinful flow. Jesus has the power to overcome brokenness in your life. Sin pulls us away from wholeness in our hearts. Sin also set into motion the tendency toward disorder and disintegration we see in the natural world; scientists refer to this deterioration as the second law of thermodynamics. When we shake a puzzle box and then drop the pieces to the floor from a few feet above, the pieces land randomly – scattered all about. The more we shake the box and the higher from which we drop the pieces, the more randomness and separation we observe.

Picture your heart as those puzzle pieces. Left to sinfulness without Jesus, our hearts – our lives – fall shattered, making no sense. However, if Jesus shakes your heart, the unexpected happens – the pieces fall out and are fully connected! He overcomes the natural, and forms the whole picture, causing things to make sense! He fixes us – against every plan of the enemy and every apparent triumph of wrong.

We need to reflect our Savior in shaking the world in which we live. We need to pursue the wholeness Jesus intends. We need to go against the flow.

Upset your world with a heart of service instead of a heart of power, private integrity in place of facade, kindness in the midst of attack, value of prayer and Bible study above entertainment, truth-telling though it cost much, giving of resources in the midst of selfishness, gentleness though surrounded by harshness, forgiveness when revenge is easier, sacrifice of time for those in need, and love of God above love of all else.

May Christians be accused as Paul and Silas were – of upsetting this world.

Need a Better Word than the Word of Guilt?

But you have come to . . . Jesus the mediator of a new covenant, and to the sprinkled blood that speaks a better word than the blood of Abel.
Hebrews 12:22, 24 (NIV)

Many people are familiar with the biblical fact that Cain killed his brother, Abel. The physical act of murder being a sin most people do not commit, the story is sometimes incorrectly dismissed too quickly. This account has everything to do with me – and you.

First, God makes clear that from the start Cain did not have faith in His holy Creator. Hebrews 11:4 (NIV) declares that it was "by faith Abel offered a better sacrifice than Cain did." For purposes of space and time, I choose not to diverge here in a detailed discussion of why Abel's animal sacrifice was of faith, while Cain's offering from his crops was not. However, the status of the hearts of both men is what was critical to their giving. This is always the case. Physical actions and spoken words brought from a wrongly motivated heart are ugly in the sight of God, and often in the sight of men. Clearly, of the myriad of things that might have motivated Cain, faith in God was not it. What a curious and critical insight. Many motivations of the heart stand wrong before God, and only one stands right – faith (Hebrews 11:6).

After having acted wrongly from his heart in regards to his offering, Cain was warned by God that the practice of sin leads to further practice of sin. In fact, God clearly informs, "But if you do not do what is right, sin is crouching at your door; it desires to have you, but you must master it" (Genesis 4:7, NIV). Instead of heeding God's warning, Cain chose to focus on his discontent and the perceived reason for his discontent – Abel. Mind you, the true source of Cain's unrest was his wrong standing with God. Had he run to God in repentance rather than to man in frustration, things would, no doubt, have turned out differently.

Standing in a field, with jealousy and the restlessness of rebellion against God in his spirit, Cain allowed sin to move from a crouched position to an all-out attack stance. Sin was no longer at the door; its damning fingers now crawled all over Cain's back. He murders his brother.

And so do we; for, Jesus proclaims, "You have heard that it was said to the people long ago, 'Do not murder, . . . But I tell you that anyone who is angry with his brother will be subject to judgment'" (Matthew 5:21-22, NIV). The anger and discontent and jealousy in our hearts that leads to anger toward others is in the sight of God subject to spiritual judgment just as murder is.

Wow. It seems a hopeless situation. So sad is it that God said to Cain, "What have you done? Listen! Your brother's blood cries out to me from the ground" (Genesis 4:10, NIV). And so it is with me. The blood of Abel cried out loudly about Cain, "You are guilty! You are condemned!" The results of my sin cry out loudly the same thing, "You are guilty! You are condemned!" Can you hear it? It drives us insane if we understand its implications. Hopelessness is all that stands before us if this is the final and strongest cry.

Enter Jesus! Blessed, wonderful, loving Jesus! Hear the Word of God, "But you have come to . . . Jesus the mediator of a new covenant, and to the sprinkled blood that *speaks a better word than the blood of Abel*" (Hebrews 12:22a, 24, NIV, emphasis mine).

Did you hear that? The blood of Jesus speaks a better word than the blood of Abel! Abel's blood cried out the horror of guilt and condemnation, but Jesus' blood proclaims forgiveness! So powerful is Jesus' blood to cleanse the human heart that the original languages tell us His blood simply "declares" its power, while Abel's blood "cried out." My friend, when your lack of faith, your sin, and your humanly-wrought disaster cries loudly your condemnation, let the blood Jesus shed on the Cross decisively and authoritatively declare, "You are forgiven."

Do you need a better word than the word of sin and guilt? Jesus is the Word you need.

Blessed versus Happy

> Blessed is the man who walks not in the counsel of the wicked.
> Psalm 1:1 (ESV)

While the world chases circumstantially-rooted happiness, we ought to be pursuing the blessing of God. To have our Creator pleased with our existence – rejoicing in the substance of our life – this is the rock-solid foundation of fulfillment and peace.

To be blessed is to stand strong. To be blessed is to know that all is well despite difficulty and heartache because we have invited God into every facet of our lives. To be blessed is to be wholeheartedly engaged in living because the Holy Spirit speaks and moves continually in our hearts and minds. To be blessed is quite the opposite of being bored, being drained, being lonely, or fighting to keep our head above water. To be blessed is to live vibrantly, with hope as a backdrop that never dissipates because Jesus Christ has risen from the dead and conquered the sin that used to bind us and the death that used to overshadow us.

As mentioned at the outset, worldly happiness sits juxtaposed with this state of Christian blessedness. Worldly happiness derives from a mindset of materialism. For people enslaved in the pursuit of happiness, the world is very small, and yet mysteriously elusive.

Therefore, the Psalmist says we ought not live according to the counsel of the wicked. The mindset of ungodliness tells us we must seek many things to be happy: entertainment no matter the cost to our morality or pursuit of intellect; fast-paced living in order to keep up with what is expected no matter the cost to health or sanity; gadgets, appliances, and vehicles no matter the cost to a reasonable financial plan or the amount of time needed for maintenance; a youthful look no matter the price tag or investment of valuable energy and resource; incomes that keep us on par with others' standards no matter the cost to relationships and emotional stability. And the greatest cost of this chasing of happiness is that it steals from us our commitment – our true relationship – with God Himself.

Happiness cannot be found by human effort. Rather, blessedness is bestowed by God as our heart turns genuinely and unabashedly to Him in a world gone mad. The man or woman is truly blessed who stays alert to discern worldly thinking from biblical thinking. The person on whom the favor of the Maker of the Universe rests is the one who measures every thought and motivation against the Word of the Lord. The blessed person is secure and full of hope not because of fleeting circumstances, but because of walking moment by moment with unchangeable, unshakeable, unfailing Jesus.

See to it that you are blessed of God and not merely happy. See to it that you make His approval your aim. For, the blessed person will remain, while the wicked in pursuit of worldly happiness is soon destroyed in his or her own way.

Nasty Doesn't Stop God

> The record of the genealogy of Jesus the Messiah, the son of David, the son of Abraham: Abraham was the father of Isaac, Isaac the father of Jacob, and Jacob the father of Judah and his brothers . . . Salmon was the father of Boaz by Rahab, Boaz was the father of Obed by Ruth, and Obed the father of Jesse.
> Matthew 1:1-2, 5

Selfish and hateful brothers, a woman from an idolatrous nation of child sacrifice, and a prostitute – these characters are all found in the genealogy of Jesus, the Messiah. Can God use anyone or anything for His glory and His plan? The answer comes back a resounding "Yes, He can!"

Grace is unmerited favor; it is blessing straight from God that is in no way earned or deserved. Through the human lineage of Jesus, God is demonstrating His unfathomable willingness to work with people the world views as most repugnant. He highlights His mysterious motivation to work through pitiful and devious people in order that His salvation may emerge at the forefront and do what only a holy God full of grace is able to do – change pitiful and devious people!

The snapshot of Jesus' ancestry holds forth to us a picture of the hope we have in God despite our sinfulness. Matthew 1:1-2 says, "The record of the genealogy of Jesus the Messiah, the son of David, the son of Abraham: Abraham was the father of Isaac, Isaac the father of Jacob, and Jacob the father of Judah and his brothers." Immediately we see in the list of early ancestors that Abraham fathered Isaac, who fathered Jacob, who fathered Judah and his brothers. Stop there and consider Judah and his brothers and to what evil their envy led them. These are the men who threw their own brother, Joseph, into a pit after contemplating

Living in Awe!

the possibility of murdering him outright. These are the ones who then sold Joseph as a slave to a band of traders.

Have we ever been jealous of someone as these brothers were? Have we ever wished or acted evil on another? Have we ever abandoned someone we should have helped? Have we ever been a part of watching someone – even a loved one – venture into a bad place? If so, we can symbolically place ourselves in this part of the genealogy of Jesus.

Let us now examine Matthew 1:5, "Salmon was the father of Boaz by Rahab, Boaz was the father of Obed by Ruth, and Obed the father of Jesse." Remember Rahab? She was a public prostitute of the Canaanites who decided to believe in the one, true God of the Israelites. And what about Ruth? Though she chose to go to Isreal and worship the real God of the universe; she had been a citizen of Moab, a nation that worshipped the false god, Chemosh, and offered children as sacrifices to that idol.

Have we ever committed sexual sin in action or in thought? Have we ever remained among idols of our own making? Have we ever not honored other adults or children as we should? Have we devalued humans? If so, we can identify with this section of the lineage of Jesus.

God did not abandon humanity when we ridiculously rebelled against Him to our own demise. Though we have sinned against our holy Creator, He has determined to give us a second chance. He sent Jesus even though the God-Man had to come in human flesh. God did not allow the ugliness of sinful hearts to stop Him from offering salvation. It is as if He stepped back from the conglomeration of misery and selfishness and said, "I still choose to save those who believe; I will not abandon those whom I have made, but I will offer salvation."

God said to Joseph about the Messiah, "Do not be afraid to take Mary as your wife; for the Child who has been conceived in her is of the Holy Spirit. She will bear a Son; and you shall call His name Jesus, for He will save His people from their sins" (Matthew 1:20-21). Thank you God, for sending your Son! Thank you, Holy Spirit, for working tangibly in this world to effect your plan!

Let us no more say that genealogies are boring. The lineage of Jesus is a reminder of God's willingness to work with the nasty world. Our responsibility is to react to His work on our behalf. We need to believe and let God save us through the sacrifice of Jesus and the renewing work of the Holy Spirit. No matter the depth or nature of human sin, God can redeem!

Inverting the Flow of Life

Devote yourselves to prayer, being watchful and thankful.
Colossians 4:2 (NIV)

We have things a bit turned around in our world, inverting the proper flow of life. It seems some of us Christians seek to accumulate earthly goods, access many avenues of entertainment, secure successful career paths, and fill our families' lives with countless activities which are meant to lead to healthy self-esteem and proper socialization. These pursuits appear to come first, followed by the occasional or regular prayer to invoke the blessing of God on the myriad endeavors. We, as good Christians, seek the Lord to bless our fast-paced, culture-driven lives.

Starkly contrasted to this rhythm, the heart of the endeared apostle Paul streamed in the opposite direction. He spoke clearly in Colossians 4:2 (NIV), "Devote yourselves to prayer, being watchful and thankful." Paul endured the gloom of Roman imprisonment when he penned this directive, and his heart was sure of one fact – all of life and its activities follow after a soul fixed on God's ideals. We ought to have a permanent bent in our attitude. We ought not to jump from one pursuit to the next event without knowing our very heart is stayed on God. Do we arise in the morning clearly cognizant of His Lordship and His promises? Are we determined to know His Word in such a way as it boldly jumps to the forefront in our moments of rest and moments of work?

Lips moving and words spoken are one way to pray – and a pivotal one. However, prayer is also a state of mind. The God of all reality should be the most important consideration in all things. Am I devoted to prayer, or am I devoted to an "acceptable life"? Am I devoted to prayer, or am I devoted to success? Am I devoted to prayer, or am I devoted to busyness? Am I devoted to prayer,

Living in Awe!

or am I devoted to the escape from boredom? Am I devoted to prayer, or am I devoted to me?

Without basic freedom and suffering for His faith in Jesus, Paul pronounces that prayer is to be coupled with watchfulness and thankfulness (note again Colossians 4:2 . . . "Devote yourselves to prayer, being watchful and thankful"). Even while jailed, Paul recognizes the need to be vigilant – to refuse to drift through life or allow circumstances to pull us along. Rather, we must remain alert, aware of the human tendency to drop to the status quo – mediocrity. We are to be consciously aware of the condition of our heart and the spiritual realm surrounding it. Life is so much more than what we eat and drink and watch on television. We are to be constantly asking, "What is God up to?" and "How are the spiritual forces of wickedness seeking to divert God's work in my life?"

When Jesus' own disciples fell asleep just hours before His arrest, Jesus told them, "Watch and pray so that you will not fall into temptation. The spirit is willing, but the body is weak" (Matthew 26:41, NIV). As the disciples dozed, Jesus was getting ready to change eternity by His death and resurrection. Could they not stay alert? Realizing our bodies tend to spiral downward in devotion, Jesus emphasized the spirit's dominance and agrees with Paul in declaring we need to watch and pray. Amazingly, Jesus is about to change eternity again by coming back to this earth to gather His own people to Himself and usher in His grand remaking of heaven and earth. When He returns, will we, too, be sleeping and resting? Are we so slothful and unaware of God's working in the world? We have it backwards. Life is not about the filling of moments with our own plans and procedures, but a focus on God Almighty, whose plan overpowers all!

We notice Paul adds thankfulness to his watchful and prayerful demeanor. We note so little gratitude among people in today's world – even believers. Perhaps we are not thankful because we are focusing on our own work rather than the mysterious work of God. My preoccupation with myself does not make me thankful, but my meditation on the moment-by-moment, righteous working of God causes my heart to leap! Things may not always truly be as they appear. Yes, Paul was in prison, but God's inexplicable joy and future hope pervaded Paul's soul. The Gospel rang out loudly to innumerable people. We, too, may live in muddled times. The answer is not changed circumstances, but a heart devoted to prayer with watchfulness and thankfulness.

Jesus With Me

Never will I leave you; never will I forsake you.
                                    Hebrews 13:5 (NIV)

Clouds above me,
Grass below me,
Jesus with me.

Friends embrace me,
Friends forsake me,
Jesus with me.

Rejoicing in clarity,
Surrounded by mystery,
Jesus with me.

Good news floods in,
Good news floods out,
Jesus with me.

Sensing His nearness,
Imagining a distance,
Jesus with me.

My faithfulness abounds,
My faithfulness wanes,
Jesus with me.

Seasons of triumph,
Seasons of loss,
Jesus with me.

Living in Awe!

Body is strong,
Body is weak,
Jesus with me.

No matter what,
No matter when,
Jesus with me.

This world begins,
This world ends,
Jesus with me.

New world begins,
New world endures forever,
Jesus with me.

Living in Awe!

Inside-Out God

> And she gave birth to her firstborn son and wrapped him in swaddling cloths and laid him in a manger, because there was no place for them in the inn.
> Luke 2:7 (ESV)

> Then I saw a great white throne and him who was seated on it. Earth and sky fled from his presence, and there was no place for them.
> Revelation 20:11 (NIV)

God has a magnificent ability to turn things inside out. How often it appears that evil prevails, when all the while God stands in full control, ready to unravel a plan that sets righteousness at the forefront. Working at times in paradoxes, God tells us that we need to give up our life to Him in order to save it (Luke 9:24). He assures us that though we suffer earthly discomfort and loss for His sake, we gain eternal, heavenly reward (Matthew 5:11-12). Most prominently, it is the message of the cross that is the very power of God! (I Corinthians 1:18)

Having studied God's paradoxical workings for many years, none seemed to crystallize the overall hope we have in Him more than the one I discovered months ago. In preparing to share a Christmas sermon with people of all ages, I came across the famous Luke 2:7 (ESV), "And she gave birth to her firstborn son and wrapped him in swaddling cloths and laid him in a manger, because there was no place for them in the inn." We recognize the well-known problem Mary and Joseph faced as they looked to rightly comfort their newborn child, our Savior. Ironically, Jesus Christ – the Creator of the Universe – found no place to rest in one tiny spot on the face of the earth He created!

Ponder for a moment . . . Jesus is the Everlasting God. He chose to put on flesh and blood to come and save us from our sin (Hebrews 2:14-15). He entered the womb of a woman, even

Living in Awe!

though He is infinite. Despite the fact that everything, everyone, and every place derives from Him and ultimately depends on Him for existence, Jesus limited Himself in this way to freely come to us in human flesh. After growing in Mary's womb for one or two months, Jesus would have been about as big as your pinky fingernail! God . . . that big for our sake!

He came to this universe, to this particular solar system, to this specific planet, to one continent, to a humble town in the Middle East, to one simple house of lodging, and . . . He could not find a place there! Unbelievable! His parents then laid His tiny body in an animal feeding trough, because there was no place for Him in the inn.

May I introduce you to the irony of all ironies? In Revelation 20:11 (NIV), the apostle John is speaking of the vision he was given of Jesus in the future, "Then I saw a great white throne and him who was seated on it. Earth and sky fled from his presence, and there was no place for them." Did you catch that phrase about the earth and heavens? There was no place for them! When Jesus Christ finally steps to the throne of His judgment at the end of time as we currently know it, His awesome holiness will force even the earth and sky to flee; and when they run, they can find no place to be!

Though Jesus found no suitable location the first time He came to this space-time continuum, He will overtake all locations when He comes back again! The first time, He came as a Servant to bear the penalty of our sin (II Corinthians 5:21). The second time, He will come to judge all of creation and make it right. As Romans 8:21-22 tells us, even this old earth knows it needs remade by its Creator; it needs set free from the curse of sin. As Romans 8:23 and Philippians 3:20-21 informs, we, too, are waiting for Jesus to remake our pitiful bodies into glorious ones.

Jesus Christ will utterly turn things inside out. He who was despised by those He came to save and rejected at the outset to the point of resting in a feeding trough because there was no place for Him . . . this same Jesus will overtake all places in order that He may prepare them for His redeemed people. Remember John 14:2 (emphasis mine), "In My Father's house are many dwelling places; if it were not so, I would have told you; for I go to prepare *a place* for you."

If you have not repented of your sin and yielded your life to Jesus, take no comfort in a situation that makes it appear God has no place. No, friend, please understand He rightfully owns all places, and He is coming back to make that clear. If you do now walk with Your Savior, Jesus, take heart! He Who had no place, will take all places, and we shall walk with Him unhindered throughout the world He made!

Notes

Riding the Updraft

Reference: Christopher M. Perrins & Jonathan Elphick. The Complete Encyclopedia of Birds and Bird Migration. (Edison, NJ: Chartwell Books)

Deep Waters of the Heart

Reference: oceanservice.noaa.gov/facts/exploration.html Accessed 01/26/12

Which Fire?

Reference: Francis Chan, Erasing Hell (Colorado Springs, CO: David C Cook, 2011)

The Vital Connection Between Learning and Humility

Reference: Bauerlein, M. (2008, February). Too dumb for complex texts. Educational Leadership, 68(5), 28-32.

Wait.For.It. (Cognitive Wait Time in a Rapid-Fire World)

Reference: Sprenger, Marilee. 2005. How to Teach so Students Remember. Alexandria, VA: Association for Supervision and Curriculum Development.

Pondering Stephen Hawking's Statements

Reference: Carlos Eire, A Very Brief History of Eternity (Princeton, NJ: Princeton University Press, 2010)

Dendrites and Deuteronomy: The Alignment of Brain Research with the Timeless Word of God

Reference: Judy Willis, M.D. (2006) Research-based strategies to ignite student learning. Alexandria, VA: Association for Supervision and Curriculum Development.

What Fallen Bridges Tell Us About God

Reference: Dean, K. C. (2010) Almost Christian: What the Faith of our Teenagers Is Telling the American Church. New York, NY: Oxford University Press.

Topic Index

Change 170, 196
Commitment 15, 78, 85, 120, 131, 145, 152, 159, 173, 191, 214
Confidence 126, 191
Contentment 36, 152
Death 106, 163
Difficulty 49, 91, 99, 193
Discernment 168
Distraction 85
Education 64, 75, 131
Endurance 78, 81, 99, 143
Eternal Life 159, 199
Fear 104, 148
Forgiveness 58, 129, 161, 165, 206
God's Leading 196
God's Love 33, 39, 165
God's Plan 31, 44, 68, 168
God's Presence 20, 13, 56
God's Reliability 20, 36, 91, 137, 173, 181, 185, 193
God's Strength 11, 61, 87, 110, 148
God's Timelessness 170
God's Wrath 117
Grace 211
Heaven 28, 33, 78, 87, 89, 94, 106, 113, 120, 181
Hell 49, 94

Hope 18, 70, 99, 120, 165, 176, 181, 211
Humility 64, 137
Identity in Christ 44, 126, 155, 191
Jesus' Deity 104
Jesus' Faithfulness 53, 75, 217
Jesus Our Savior 83, 117, 122, 219
Jesus' Return 89, 124, 188, 214, 219
Jesus' Sacrifice 31, 46, 70, 113, 176, 188
Joy 56, 209
Judgment 46, 49, 94, 124, 145, 159
Kingdom of God 28
Peace 20, 13, 39, 68
Pleasing God 15, 102, 145, 203
Prayer 150, 179, 214
Priorities 41, 89, 102, 163, 179
Promise for the Future 23, 44, 70, 73, 117, 143, 185
Rest 11, 36, 122
Restoration 53
Right Focus 18, 131, 140, 181, 209
Sin 31, 129, 161, 211
Trouble 87, 97, 217
True Beauty 25, 113, 161
Worry 25, 73

225

Title Index

A Deep Greeting 91
A Good Captivity 102
A New Song 68
A Warning with an Astonishing Promise 179
Actually Finding Life 159
Are You Drained? 129
Blessed versus Happy 209
Blown Out of the Water 104
Chokehold or Mercy? 58
Close to His Heart 39
Counting Trials as Joy 99
Deep Waters of the Heart 20
Dendrites and Deuteronomy:
The Alignment of Brain Research with the Timeless Word of God 131
Devilish Pondering 31
Dingy Socks 161
Distracted to Death 85
Do My Eyes Deceive Me? 168
Does God See My Couch? 13
Embarrassed? 191
Endure 81
Enduring and Moving 196
Equipped 126
Far Beyond Gasoline Prices 163
Get a Taste of This Kingdom! 28
God of the Lilies 25
God of the Means and the Extremes 36
God on Good and Bad Days 193
Greater than a Fairy Tale 176
Imperishable Seed Beyond the Boundary of Science 199
Inside-Out God 219

Integrity, the Second Law of Thermodynamics, and Jesus	181
Inverting the Flow of Life	214
Jesus With Me	217
Leaving Space	41
Life-Building: Will You Crash or Stand?	145
Like Water Through My Fingers	152
Living in Heavenly Places	140
Most Bosses Don't Listen, But . . .	137
My King Is In the Pit	97
Nasty Doesn't Stop God	211
Need a Better Word than the Word of Guilt?	206
Outside the Box	33
Plunging Up Through a Mound of Dirt	143
Pondering Stephen Hawking's Statements	106
Regular Miracles	185
Rescue from the Wrath to Come	117
Rest, Not Religion	122
Riding the Updraft	11
Seasons and Changes UNDER Heaven	170
Sinking and Swimming	53
Soul War	15
Spanning the Gap	73
Swordtails and God's Sleeve	83
The Answer to Self-Esteem Issues	44
The Cup and this Pitiful Creature	188
The End of the World as We Know It	89
The Operative Word	150
The Paradox of Life	78
The Real You and the Plans of God	155
The Verse AFTER the Favorite Verse	18
The Vital Connection Between Learning and Humility	64
The Weakness of God	61
Truly Wonderful	113
Upsetting the World	203
Wait.For.It. (Cognitive Wait Time in a Rapid-Fire World)	75
What About Your Legs?	110
What Do Swaddling Cloths Have to Do with Anything?	70
What Does It Mean to Live, and What Does It Mean to Die?	120

Living in Awe!

What Fallen Bridges Tell Us About God	173
What If Every End Were a Beginning?	23
What if the Sun Went Dark?	124
What Is the Good Life?	56
What the Stars CAN Tell Us	148
When the Walls Come Crumbling Down	87
When We Almost Can't Believe God Would Still Love Us	165
Which Fire?	49
Why Doesn't God Do Something?	46
Will Christians Have Knowledge of the Great White Throne Judgment?	94

About the Author

Shelli Prindle is known for her passion, joy, and integrity. She clearly articulates biblical truth in a down-to-earth fashion that inspires people to practically apply it to their lives. As a writer, educator, and speaker she engages the intellect and presents a message of true hope to her audiences. Those who hear her messages often say they have an increased longing to dig deeper into God's Word on their own.

A graduate of Seton Hill University (B.A., Mathematics) and Crown College (M.A., Educational Leadership), Shelli spent more than a decade teaching math and Bible in Christian high schools in the Pittsburgh area. She has served as principal/administrator of two Christian schools and has consulted with the Association of Christian Schools International (ACSI) as a conference speaker, curriculum developer, and seminar leader. Currently she is serving as Director of Youth and Young Adults for Norwin Alliance Church in North Huntingdon, PA.

In 2007, Shelli founded Hope & Passion Ministries as a vehicle through which to share her passion for God's Word and His people. Sharing a Jesus-view of reality that produces true hope and passionate living is the vision of Hope & Passion Ministries, Inc. This vision is realized as she teaches and speaks at churches, retreats, seminars, and conferences. Hope & Passion Ministries stands on the truth that "all things were created by Him and for Him, He is before all things, and in Him all things hold together." (Colossians 1:16b, 17) Jesus created and sustains all reality, provides true redemption, and offers abundant life as we await His glorious re-creation of this world.

In addition to her speaking engagements, Shelli has also produced many original works including Apologetics Activated!, a ten hour practical primer on Christian apologetics and The Heaven Event, a half-day presentation on the rock-solid nature of our eternal home. She published her first book, Real Life, Real God, Real Hope!, in 2011. It has inspired people of all ages to live passionately, knowing Jesus is over all!

If you would like more information about Hope & Passion Ministries or would like to consider Shelli to speak at your event, please visit the website at www.hopeandpassion.org.